TWO SIDES

SUNY Series in Oral Public History
Michael Frisch, Editor

TWO SIDES TO EVERYTHING

The Cultural Construction of Class Consciousness in Harlan County, Kentucky

by

SHAUNNA L. SCOTT

State University
of New York
Press

Acknowledgment is given to Chronicle Features for providing a Gary Larson "The Far Side" cartoon, 1994.

Published by
State University of New York Press, Albany

Production by Susan Geraghty
Marketing by Dana Yanulavich

Printed in the United States of America

For information, address State University of New York Press, State University Plaza, Albany, N.Y., 12246

Library of Congress Cataloging-in-Publication Data

Scott, Shaunna L., 1960–
    Two sides to everything : the cultural construction of class consciousness in Harlan County, Kentucky / by Shaunna L. Scott.
      p.   cm.—(SUNY series in oral and public history)
    Includes bibliographical references and index.
    ISBN 0-7914-2343-3 (alk. paper).—ISBN 0-7914-2344-1 (pbk. : alk. paper)
    1. Harlan County (Ky.)—Social conditions. 2. Class consciousness—Kentucky—Harlan County. 3. Coal miners—Kentucky—Harlan County—Social conditions. I. Title. II. Series.
HN79.K42H377 1995
305.5' 09769' 154—dc20   94-13464
                                                CIP

10 9 8 7 6 5 4 3 2 1

TABLE OF CONTENTS

LIST OF TABLES AND

FIGURES

ACKNOWLEDGMENTS

I would like to express my gratitude to Professors Jack M. Potter, Herbert Reid, and Susan Abbott for mentoring me through my academic infancy so that I could see a project of this nature through to completion. In addition, this project would not have been possible without the financial support of the University of California, Berea College, and the University of Kentucky. I am very grateful. The advice of Professors Dick Walker, Michael Burawoy, Gerald Berreman, and Aihwa Ong were instrumental during the early research and writing process. For granting me expanded access to the oral history archives and photographic collections at Southeast Community College during my research project, I owe a debt to Professor James Goode. Thanks to Meredith Redlin for assistance in index preparation. And special thanks go to my colleagues Professors Dwight Billings and Kathleen Blee, who have proven invaluable to the final completion and ultimate publication of this book.

As is always the case, the comments of anonymous reviewers and the assistance of editors, Chris Worden, Susan Geraghty, and Wendy Nelson have played a major part in the final product and its readability. I am also grateful for the support and advice of Professors Milton Cantor, Stephen Fisher, Roger N. Lancaster, Sally Maggard, Alessandro Portelli, and Michael Yarrow. Thanks, also, to Tom House and Kate Black for their assistance in locating the historical photographs that appear on the cover and in chapters 1 and 2, all of which came from the University of Kentucky Photo Archives. The photographs of underground miners, in chapter 3, appear courtesy of the Kentucky Coal Association. (All other photographs appearing by this book are the property of the author.) Harlan County memorial designer, David Harp, and poet John Deaton, Jr., kindly allowed me to reprint the fruits of their artistic labor in chapter 7. I thank them both.

Finally, I owe an incalculable debt to my tireless and generous parents, Sally and Phill Scott, who helped care for my daughter,

Hannah, while I completed revisions on the manuscript. This work stands, not only on their shoulders, but on the shoulders of my grandparents, Emma Grace Blackburn Blankenship, Opal Rutherford Scott, Mallie E. Scott, and George T. Blankenship. In addition, I thank my husband, Keith Barton, for his care and patience, for agreeing to delay our marriage so that I could prolong my stay in Harlan, for arranging his career path around mine, and for consistently struggling against the patriarchal cultural grain. But, most of all, I would like to thank my friends in Harlan County for allowing me to share their lives for a time that I shall always cherish.

ABBREVIATIONS

BCOA	Bituminous Coal Operators' Association
HCCOA	Harlan County Coal Operator's Association
HDE	*Harlan Daily Enterprise*
KFTC	Kentuckians for the Commonwealth
NMU	National Miners Union
SECC-OHP	Southeast Community College Oral History Project
SLU	Southern Labor Union
UMW	United Mine Workers of America

FOREWORD: HALF-TRUTHS AND GOOD INTENTIONS

In January 1987, I returned to Berkeley, California, after eighteen months of residence in Harlan County. With thousands of pages of field notes, dozens of interview tapes and transcripts, and countless additional documents in tow, I faced the nearly impossible task of rendering the complexity, beauty, and hardship of life in Harlan in an ethnographic manuscript that was to serve as my doctoral dissertation in anthropology. In the midst of this daunting task, I went to see the movie *Matewan* in nearby San Francisco. I had been following the production of this historical dramatization of the unionization of West Virginia with great interest, not only because it was an important period of Appalachian labor history, but also because members of my family had participated in it. The director and producer, John Sayles, had chosen to film on location near my family's home place, and my grandmother kept me apprised of the local reactions to and participation in the film production. I had been awaiting the movie eagerly.

Various relatives had told me the story of "the Matewan massacre" when I was a child. In my family's version, my great-grandfather, the sheriff of Mingo County, always appeared to be a fair and courageous law officer, as committed to protecting the rights of miners as to protecting those of the mine owners. I suspected that my family had romanticized its account. Don't we all like to think of our ancestors as heros? My great-grandfather's alleged neutrality, his commitment to law, order, and justice, and his active protection of the miners clearly differentiated him from his counterpart in Harlan County, where I had done my research. This added fuel to my skeptical fire: this great-grandfather of mine seemed too good to be true. With the release of *Matewan*, however, came the opportunity to see the results of a disinterested outsider's perspective on these figures and events. And because I had always admired Sayles' work, politics, and philosophy, I could not dismiss his representation out of hand. So I was nervous when I went to the movie's opening. In fact, I felt as if I was being tried for a serious crime rather than going to an afternoon matinee. By the end, however, I was quite satisfied. My family's portrait of its upstanding patriarch had been affirmed by the filmmaker. I was so proud that I felt the urge to announce to the entire audience, "That was my great-grandfather up there!"

My encounter with the film *Matewan* offered me a taste of how Harlan County readers might feel in approaching this book—how nerve-racking, frightening, and alienating the experience of reading it might be. It is difficult to have one's personal life, family, and community serve as the raw material for someone else's book, as ethnographers and oral historians have become increasingly aware (Clifford 1986; Hastrup 1992, 122–24; Stacey 1991). On several occasions, those who consented to be interviewed and observed for this project expressed their misgivings to me, either directly or indirectly. Most commonly, they complained about stereotypical depictions of Harlan County and Appalachia that have appeared both in scholarly works and in the national media. Had I come to Harlan County just to make fun of people? they asked. One person accused me of being just another outsider, "up to no good." And the local newspaper editor, Ewell Balltrip, told me quite bluntly that he thouught the place had been "studied enough." Most of the time, however, this uneasiness was expressed through humor: People would introduce me to their friends with precautionary edicts like "Watch what you do around her. She's observing us, you know"; they brought me a "Far Side" cartoon of naive anthropologists being misled by savvy "natives" who maintained their image as quaint and exotic only by hiding their modern technology from view (see Figure F.1). Like the "Far Side" "natives", they would offer to stage "quaint" and "exotic" scenes—suggesting that they should dress up in denim overalls to pose for my photographs, for instance.

On these occasions, I tried to respond in kind, with a good dose of humor. I also reminded them that I, like them, had been born and raised in the mountains of eastern Kentucky, just two counties away in Pikeville. As a "hillbilly" myself, I had no intention of perpetuating negative stereotypes of mountaineers. If anything, I hoped to combat oversimplified, negative stereotypes with an ethnographic portrayal that emphasized the complexity, diver-

THE FAR SIDE   By GARY LARSON

"Anthropologists! Anthropologists!"

sity, and dignity of the Harlan community. My claim to "insider status" and declarations of good intentions assuaged their fears, but never completely eliminated them. And rightly so. No matter how vigorously I had tried to minimize our differences, class, gender, and age set me apart from the people whom I had come to interview. They were working-class miners; I came from a middle-class family of teachers and managers. Most of them were men, ranging in age from 33 to 85; I was a 25-year-old woman. None of them had graduated from college, and some had not graduated from high school; I was a Ph.D. student.

I frequently told myself that this marginal, half-insider and half-outsider position provided me with the ideal ethnographic perspective (see also Michrina 1993, 164–78). I could blend in and speak the dialect in an eastern Kentucky accent, yet I could achieve an analytic distance from the subject at hand. In these more self-assured moments, I was optimistic that my ethnography would capture some fundamental truths, truths that would satisfy both the academic and the native Appalachian in me. Such an ethnography would undoubtedly please my dissertation committee and my friends in Harlan County. With the lofty goals of accuracy and respect ever at the forefront, I grew weary of addressing the misgivings and distrust expressed by some of my informants. After several months, I felt that I had earned their trust. I certainly had made no secret of the fact that I was an anthropologist studying Harlan County. In fact, I shared ideas, interpretations, and opinions with them throughout the research process and, more formally, during classes that I taught at Southeast Community College and in presentations at the local public schools. I participated in the community, through volunteer work at the hospital and nursing home, in the church, and in civic organizations like the Harlan Jaycees. I thought that surely they would recognize my good intentions and come to trust me in time. I was not completely mistaken in my prediction. Many people did come to trust me very much. But no one trusted me completely.

In retrospect, I have come to admire my Harlan County friends for their tenacity in reminding me of something that I knew, intellectually, but was not to experience until the following year when the movie *Matewan* was released: representations have important political and personal implications. Movies and dissertations contribute to politically charged discourses that define and assign meaning to people, events, and reality itself. They knew that my research project, if successful, would be stamped with "expert" credentials by the University of California and find its way to a library shelf. It would become part of the permanent record on Harlan County. If published, it would gain an even wider audience, a wider audience than my subjects could reasonably hope to command. It is little wonder that people sometimes worried about the project, that they cajoled me, and that one woman constantly used the phrase "And you can write *that* in your book!" to underscore certain points in her narratives (Scott 1991). She hoped that I would not overlook elements that were important to her story. But, in the end, she depended upon me to relay that story. She occupied this dependent position uneasily.

And why not? Our relationship was inherently unequal and

unavoidably exploitative. I did not dwell on this fact while I was in Harlan County because I found it to be both personally painful and politically difficult. But, in pouring over my field notes, listening to my tapes, interpreting, and "writing up" my Harlan County experience, this dimension of ethnographic field work troubled me more and more. Like other ethnographers who have fretted over this matter (Borland 1991; Clifford and Marcus 1986; Frisch 1990; Michrina 1993, 164–78; Okley and Callaway 1992; Marcus and Fisher 1986; Rabinow 1977; Stacey 1991), I can offer no simple solutions to the ethical dilemmas of ethnographic fieldwork. In spite of its lofty goals, good intentions, and more recent feminist and postmodern debates on self-reflexivity, cultural critique, rhetorical strategies, and giving voice to the "Other," ethnography remains a dangerous and messy business that inevitably positions the ethnographer in the "expert" role, privileging her/his voice over the voice of the marginalized "other." I can but acknowledge this fact and discharge my duties with the hope that this text produces more truth than falsehood, more good than harm.

Harlan Countians who read this book will inevitably be disappointed by it. Such disappointment will stem many factors, not the least of which is expressed by two local sayings: "There are two sides to everything" and "You can't please everyone." The barriers to local popularity are further multiplied in this particular book because it focuses upon divisive issues, such as labor-management conflict, local politics, and the cultural construction of class and community identity. I fear that this ethnography, by virtue of its orienting questions, may contribute to the negative stereotype of Harlan County as a overly violent, class-polarized community. I know that, by bringing up a painful past, I run the risk of rubbing a collective sore spot in Harlan County, a place that has been irritated and "picked on" enough. And even though I regret this fact, I have elected to proceed with this project. I do so, *not* because I dislike Harlan or view it aberrant, but because I value Harlan and see it as representative of small-town and rural America, where many communities face the interrelated social and domestic problems of stagnating economies, poverty, out-migration, shrinking tax bases, gender-role transformation, community and family conflict, rise in divorce, and changing kinship structures (see also Bluestone and Harrison 1982; Gaventa 1990). In short, I believe that Harlan has much to teach us about our nation and the dynamics that propel it into the future.

No ethnography can provide a realistic picture of a whole society, a community, or even a family. Each is necessarily limited by the experiences, perceptions, social position, and interests of the ethnographer. I have already pointed out that my class position, educational background, gender, and Appalachian identity affected my relationship with my Harlan informants, particularly around issues of trust and solidarity. This study was, of course, further circumscribed by my research questions. I went to Harlan County, not simply to describe and interpret anything and everything I witnessed there, but to investigate two overarching problem areas.

My first area of interest concerned the contradictory image of Harlan Countians and other Appalachians as political actors. On the one hand, there is the popular image of Harlan County as a place where militantly pro-union miners battle entrenched anti-union coal operators. The Harlan labor organizing song "Which Side Are You On?" and the Academy Award winning documentary film *Harlan County, U.S.A.* have contributed greatly to this widespread notion, as have scholarly studies, journalistic exposés, and biographical memoirs (see, for example, Dreiser 1932; Ewen 1979; Forester 1986; Hevener 1978; Jones 1985; Portelli 1991; Titler n.d.; see also Batteau 1990:102–26). The titles of these works, alone, suggest a Harlan County history that is fractious, violent, and rent with hardship. The titles *Which Side Are You On?* (Hevener 1978), "No Neutrals There" (Portelli 1991), *Hell in Harlan* (Titler n.d.), *Growin' Up Hard in Harlan County* (Jones 1985), *Harlan County: The Turbulent Thirties* (Forester 1986), and even my own 1988 dissertation title "Where There Is No Middle Ground" evoke an aura of struggle. This image of Harlan County sets it apart from the rest of the United States, a nation noted for its lack of working-class activism. This image of militant miners also stands in marked contrast to the predominant stereotypes of Appalachians as passive, fatalistic, individualistic, and unwilling to cooperate in community endeavors (Weller 1965) and, furthermore, contradicts much of the academic literature that portrays mountain unionists as more reform oriented than revolutionary (Corbin 1981; Gaventa 1980; Hevener 1978; Shifflett 1991; Yarrow 1982). But before we dismiss the image of Harlan as more "media hype" than reality, we had best consider a legacy of Appalachian dissent and political activism, including unionization struggles, "wildcat" strikes, welfare rights organizations, strip-mine protests, environmental activism and tax reform movements (Fisher 1992; Gaventa, Smith, and Willingham 1990). This evidence suggests that the question of Harlan County and Appalachian political activism and class conflict can be quite complicated.

Prior to my arrival in Harlan I had, of course, read many fine ethnographies and social histories of Appalachian communities. Focused on their own research agenda, the authors did not resolve the contradictory image of mountain people as passive fatalists and militant radicals, but only further piqued my interest in exploring this issue. Ethnographies of nonmining communities, for example, generally emphasized family, religion, and community (Beaver 1986; Foster 1988; Hicks 1976; Pearsall 1959; Stephenson 1968), while studies of coal communities concentrated upon labor unions and class struggle (Corbin 1981; Gaventa 1980; see also Yarrow 1982).[1] My reading of them, then, left me with a rather disjointed sociological map of Appalachia as a place where kin-structured agricultural communities stood alongside, or were supplanted by, class-structured coal-mining communities. I was not at all satisfied with that portrait. I furthermore suspected that the key to reconciling contradictory images of Appalachians might be found through a systematic examination of the linkages between class, kinship, community, and religion.

I started graduate school in 1982, a time when more-established Appalachian scholars were also scrutinizing the neat analytical separations and dichotomous oppositions that had previously organized their disciplinary discourses. Allen Batteau, for instance, questioned scholars' "either-or" treatment of Appalachian regional development, as represented by the debate between the "culture of poverty" and "internal colonialism" models (Batteau 1983, 142; 1982a; 1982b). Rather than separating and examining social forces as if they operated within a vacuum, these scholars increasingly sought to make sense of the complex relationships and interactions among them—those of class, race, gender, kinship, and religion, for example. (Billings 1990; Graves 1993; Lewis 1987; Maggard 1985, 1988; Shifflett 1991; Trotter 1990; and Yarrow 1985 all attempt to relate two or more of these elements; see also Lewis, Johnson, and Askins 1978, 113–40, as an early example of this trend.)

This ethnography participates in the movement to integrate

seemingly disparate sociological categories. In this case, I was initially interested in the ways in which class articulates with kinship, family and community identity, and religious belief. After several months in Harlan County, I realized that I must incorporate gender into my analysis, in spite of my fears that my investigation would lose its focus and be impossible to present in a coherent form. As a historical materialist proceeding from a "cultural Marxist" or neo-Marxian tradition (Marx 1967, 1975; and, later, Gramsci 1971; Thompson 1966; Hall and Jefferson 1976; Nash 1979; Willis 1977), my first task had been to describe and understand Harlan County miners in their historical context. Gender, as it turned out, was so central to the understanding of occupational identity and class solidarity among coal miners that it simply could not be ignored.

So, like any ethnographer, I changed my plans and shifted my emphases in response to what I had learned in the field. Of course, there are limits to how many leads an ethnographer can follow, how many new directions can be taken, or how many additional topics can be addressed. One must make careful, strategic decisions about whom to interview and what kinds of data to collect, unless one expects to remain in the field forever. Fairly early in my fieldwork, for instance, I elected not to make race a primary focus of study, largely for pragmatic reasons: I did not have the time to pursue the topic adequately and feared that I could not integrate it into my complicated schema. I will reflect upon this regrettable decision further, in the concluding Afterword. For now, suffice it to say that this book focuses almost exclusively on the experiences and ideologies of White miners in Harlan County.

I went to Harlan County to investigate not race or gender, but the interlinked topics of class conflict and political struggle. I chose these topics, in part, because I was dissatisfied with some of Marxian theory's deterministic, undialectical oversimplifications. Particularly troubling were unilinear evolutionary notions about the revolutionary potential of the working class and an oversimplified grounding of class solidarity in work experience. Still, I was not prepared to throw the baby out with the bath water. Instead, I elected to observe and speak with a group of workers who could shed some light on such theoretical dilemmas (not unlike Thompson 1966; Hall and Jefferson 1976; Nash 1979; Willis 1977).

Michael Burawoy (1991, 10) calls this mode of sociological inquiry "theory reconstruction." In theory reconstruction, one seeks to improve a theory by being critical of it—that is, by identifying and addressing its gaps, contradictions, and anomalies. While theory reconstruction is by no means the only way in which social scientists conduct research and elaborate theory, this dialectical interchange between theory and experience has always come most naturally to me. It is the way I have proceeded with this, and most of my intellectual tasks: first by locating a theoretical problem or question; then exploring the treatment of that problem or question in the academic literature; then conducting my own original ethnographic study; and, finally, modifying, elaborating, or rejecting a theory or its propositions in light of the evidence from the literature and the field. This is not, as critics of qualitative research may suggest, an effort to erect complex theoretical arguments on the foundation of a single, limited, and, perhaps, atypical case study. Rather, it forms part of an ongoing intellectual discourse concerning thousands of "case studies" that have been done over the last 130 years or so.

Just as there are several approaches to conducting social research, there are several varieties of Marxian theory, each of which traces its roots to some element in the complex philosophical legacy of Karl Marx. Because of this, and also because Harlan County workers have historically had a problematic relationship with Marxian thought, it is necessary for me to clarify my usage of the term. Oddly enough, I doubt that my central premises will shock Harlan County readers, despite their antipathy toward Marx and their opposition to authoritarian regimes that have claimed him as an inspiration (see Forester 1986). In fact, there appears to be considerable overlap between a materialist epistemology and what my Harlan County subjects might call old-fashioned "common sense." The most basic assumption of the materialist position is that material and social reality exist independent of cultural meaning and, therefore, sociological analysis should begin with the spheres of production and reproduction—that is, how biological and social life is maintained across time.[2] Having said that, however, it cannot be denied that human beings are, after all, symbolic creatures; they make meaning. And, in interpreting reality through interactive symbolization, reflection, and dialogue, we also mold and transform it. It is through symbolic and linguistic processes such as these that people collectively reach an understanding of reality that then informs their actions.

This brings us back again to the question of the consciousness and transformative potential of the working class. Debates about class consciousness have raged in Western social theory for well over a century now (to chart the terrain of the debate, see, for instance, Althusser 1969; Calhoun 1982; Lukacs 1971; Mann 1987; Marx 1967; and Thompson 1966) with no definitive resolution in sight. Many questions remain, including (1) how to define and assess class consciousness; (2) the relative importance of material forces of production, class struggle, life experience, and culture in promoting class consciousness; (3) when, where, and among whom has class consciousness developed; and (4) the role of class consciousness in promoting revolutionary social change. Interest in these issues provides the guiding impulse for much sociological inquiry (direct inspirations for this work include Calhoun 1982; Corbin 1981; Gaventa 1980; Hopkins 1986; Nash 1979; Ollman 1987; Taussig 1980; and Yarrow 1982).

This ethnography investigates two subsections of the contentious area of debate around class consciousness and political ideology. First, it seeks to characterize the political ideology of contemporary white Harlan miners, using both their words and their actions as indicators. How did miners explain their political, economic, and social past and present? What actions did they take? What did they see as their future, and by what means did they plan to arrive there? More broadly, what principles and values did they identify as guides to action (see also Foley 1989; Nash 1979; Wilentz 1984)? To what extent did their actions conform to their stated goals? And, finally, what was their vision of an ideal community or society? I spent much of the eighteen months in Harlan engaging miners and owners in conversations around these topics, both informally and through tape-recorded interviews. Local oral history interviews (SECC-OHP), the Harlan newspaper, and locally produced histories (Forester 1986), memoirs (Garland 1983; Jones 1985), poetry, music, and memorials offered a rich public discourse for analysis as well. Last, but not least importantly, I observed people's actions as I participated in the community, as a churchgoer, club member, hospital and nursing home volunteer, and a community college instructor. Throughout this process, I sought to determine the salience of class to identity, ideology, and action. How important was class in understanding the political dynamics of the local community? How did class relate to the other important social structural and ideological forces in Harlan County, such as kinship, community, religion, and, later, gender? And, finally, are contemporary Harlan County miners class conscious; do they identify by class and use this identification as a basis for collective action?

The title "Two Sides to Everything," taken from my interview with a woman miner, foreshadows the ethnographic material and interpretations that follow. "There's two sides to everything," she told me. "And I try to look at both sides." Her remarks were in keeping with much of the public discourse in Harlan County: it recognized the reality of political conflict yet concentrated upon creating community harmony, mitigating the negative effects of past conflicts, and forging a consensus between old adversaries. This was a theme repeatedly sounded during interviews and conversations. A pro-union miner might recall events leading up to a strike and then offer his recollection of the management's perspective, giving a sympathetic account of the market and organizational binds of his bosses. Likewise, the president of the Harlan County Coal Operators' Association would tell me that the miners' unionization movement had been both proper and necessary. It had countered the abuses of a previous generation of coal operators and had benefited not only the miners but the community and the industry. The tension between cooperative political discourse and action, on the one hand, and conflictual discourse and action, on the other, posed an interpretational challenge, to both the ethnographer and her subjects, as will be apparent throughout this book. For now, let me suggest that more research should be done on the structural and ideological contradictions that give rise to this interplay between conflict and cooperation, a dynamic that does not set Harlan apart from other American towns (see Greenhouse 1986; 1992, 247).

In analyzing this ethnographic material, I have found certain concepts to be indispensable. So, in spite of my recognition that disciplinary jargon often serves as a barrier to enjoyable reading, I have continued to utilize them. The following dicussion is offered to assist the reader in making sense of these concepts. My apologies to its resemblance to a textbook glossary but, because the project was so heavily inspired by theoretical concerns, it should come as no surprise that it should be somewhat constrained by such terminology. The first important concept is "dialectic," a term that I have already utilized in describing my research process as a dialectic between theory and experience (or, in Marxian terminology, practice). The term *dialectic* denotes the interpenetration and interaction of social elements that have been separated only for heuristic purposes. These "separate" elements include topical foci, such as economics, politics, religion, and the family, as well as more general oppositions between theory and practice, the material and the ideological, individualism and corporatism, and masculine and feminine. The term *dialectic*, then, serves to direct the reader's attention to the interactions and mediations between phenomena that are *really* connected, even though they may be separated for analytic purposes.

A second central concept, "discourse," refers to linguistic or dialogical constructions of material and social reality. Following Marc Steinberg (1991, 197), I define discourse as "the process through which actors create propositional or evaluative accounts of the relations between themselves, other actors and situations, and larger social processes." Much of this text, particularly the final chapter and epilogue, concerns public verbal discourses that I have identified as relevant to class consciousness and conflict. The concept of discourse, however, is not confined to verbal communication but also applies to written texts, symbols, and ritual practices. Regardless of its form, any such "process of meaning production is itself always governed by systems of rules delineating the use of the symbols that convey meanings (signifiers), the meaning attributed to them, and restrictions on those who engage in the process. Discourse is thus viewed as a productive process, with certain homologies to other forms of production" (ibid., 197). Defining discourse as a "productive process" emphasizes the "back-stage" (Goffman 1959) labor devoted to meaning-making while highlighting its role in securing ideological dominance and public consensus. My analysis of discourse is more reminiscent of Habermas (1987) than of Foucault (1982), inasmuch as I concentrate upon the subject's construction of discourse more than the discursive construction of the subject.

Antonio Gramsci's concept of hegemony, the "unrecognizable shaping of alternatives" that makes noncoercive governance possible (1971, 257–64), is also important to this analysis. The process of shaping alternatives can be seen as a discursive endeavor that, by virtue of its premises, logic, and rules, equates class interest with the overall social good. It involves both conflictual and cooperative processes of interpretation and persuasion. Once it is established, hegemony must be constantly rearticulated or reconfigured to meet the challenge of counterhegemonic ideologies, internal ideological contradictions, and changing material conditions.

Although the consolidation of class hegemony is primarily a discursive endeavor, the concepts of discourse and hegemony should be differentiated. *Discourse* refers to a broader, more diffuse process that encompasses the dialogical, symbolic, and interpretive constructions of reality, in addition to the construction of hegemony. Furthermore, discourses generally accomplish many tasks simultaneously—not simply the construction of class identity or ruling-class dominance, but also the construction of gender, race, community, region, body, and self. Texts, such as this ethnography, cannot represent the discursive arena in its complexity; they are, by necessity, simplified and selective.

The next concept, ideology, has found a niche in vernacular English and, hence, is the most difficult to define and control. Here, the term *ideology* is meant to refer to the symbolic realm of ideas as opposed to the material arena of physical and biological reality. The selection of the term *ideological,* over alternatives like *ideal, ideational,* or *symbolic,* highlights the political implications of socially constructed representations, even those called "knowledge" or "truth." Unfortunately, ideology has often been confused with propaganda, the self-conscious and deliberate dissemination of information or arguments designed to advance an interest or cause. But, in this text, *ideology* refers *not* to the manipulative spread of (mis)information, but rather to a diffuse, ubiquitous, unconscious, and unavoidable consequence of human thought and interaction.

Like other cultural Marxists, I find the classical Marxist concept of "false consciousness" to be of little utility. The employment of such a concept necessarily implies that the scholar is uniquely capable of differentiating truth from falsehood and that she/he is either more intelligent or less socially constrained than those about whom she/he writes (see also Burawoy 1991, 4–5; Gouldner 1970; Hall 1988, 44). Such an idea contradicts the central materialist and realist premise that all knowledge represents an approximation to reality—neither completely true nor completely false. The difference between truth and error, in the end, is a difference of degree (Sayers 1985, 167).

Having gotten this definitional task out of the way, we can now turn our attention to a brief overview of the book itself. It is divided into seven chapters, starting with three chapters that present a historical narrative of Harlan County as told through the "Norton" family. Although based upon actual persons, this family, their friends, neighbors, co-workers, and associates have all been given pseudonyms. In addition, I have changed elements of their biographies in order to protect their anonymity. Chapters 1 through 3 concentrate primarily upon three generations of the Norton family (from 1910 to 1986) and represent much of the historical and ethnographic data upon which my interpretations analyses are based. Interspersed throughout Chapters 1 through 3 are personal recollections of our time together and a few preliminary analytic comments, as well. As a compilation of facts, stories, memories, and preliminary interpretations, these three chapters more faithfully represent the dialectical and dialogical nature of my fieldwork encounter than one in which the author has exorcised herself and the academic literature from which her representation has emerged (see, for instance, Clifford and Marcus 1986; Frisch 1990; Okley and Callaway 1992).

Chapter 4 discusses the personal, social, and ideological importance of kinship in Harlan County. I argue that ideals about community behavior represent an extension of the kinship ideology, which in turn provides an important basis of class identity. Kinship ideology also informs local critiques of capitalism. Yet because kin and community ties crosscut class allegiances, this sort of solidarity simultaneously undermines class identity and solidarity. This chapter briefly explores some of the structural and ideological forces that divide classes internally, a phenomenon that is too often ignored in simplified statements about how ruling ideas reflect the interests of a monolithic ruling class (Marx and Engels 1942; see also Hall 1988, 35–57).

Chapter 5 explores the political ideology of the Harlan miners who participated in my research, with particular attention to its critical elements and transformative potential. Such an exercise, while potentially constructive and enlightening, turns out to be quite treacherous, in light of the variations within the political ideologies of this group of miners, generational shifts in their politics, experiences, and economic contexts, and the historical ebb and flow of Harlan County labor militance. This chapter offers a carefully considered set of speculations and interpretations, which are inevitably tentative and potentially controversial.

Chapter 6 considers the ambiguous relationship between religion and class consciousness, drawing from twelve months of observation and worship in a rural, working-class, Southern Baptist church as well as a three-week visit to a Pentecostal revival. Classic Marxian dismissals of religion as an "opiate of the masses" and portrayals of Appalachian religion as "fatalistic" (see especially Weller 1965, 37–40) are discussed in light of historical and ethnographic evidence from Harlan County. For the most part, however, this chapter elucidates the dialectic between religious discursive constructions of class, community, and gender with contemporary material and social structural contexts. It does not seek to document regional church history or to provide a semiotic analysis of ritual practices or speech, as laudable as those projects may be (Dorgan 1987; Titon 1988; see also Sovine 1979). In this chapter, more than others, gender provides a primary analytic focus.

Chapter 7 examines the Harlan Miners' Memorial as an *object* that enscribes collective memory about the past, and as a *process* by which such memory is constructed. Once again, this chapter highlights the contradictions between communal harmony and class division, as they relate to class consciousness among miners in Harlan. The chapter then closes with an update on the fate of the monument since its dedication, a reflection of the ongoing dialectic of class conflict and community solidarity in contemporary Harlan County. In a closing Afterword, I offer a brief enumeration of the central arguments and observations made in this book and then reflect upon the shortcomings and insights of the work it represents.

CHAPTER 1

Of Bellies and Hearts

When I arrived at graduate school, my advisor presented me with the gift of a book called *The Sociological Imagination* (1959) by C. Wright Mills. The primary task and promise of social science, Mills argued, was to explore the intersection of individual biography, history, and society (6) in such a way as to distinguish between personal "troubles" and social "issues" while simultaneously recognizing the connection between the two (8). When I read Mills's work, I had just begun to reinterpret my own experiences of marginality in light of a broader social and historical context. I had previously felt embarrassed by the ridicule my Appalachian accent often inspired, ashamed about my ancestors' involvement in the Hatfield-McCoy feud, and uneasy about TV shows like "The Beverly Hillbillies" and movies like *Deliverance*. But books like Helen Lewis et al.'s (1978) *Colonialism in America: The Appalachian Case,* Henry Shapiro's (1978) *Appalachia on Our Mind,* and David Whisnant's (1983) *All That Is Native and Fine* helped me to see how mainstream America's stigmatization of Appalachia and its people might be linked to a history of economic exploitation and political domination of the mountain region as well as the nation's own fledgling efforts to forge a coherent cultural identity and consolidate its capitalist economy (see also Batteau 1990; Foster 1988). All of these books have influenced my work but Mills, in particular, has inspired chapters 1 through 3, which interweave the "history" of Harlan County with the stories of the Norton family and their friends, neighbors, and in-laws.

I have placed the word *history* in quotation marks to remind the reader that history, in this case, is nothing more than the representation of past experience and, as such, it is an important exercise in meaning-making that informs collective and personal identity. This particular history is based upon eighteen months of participant-observation and archival and oral history research in two Harlan County coal-mining communities. In addition to hundreds of conversations and observations documented in my field notes over the period, thirty-seven locally collected oral histories provided the database for this project. These were supplemented and cross-checked with information available from the local newspaper, census data, the Harlan Public Library's genealogical collection (see especially Burns 1870), and histories and memoirs written by people who lived and worked in the area, including William D. Forester, Jim Garland, G. C. "Red" Jones, and George Titler.

In constructing the narrative shape and emphases of this particular history, I have tried to follow the leads of the Harlan Countians whom I knew and interviewed for this project. However, I have also interspersed my own observations and reflections, as well a few preliminary analyses in these introductory chapters. This writing strategy, I think, more accurately reflects the dialectical nature of the ethnographic enterprise than would completely segregating "ethnography" from "analysis." In the interests of clarity, however, I have concentrated much of the analysis in the second half of the book, chapters 4 through 7. Let us now turn to the Norton family.

è♣

My primary daily connection to the Norton family was not through its patriarch, retired coal miner Ernie Norton, but through his adult daughter Cindy Norton Carson. Cindy and I met about three months after I moved to Harlan in 1985. We were introduced by one of her husband's friends, who had kindly invited me to go "four-wheeling" and picnicking with them in the mountains. She and I became close friends almost immediately. She was only five years my senior and could have been the sister I never had. We talked and laughed. We went "driving around town," shopping, and bowling. Sometimes we stayed up late watching videos and eating nacho cheese Doritos. After about six months, I moved to the community where Cindy had grown up and began regularly attending her family's church. That spring, we worked together on the Harlan Miners' Memorial Project, which is described in some detail in chapter 7. But if Cindy was like a sister to me, she was definitely an *older* sister, or perhaps an aunt. She was solicitous toward me, often pointing out what an easy life I had and how naive I could be. Maybe she "mothered" me because she was so used to taking care of her daughter, Julie. More likely, however, she guided and protected me because I was an outsider, dependent upon her for knowledge, interviews, and social contacts.

Her parents played a similar role in my life. Her father, whom I had interviewed on a preliminary research trip to Harlan in the summer of 1984, helped me find an apartment in Ages when, after six months, I decided that my original residence did not provide the optimal base for the type of participant-observation research I wanted to do. Cindy's mother offered me home-cooked meals after church every Sunday. She was a good cook; I gained twelve pounds in the year I lived in Ages! In retrospect, I think my status as a single woman, with no children, contributed to my subordinate, dependent position. It seemed that the Nortons did not regard an individual, particularly a woman, as a full adult until they married. Even though I was 25 years old, living independently, engaged to be married, and gainfully employed, they thought I needed the guidance and protection of parents. Although I sometimes found their protective attitude toward me amusing and ironic, I did not consciously resent their solicitous attitude. After all, I really did need them to help me: to share information, tell me about their lives, introduce me to people, and give me directions when I got lost in the unfamiliar terrain of Harlan County.

The Nortons seemed to know a lot about Harlan County: the best routes to take to any destination, who the "movers and shakers" were, where to find the best food, which high school team would win on Friday night, which churches handled snakes, who was sleeping with whom, who was "no account" (lazy, dishonest, drank too much, took drugs, beat their wives and kids), and whom to consult on almost any topic. But they were sorely lacking in knowledge of their family's history beyond the grandparental generation. I encountered the same shortcoming among community college students when I asked them to complete a family genealogical chart and compile and analyze their family histories. Few could record more than two or three generations without consulting parents, grandparents, and family Bibles. While most people knew their first cousins quite well, all others were lumped together into an undifferentiated, nebulous category of "second cousins" or "some kin to me."

This should not have surprised me since I myself could not name each of my great-great-grandparents, much less remember where and when they were born. I also have the same mental block about cousins that plagued my students. I do my best to be specific, however. Midge is my maternal grandmother's first cousin, I say. Or L. R. is my dad's first cousin. Nevertheless, I unreasonably expected more from my eastern Kentucky neighbors than I had from myself. Perhaps my misconceptions sprang from my highly selective reading of Appalachian ethnographies attesting to the social and personal salience of kinship. Perhaps I thought that the subjects of these ethnographies just reeled off lengthy family histories and complex kinship connections from the tops of their heads. Maybe I thought that this kinship data had leaped on to these authors' pages, fully assembled and articulated. My experiences in Harlan County disabused me of any such romantic notions. Yet even though compiling the Norton family history took more detective work than I had originally imagined, it was well worth the effort.

❧

Ernie Norton's mother's paternal great-great-grandparents, Samuel and Rebecca (Niles) Brown, came to Harlan County around 1807, arriving with other Euroamerican settlers who settled the region in the post–Revolutionary War era. In this initial settling period, Harlan's communities remained small and relatively isolated. Travel in the rugged terrain was difficult and time consuming. Mule drivers brought supplies to local merchants from Hagen, Virginia, along the treacherous trail on Stone Mountain where Cindy and I first met "four-wheeling" and picnicking. But many of life's necessities were produced locally by subsistence farm families.

The county's first Euroamerican settler, Samuel Howard, arrived in Harlan County in 1795, five to fifteen years before the Browns did. All of the founding families—the Howards, Skidmores, Turners, Lewises, Smiths, Jones, Farmers, and Brittains—had arrived in 1819, when the state legislature created the county from portions of Floyd and Knox counties. They named it Harlan, after Major Silas Harlan who died in the Battle of Blue Licks, one of Kentucky's Revolutionary War battles. Harlan was one of several Kentucky counties carved out of larger administrative territories during the nineteenth century. Mountainous terrain and lack of transportation networks account, in part, for the proliferation of Kentucky counties in this era. But other factors played a role as well. Most important among these were the political ambitions of early settler families. These "first families" sought to consolidate their political power by creating new counties to command from administrative town centers that they already dominated (Ireland 1977, 140–50).

Until the 1910s, Harlan County's communities were composed of expanded kin networks, with households connected to another by blood and marriage ties. Many communities were named after the families that originally settled, organized, and dominated them: Smith, Cawood, Rosspoint, Jones' Creek, Hensley Settlement, and Holmes' Mill, where Cindy's ancestors lived, serve as a few examples of such kin-based, agricultural communities. Communities like these were relatively small, consisting of only a few hundred residents (*Census of Population* 1830). The population of Harlan County's six hundred square miles did not exceed 6,200 throughout the entire century, about ten people per square mile (table 1.1).

TABLE 1.1
Population of Harlan County
1820–1990

Year	Population
1820	1,961
1830	2,929
1840	3,015
1850	4,268
1860	5,494
1870	4,415
1880	5,278
1890	6,197
1900	9,838
1910	10,566
1920	31,546
1930	64,557
1940	75,275
1950	71,751
1960	51,107
1970	37,370
1980	41,889
1990	36,574

Source: Census of Population, Harlan County 1830–1990.

Among these residents were members of the Brown family, a family that had done well for itself in those early agricultural days. By 1830, members of the Brown family were represented in 5 of the 308 Harlan County households engaged in full-time farming (*Census of Agriculture* 1830). Rebecca Brown had died in 1820, after having born Samuel five children. Together they had amassed over four hundred acres of land. Much of it was uncleared mountain-side. The Brown family tended the flattest sections in cornfields and vegetable gardens and kept livestock in the hills. They planted corn as far up the slopes as they could. Several local jokes persist to attest to the difficulty of such hillside farming. Mountain farmers are said to have one leg longer than the other from plowing their fields. Or did you hear the one about the farmer falling out of his cornfield and breaking his collarbone?

All but one of the Brown children had married by 1832, when Samuel Brown deeded a plot of land to his eldest son as a wedding gift. He did the same for his second daughter. Two other daughters had married men from other nearby communities and had moved off the old place. And the "baby" of the family, George, stayed in his father's home even after he married in 1832. When Samuel Brown died, he left the original house and 120 acres of the best farm land surrounding it to George. George and his wife, Elizabeth, had seven children, three of whom survived to adulthood. Of them, only the eldest son, William, remained in the community to farm the land. The ultimate destination of the other two children is unclear. Both had initially headed for neighboring Letcher County. The family has not since kept up with these two branches of Browns.

William and his wife, Mary, had six children. This time the land went to their youngest child, Clarence, who married Cora in 1909, two years after his mother's death. The remaining descendants moved off the farm. Two became tenant farmers in the Holmes' Mill community.[1] One became a logger in Knott County. The fate of the other child is not known, but he seems to have left the state of Kentucky altogether. This pattern of geographic mobility does not appear to be unusual for either the region or the period (see Corbin 1981; Egerton 1983; Shifflett 1991), as Appalachian farmers sought better plots of land or were displaced from their land by debt, estate conflicts, inadequate farm land, unclear title, failure to pay taxes, lawsuits (see especially Waller 1988), and pressure from land speculators and railroad, timber, and coal companies. As one Harlan County out-migrant recalled, "I was ready to leave Harlan County. We had lost our land, didn't get a dime for it. I couldn't see nothing to hold me in Harlan County. The way it all turned out, I never was sorry I left" (Egerton 1983, 86).

Ernie Norton remembered quite clearly the generation of his family that included his grandparents, Clarence and Cora Brown. He had spent a lot of time with these folks during his childhood. Growing up in the coal community of Ages, Kentucky, he had visited his Grandmother Cora almost every day when his mother was busy with chores and wanted keep him "out from under foot." When his parents temporarily separated in 1932, Ernie and his mother moved in with Clarence and Cora Brown. They were like "second parents" to Ernie, he recalled.

It was Clarence and Cora Brown, Ernie's fondly remembered grandparents, who made the transition from agriculture to coal mining. It was an important shift for this line of the Brown family. As Ernie recalled, his grandfather regretted this turn of events, although not bitterly. For many years, he struggled to make a decent living for his family. He always "came up short." He could not see how his increasingly infertile land could support his six children, so, finally, in 1924, he agreed to sell the land to a distant cousin, a Holmes' Mill storekeeper and part-time farmer. Even after he became a coal miner and moved his family into a coal camp, Clarence continued to tend a vegetable garden on the old Brown home place. His cousin, who was not farming the land, did not object. He was earning a healthy income from his store and the sale of timber and mineral rights. Financially more prosperous and independent than Clarence, this particular cousin proved to be an important source of support and refuge during the 1930s, when labor-management violence and economic decline threatened Clarence's family.

The Brown family's move, from farming to coal mining, was part of a local and regional trend during this period. From 1910 to 1930, the number of farms in Harlan County decreased from nearly 16,000 to 786 (Banks 1983–84, 90). By 1985, there were no full-time farms there. Farming provided only 0.06 percent of the personal earnings for Harlan residents compared to the 31.4 percent of the residents' personal earnings provided by coal mining (Bureau of Economic Analysis [BEA] 1991). By then, coal mining had replaced agriculture as the mainstay of the local economy, providing the productive base for a host of related enterprises, from retail to construction to service industries. Accompanying this decline of agriculture was a general shift in the pattern of land ownership from county- to absentee-controlled, a pattern that was common throughout the mountain region (see Appalachian Land Ownership Task Force 1980).

A number of factors combined to push the Browns out of agriculture in the opening decades of the twentieth century. The steep terrain made farming difficult anyway; but by then erosion and decreasing soil fertility had decreased their yields. The situation deteriorated throughout the late nineteenth century, as the population increased and land was subdivided for each succeeding generation (see table 1.1). With so much pressure on the land, farmers could not leave fields fallow long enough to recover their fertility. By the end of the nineteenth century, the subsistence agriculture economy was in crisis (see also Arcury 1990; Kephart 1913, 35; Pudup 1990a; Waller 1988, 35–40).

Things were not always so bleak for Harlan County farmers, even though they worked in some of the highest, steepest mountains that Central Appalachia had to offer. In the early years, farmers sold livestock in lowland Southern markets to meet the demands of plantations engaged in commodity production. Mountain farmers, like others in Kentucky, were hampered by the state's unwillingness to invest in the construction of roads, canals, and railroads. Harlan County farmers, lacking a navigable waterway and failing to generate enough capital locally to fund transportation developments, eventually lost in a market competition with lowland producers, especially those in the Midwest (Pudup 1988, 23, 98–101). Although mountain agricultural communities were by no means identical in their adaptations or links to commodity markets (Arcury 1990; Blee and Billings 1992; Weingartner, Billings, and Blee 1989; Dunn 1988; Pudup 1990a), by the late nineteenth century, Harlan County had settled into a subsistence pattern that was to last well into the twentieth century (Eller 1979, 92; Pudup 1986 115–17).

In Harlan's 1860 census, for example, 32 men out of a total population of 5,371 claimed to be professionals. Among them were six merchants, four lawyers, two political officials (a sheriff and a jailor), one doctor, one teacher, ten clergymen, three blacksmiths, one wagonmaker, one millwright, one mechanic, one hatter, and one basketmaker (Census of Population 1860). These professionals comprised only 3.8 percent of the male population; all of them farmed part-time. The situation had not changed significantly by 1880, when there were five merchants, one lawyer, three political officials (two court clerks and a jailor), one doctor, one miller, and one blacksmith (Census of Population 1880).

This relatively undiversified economy and undifferentiated occupational structure does not indicate that there was no social stratification in the area, however. Some Harlan families ultimately lost their land and either moved away from the county or were forced into tenancy or wage work (see also Dunaway 1993; Pudup 1988). At the other end of the social spectrum, however, there were merchants, lawyers, doctors, and politicians whose social status and wealth secured for them positions of dominance in local politics and society. Many of these people sought education outside the mountain region, where they formed business and political alliances through marriage and friendship. Starting small-scale businesses in timber harvesting and investing in real estate, commerce, and sawmills, this elite played a pivotal role in the industrialization of Harlan County (Pudup 1986, 216–17; 1989; 1991). When capitalist developers and speculators called, the elite was more than ready to answer.

≥♦

Because of its isolation and inaccessibility, Harlan County's elite had to wait a long time, even by Appalachian standards, to reap the benefits of capitalist expansion. The process was begun in 1905, when the Kentennia Corporation, representatives of northeastern business interests, began acquiring land, timber, and mineral rights in Harlan County. Stockholders in the company included Franklin Delano Roosevelt's uncle Warren Delano. Franklin Roosevelt himself journeyed on horseback to Harlan County to assist in surveying. He wrote to his bride, Eleanor, of the harsh terrain, beautiful forests, and bountiful farms he visited in Harlan County (Caudill 1983, 88–89). Six local businessmen obtained seats on Kentennia's board in return for their investments and assistance in facilitating the company's operations. They were Marion Smith, Daniel Skidmore Farmer, William Watkins Noe, Arthur Blankenship Cornett, W. W. Lewis, and William T. Rice, all featured prominently in advertisements the company placed in the local paper (*Harlan Daily Enterprise* [HDE] Supplement, 4 October 1908).

The tasks of surveying land and clearing property titles in Harlan County was complicated by competing claims, unclear boundaries, and inadequate record keeping. This worked to the advantage of land speculators. Unlike most local farmers, land companies could afford to hire surveyors and lawyers to document and research property titles. In many cases, they acquired a "cash poor" farmer's property in return for paying the "back taxes" he owed. Some farmers were in Clarence Brown's position, however: they saw no alternative to selling the farms that could no longer support their families. Others, like Clarence's cousin, chose to sell off their mineral and timber rights while retaining possession of the surface area.[2] Still others sold their land with the hopes of using the proceeds to purchase more-productive land elsewhere (Egerton 1983).

In addition to surveying and clearing land titles, early land speculators promoted the construction of railroads in the county. Unfortunately for Harlan County speculators, the Louisville & Nashville Railroad (L&N) bypassed Harlan in order to construct a link to serve Middlesboro, an elaborate town constructed by the British firm American Association, Ltd. (see Caudill 1983; Gaventa 1980). In 1912, an impatient Dr. Thomas Jefferson Asher of Bell County, eager to take advantage of wartime coal demand, built his own twelve-mile railroad spur into Harlan County. The L&N followed his lead shortly thereafter.

Accompanying the new railroad were Ernie Norton's paternal grandparents, Henry and Mary Norton of Clark County, Kentucky (see figure 1.1). The Nortons were tenant farmers whose failed efforts to secure a stable livelihood farming had sent them to seek their fortunes as wageworkers. Henry's brother, an employee of the L&N railroad, had told them that Harlan County looked to be a promising place to start over. He was simply echoing the forecasts of other observers, for the mood of the times was optimistic. As one journalist forecasted, "One can scarcely predict the possibilities of Harlan—a primeval country, rich beyond belief" (HDE Supplement, 31 October 1986, 9–10).

Others joined them in the move to Harlan County. Some, like the Nortons, were farmers "down on their luck." Others had been encouraged, by state and corporate advertising campaigns designed to supplement the low supply of local labor. The stream of

FIGURE 1.1
Norton Family Genealogical Chart

			Samuel Brown 1782–1835	=	Rebecca Niles 1788–1820
			George Brown 1812–79	=	Elizabeth Gilbert 1820–99
			William Brown 1833–1901	=	Mary Skinner 1849–1907
Henry Norton 1883–1958	=	Mary Boone 1892–1963	Clarence Brown 1888–1943	=	Cora Jones 1896–1951
Will Norton 1906–87			Jess Norton 1908–69	=	Janie Mae Brown 1914–89

Ginny Henderson = Ernest Norton   Daniel Norton   Edith Norton
    1934–   1930–   1933–   1935–

Ernest Norton, Jr.   Cindy Norton   =   Bobby Carson
    1958–   1955–   1953–

Julie Norton
1977–

in-migrants included recently released convicts, Black tenant farmers and miners (mostly from Alabama), and European immigrants (primarily from Italy, Russia, and eastern European countries). Together, they accounted for the largest population increase in local history. Harlan County's 1910 population of roughly 10,000 tripled in just 10 years. By 1930, the population reached its peak of over 64,000 people (see table 1.1).

Much of the new population was involved, directly or indirectly, in coal mining. Coal production expanded from 17,860 tons, in 1911, to 14.5 million tons, in 1928 (Hevener 1978, 3); and the number of local coal mine employees went from zero, in 1910, to 11,920 in 1930 (Banks 1983–84, 91). The new residents brought an increased demand for public services, housing, and consumer goods, which local government and communities were ill-equipped to serve. Much of the burden fell to the coal companies themselves, ninety-two of whom constructed housing for their employees. In fact, they built entire towns almost overnight (HDE

Supplement, 28 February 1982, 2). These towns had many similar features but were not identical. They varied in the number, size, and quality of the homes as well as the types and range of services and amenities they offered. The small companies, most of whom sold coal on the "spot market" for heating purposes, built simple settlements with few amenities. However, large energy corporations and steel companies that produced coal for their own coking operations ("captive mines") had the capital to invest in more-elaborate accommodations to serve a larger pool of employee residents. U.S. Steel, Bethlehem Steel, and the Ford Motor Company, for example, built the larger company towns, complete with infirmaries, stores, opera houses, ball fields, clubhouses, and hotels (see figures 1.2 and 1.3).

Company towns, such as these, were built primarily to house the influx of workers into the county during the 1910s and 1920s. But newcomers were not the only ones to flock to company towns.

FIGURE 1.2
Site of company store building in Lynch, Kentucky, before construction commenced in 1917. Photograph from the Billups Collection at the University of Kentucky Photo Archives.

FIGURE 1.3
Lynch, Kentucky, after construction was completed, circa 1918.
Photograph from the Billups Collection at the University of Kentucky
Photo Archives.

Natives who had sold or were forced off marginal farmsteads also took up residence in company towns. These towns differed from the kin-based, agricultural communities that they had originally settled. For one thing, the residents in coal towns were a more diverse population than the original settlers. In 1910, for instance, Harlan County had only 9 residents of "mixed or foreign parentage" and no non-native whites. By 1930, however, there were 1,374 residents of "mixed or foreign parentage" and 822 foreign-born whites (Census of Population 1910, 1930). The proportion of African Americans had risen as well, from 5.3 percent in 1910 to 8.9 percent in 1930 (calculated from Census of Population 1910 and 1930). Race and ethnicity formed the basis for a pattern of residential segregation that continues today in Harlan County, where a dwindling African American population remains largely clustered around the towns of Benham and Lynch, where their ancestors were originally house and employed. Segregation was common *within* the towns as well. "There were four distinct sections of the town, each determined by either race or job status in the mines," recalled a Benham resident. "These included 'Smokey Row' where the blacks lived, 'New Benham' where the common laborers lived and eastern European ethnics lived including one street named for the Hungarians called 'Hunky Street.' Another section ranging from about Poplar Street to Hemlock Street was called 'Middle Benham' where non-ethnics and middle-income families lived. 'Silk Stocking Row' was where the coal officials, foremen, superintendents, etc., lived" (HDE Supplement, 31 October 1986, 14; see also Herrin 1985; Shifflett 1991; Trotter 1990). Racial segregation and hostility, it seems, were only partly mitigated by the shared work experiences, political and economic interests, and unionization struggles of Harlan's miners.

In addition to cultural diversity, the industrialization of Harlan County introduced new cleavages between local farmers and workers, on the one hand, and the local elite, on the other. Professionals and politicians, who formerly owed their economic and political success to their "farmer cousins," switched their allegiance to the more powerful coal operators (Forester 1986, 147–91; Garland 1983, 129–30, 173, 189; Hevener 1978, 106–23; Jones 1985, 130–39; Titler n.d., 48–91). Construction of coal camps and investments in Harlan's communities further differentiated Harlan's towns. The county was no longer a network of relatively equal and autonomous farming communities administered from the county seat of Harlan. By the late 1920s, Harlan, Cumberland, and Benham-Lynch had emerged as major commercial and political centers while other communities either remained the underdeveloped, dependent camps of immigrants and workers, or were abandoned altogether (Census of Population 1920 and 1930). The Browns' former community of Holmes' Mill, for example, was one of the many settlements that languished.

≈

The Brown family moved from Holmes' Mill to Brookside, a modest coal camp, in 1924. They did not think highly of coal camp life in these first years, and their reaction was not unique. Among the chief complaints registered against such towns was that the company owned everything in them and, therefore, had too much control over the miners and their families. If a miner was fired or hurt, for instance, he lost his job and his family was evicted from their company-owned home. In addition, a company could force its employees to shop at its store by issuing their wages in "scrip" that could be redeemed only by the company.

Of course, some found company homes to be an improvement over their farmsteads, and many preferred the conveniences and excitement of town life over their previous existence. Still, they generally also recognized that moving from rural farmsteads to coal towns involved a trade-off. The overwhelming majority of those I interviewed thought the price of company-town life was too high.[3] "I was pretty lucky in one way," explained one miner I interviewed. "You see, my dad moved into a camp there, in Black Joe and, see, that's how come I didn't move into a coal camp. . . . The company had rules, at that time, that they wanted you to take out an order from the store to buy your furniture and different stuff. If you didn't, they'd lay you off or fire you or something; but, since I didn't live in their camps, they couldn't put me out of their 'house row.' I didn't get involved with having to take out one of their big store orders. That was one way I dodged a whole lot of trouble."

About three-quarters of Harlan County's miners were not so "lucky": they ended up living in the company towns (Bethell 1983, xxii). Joe Phipps's father, for instance, was told by his employer that he would be fired if he did not move into the company board-ing house.[4] Phipps had been staying with his uncle in order to save money to bring his wife and children from Tennessee to join him. It was quite common for miners to become ensnared in a cycle of credit and debt at the company store. When payday arrived, many found themselves "in the hole," owing the company money for groceries, furniture, and work supplies bought in the previous month. In those days, miners had to purchase their supplies for work out of their paychecks; money was also deducted for rent and the services of the company doctor.

In a company town, the coal operator served not only as the employer, the landlord, and the merchant, but also as the govern-ment and the law. Operators hired assistants to direct, administer, and maintain order in their towns. They built their own jails, armed their own guards, and, in some cases, erected fences around the perimeters of the "communities" they had constructed (see also Portelli 1990). In times of labor unrest and union activism, compa-nies placed machine-gun and surveillance towers around their towns and expanded their cadre of private deputies (Hevener 1978; Jones 1985; Portelli 1990; Titler n.d.). Because they also owned and operated their own post offices, churches, schools, and other public spaces, operators were able to monitor communication around their towns. Mail could be opened and read before it was delivered. Guards could eavesdrop on conversations and spy on meetings. For that reason, most union organizing rallies and meetings of the 1930s occurred outside the confines of the company town.

Company control was not restricted to company towns, by any means. Even in the ostensibly independent towns of Harlan, Cumberland, and Evarts, coal operators put local democracy to the test. By 1930, the coal industry served as the driving force behind the local economy, providing the patronage and wages that kept local businesses afloat. Local businessmen-politicians could ill afford to alienate their wealthiest patrons. Some local politicians depended even more directly upon the coal operators: They were employed by the companies as doctors and lawyers; they held seats on corporate boards of directors; they had invested capital in coal companies; and, finally, some local politicians had become coal operators themselves. Coal companies, both large and small, endorsed candidates and provided much-needed campaign funds. Some said that operators "delivered the vote" more directly, by either providing their employees with a premarked ballot ("the company slate"), bribing voters, or, as last resorts, tampering with ballots and stealing ballot boxes (Forester 1986, 146–91; Hevener 1978). "They [the Harlan County Coal Operators' Association] did buy the elections," a prominent coal operator's daughter reported. "Yes, they stole the elections. They paid for 'em. They would give two dollars and liquor for their votes. . . . but I don't feel bad about it. I really and truly don't" (Sue Bassham Cudd by James Goode, SECC-OHP, 3 March 1984).

Wielding a formidable combination of political and economic power, coal operators obviously dominated the county, but not without encountering resentment and resistance from the "common folks." "They had better houses, clean and everything," complained one Harlan miner. "The workers and operators didn't have much to do with each other and their children didn't either. . . . They [operators] were treated with respect . . . because workers were afraid not to. . . . Harlan County was controlled by the coal operators" (Cecil Stallard by Tony Sizemore, SECC-OHP, 2 April 1982). Local oral history interviews (SECC-OHP; Portelli 1990, 140–42) as well as autobiographical and historical accounts of the period (Dreiser 1932; Forester 1986; Garland 1983; Hevener 1978; Jones 1985; Title n.d.) include massive amounts of testimony against coal operators and the company town system. In a few cases, local miner-activists generalized their complaints to include not just coal operators or company towns, but the entire capitalist system. Song lyrics like "Which Side Are You On?" and "I Hate the Capitalist System" suggest that some level of class consciousness was achieved by Harlan Countians in the 1930s, even if it was held only fleetingly by a small minority.

Even during the pitched labor-management battles of the 1930s, miners were far from unified in their condemnation of coal companies. And it would be a gross oversimplification to claim that nobody in Harlan County had a single fond memory of company-town life. Alessandro Portelli (1990, 140–55), for instance, has collected a number of oral history narratives from Harlan County, praising coal camp conditions, in particular the quality construction of houses and company efforts to keep the town clean and well maintained. Some company bosses—Robert Lawson from the Louellen camp, for example—appeared as benevolent father figures in miners' accounts (140–46). Coal companies brought Harlan residents increased access to professional medical care, which many saw as an improvement. Likewise, many, including the Browns and Nortons, credited coal companies with expanding educational opportunities in the county, which in 1880 had no full-time schoolteacher. Four generations of Browns had been minimally educated in Harlan County. They could at best sign or initial contracts and deeds, and perhaps read a few words from their Bible or primary reader. After moving to the coal camps, however, the Brown children and grandchildren went to school at least through the eighth grade; most went through high school (see also Dotson 1943).

The wider variety of retail goods, although they seduced some families into indebtedness and financial hardship, relieved some of the burdens on local women, who had previously formed the backbone of the home manufacturing economy. Ernie recalled that his grandmother especially liked "store-bought" dresses, preferring them to the homespun and flour-sack dresses she had worn as a child. "That woman never liked to sew—not even quilts!" Ernie would later chuckle in mock disbelief. Finally, it is important to note that coal mining compared favorably to tenancy and hillside subsistence farming in the eyes of many. Farming is strenuous and, sometimes, lonely work. Every family member worked hard on marginal hillside farms, like the Browns', and still they were barely surviving. Ernie Norton's uncle Will compared mining favorably to farming, when he observed: "Mining isn't so bad. It gets you out of the weather!"

In addition, company-town residents, in particular natives who remained in familiar landscapes and retained ties to their extended kin networks and to local churches and communities, could draw upon considerable social and cultural resources as they made the transition to life in company towns. More-specific discussions and clarifications of these resources constitute the primary goal of chapter 4, although it must be clear by now that the Browns were one such family. For the present, however, let us prolong our detour from the story of the Brown-Norton family long enough to trace some of the work-related sources of power, resistance, and collective identity that all Harlan miners shared, regardless of the racial, ethnic, and cultural differences that frequently divided them.

❧

In those first decades after the Harlan field was opened (1915–1930s), the organization of mine work, particularly labor's central role in the production process, contributed to the individual and collective strength of local miners in struggles over the contested worksite terrain (Edwards 1979). When the Harlan field was first opened in the 1910s, mine work was not highly mechanized. Workers used dynamite, augers, and picks to dislodge the coal from underground seams. Then they loaded the coal with shovels into horse- or mule-driven cars, or gondolas, which transported the mineral to the processing plant, located outside the mine, where rocks, slate, and other impurities were removed (see figure 1.4). At this time, workers utilized strength, skill, and knowledge in conducting a variety of production activities. Since work took place in areas called "rooms" that were separated by rock walls and support pillars (timbers), close management supervision was difficult, and, for the most part, miners exercised a great deal of control over the

FIGURE 1.4
Coal miner, Harry Fain, hand-loading coal in 1946. This photo was
taken by Russell Lee (Photo #12 from the Russell Lee Collection
[79PA103] at the University of Kentucky Photo Archives).

speed, timing, and direction of their work. In this regard, the underground mines where they worked stood in stark contrast to the company towns where many of them lived. Miners at work could, to some degree, escape the scrutiny of their employers.

In the 1910s and 1920s, many Harlan coal companies subcontracted sections of their operations to a worker who could hire his own assistants. This miner supervised and coordinated his work team, often composed of kinfolk, neighbors, and friends. This is how Ernie Norton's father, Jess, and his uncle Will got their start in mining as teenagers. At the ages of thirteen and fifteen, they were hired by the father of a schoolmate to drive mule-driven carts of coal out of the mines.[5] As they grew bigger, stronger, and more experienced, they moved on to more-demanding work. While this arrangement freed companies from the cost of preparing a site for production and from supervisory duties, it also increased workers' control over their time and work.

It was common for miners in this period, for example, to stop working when they had loaded enough coal to earn them their target pay. They might leave work to hunt, fish, farm, recuperate from a hard night's drinking, or start drinking again. Supervisors did not approve of such practices, as they preferred a predictable, well-disciplined workforce who would maximize production. "Their [Appalachian miners] shiftless methods of living have not accustomed them to continuous and sustained labor and very little suffices," complained one mining engineer. "In short, they resemble the negro in their desire for frequent periods of 'laying off'" (Fowler 1904, 386–87). Similar observations were made by others, who noted that "It has been his [the mountaineer's] wont to rest during the unfavorable season, or while provisions are at hand" (Schockel 1916, 130) and "Every man is accustomed to be his own master, to do his own work in his own time. . . . He has little sense of the value of time" (Semple 1961, 581). The subcontracting system, the craftsmanship of mining, and in some cases the family's continued reliance on nonwage sources of subsistence fostered a sense of independence and solidarity among Harlan's miners (Dix 1988; Yarrow 1985).

Mine operators sought to circumvent miners' control over production processes and to increase labor discipline in a number of ways during this period. Some operations, for instance, implemented "cleanup system" work organization. According to the rules of this system, employees could not stop work until all of the dislodged coal had been loaded into cars and moved out of the mine. This was to prevent miners from cutting the work shift short or leaving when they felt they had earned a fair day's pay.

Employers also attempted to control leisure activities, particularly alcohol consumption, which they saw as a deterrent to work discipline. In West Virginia, David Corbin notes, "The miner did not need any special day or excuse to drink" (1981, 35). Corbin reports the following quote from a coal company official, "I am not a prohibitionist but saloons hurt coal production. The coal states, at least, should be dry. I believe the operators are unanimous on this question" (36). Over in Harlan County, Kentucky, the situation appeared to be comparable. In fact, the most common memories of the first "boom days" of coal mining in Harlan revolved around the violence and disorder of company towns where groups of men congregated to drink, gamble, and fight (see also Hevener

1978, 23–25; Portelli 1990, 145; Shifflett 1991, 164–68). As one man put it, "They [the miners] usually had Sundays off, sometimes Saturdays. . . . There wasn't but one thing to do in a coal camp: drink. And they did it." In Lynch, where this miner lived, U.S. Coal & Coke took strong measures against such employees. "If a person lived in that coal camp [Lynch] and he was an employee of that coal company [U.S. Coal & Coke], he did work every day that the coal company deemed necessary. Even if he was home in bed with the mumps, the measles, the flu, pneumonia, spinal meningitis, or *anything* else, they came and got him with clubs and beat him to the mines. That's the 'shack rousters.' If a man did not show up for work in the morning, his only excuse was being dead," he recalled.

Geographic mobility constituted a primary form of protest against such heavy-handed management techniques, as David Corbin (1981, 40) has previously observed. Whether in search of steady work, higher wages, or better living and working conditions, Appalachian miners were a mobile group (40–41).[6] In their first ten years of mining, Ernie Norton's uncle Will moved seven times and switched employers five times. He quit one job because he believed that the company was cheating him out of wages by falsely accusing of him loading too much slate in his car. He explained, "They had rules back then. They was pretty tough on you. . . . If you had as much as a cigar box full of slate in your car of coal, the first time, you'd get a three-day layoff. The second time, you was fired. So, they caught me with a cigar box full of slate in my car and they told me I'd have to lay off three days. I told them just to write my time in. I wouldn't take no layoff. I couldn't help throwing that [slate] in there and, if I went back, I'd do the same thing. So, there wasn't no point in me taking a layoff. . . . I quit." In the following decade, local miners sought to resolve this problem by demanding the right to elect a representative to weigh and inspect their loads.

The piece-rate system had several advantages for the coal operators. First, it provided their employees with a powerful incentive to produce coal quickly: the more they produced (at twenty to thirty cents per ton), the higher their take-home pay. If only miners had worked under the same assumption of "profit maximization" as the operators, this system would have worked more efficiently. The system succeeded more clearly, however, in transferring the costs of preparatory work from the operators to the workers. If a work team had to spend seven hours driving a shaft, cleaning out the work area, and setting timbers before they could actually mine and load coal, that was the workers' problem. They only got paid for the coal they produced, not the time they spent. This put the mine foreman, who oversaw and coordinated the work process, in a powerful position. A foreman *could* use work assignments to enforce work discipline or to punish workers. "Most of the time," Ernie's uncle Will told me, foremen sent newcomers to undesirable work areas. ". . . if you was a new beginner going in, you got a place that nobody else wanted. . . . If you want to go in there and lay all this track back there. And set all the timbers, move all that rock out of the way so you could get the coal. If you wanted to do that, you'd have a job."

In 1934, unionized coal operations outside of Harlan County negotiated a contract aimed at addressing some of the problems in the piece-rate system. Only those jobs that directly produced coal were to be paid by the ton, while others were paid by the hour. The only "catch," from the workers' point of view, was that piece-rate workers were required to stay at work for a seven-hour shift—they could not leave at will. By the mid-1950s, most operations had made the transition to shift work, including those in the Harlan field, which had, by then, been organized by the United Mine Workers of America (UMW).

Underground coal mining remains a risky endeavor with higher death and accident rates than most industries (Wallace 1987). During the 1980s, 80 to 100 workers died in U.S. mines each year. At the state level, during the 1980s, approximately ten Kentucky miners lost their lives annually, with Harlan Countians accounting for two or three per year. These numbers represent an improvement over the incidence of occupational fatalities underground coal mines earlier in the century. In the first full decade of industrial underground coal production in Harlan County, for instance, 357 miners lost their lives (approximately 36 each year).[7]

Most of the miners that I interviewed recognized that the contradiction between profit maximization and worker safety placed them at risk. By this time, companies had take on the full cost of preparation work, although they had not necessarily done so voluntarily. "Old-timers" commonly related an anecdote about a foreman or an operator, usually unidentified, who showed more concern for a mule than for his employees. After all, the miner would explain, you had to buy the mule but you could always hire a new man! This was one of Ernie's uncle Will's favorite stories about the old days. He never identified the villain of the tale, however. Whether this incident actually occurred, I cannot tell; but it certainly is a common story. Michael Yarrow (1982, 217–18), for instance, reports a similar story from his interviews with miners during the 1978 strike. In the end, it matters little if we can document the facts behind the anecdote. This mining folklore continues to articulate the experience of underground coal mining for many.

એ

All things considered, Harlan coal production and work relations proceeded rather smoothly in the 1910s and 1920s. The Harlan field had been opened during a time of high coal demand, when industrial growth and World War I were in full swing. Harlan had high-quality coal, ideal for use in steel manufacturing. High-quality metallurgical coal, in combination with generally high coal demand, spurred industrial expansion in Harlan County. Operators were able to grant wage concessions to workers during this boom period; wages rose to nearly forty cents per ton.

All this changed after the war ended and demand for coal declined. In peacetime, industries required less fuel. Furthermore, American corporations and utilities had increasingly converted to oil and natural gas. American coal operators were slow to detect the reversal in their fortunes, none more so than those in central Appalachia. By 1918, the industry had an excess capacity of about 30 percent. Yet they continued to expand production until 1927, further exacerbating the oversupply problem (Bethell 1983, xi). Large corporations mechanized and cut wages to reduce the cost of mining coal (ibid, xii; Banks 1983–84, 85–102). Small operators, those who could not afford mechanization, cut wages and laid off workers. The large reserve of labor and low coal prices drove down miners' wages all over the region. Miners in other areas, most notably Illinois and West Virginia, responded by increasing organization efforts and strikes to protest and resist wage cuts, deskilling, and job layoffs (Baratz 1973; Corbin 1981).

This did not occur in Harlan County, however. Perhaps because they were new to the industry, Harlan miners lacked the experience, resources, and collective identity for such activity. Their counterparts in Pennsylvania, Ohio, and Illinois, after all, had been working underground for two or three generations, some of them having migrated from established coalfields in Europe, including Wales, England, and Germany. They had started their own fraternal organizations and benevolent societies, some of which had developed into quasi unions in their own right. Harlan miners had not. Indeed, coal operators had expanded to the Harlan field in part to escape the power of organized labor elsewhere (Baratz 1955/1973, 30–35; Bethell 1983, xx–xxi; see also Dix 1988, 191). Initially, this maneuver was quite successful. Harlan miners withdrew quickly from their first strike attempt in 1922, although this national coal strike dragged on for several months in the northern fields. The 1922 strike set the stage for the 1924 Jacksonville agreement, raising Illinois miners' wages and further accelerating southern migration of the coal industry (Baratz 1973, 59–63).

Throughout the national coal depression of the 1920s, the Harlan field remained relatively quiet. The local newspaper declared labor relations "smooth" and business "good" in Harlan County (HDE, 7 April 1922, 5 May 1922, 30 June 1922; see also Corbin 1981, 176–236). Journalists boasted that there were no starving miners in Harlan, as there were other areas. According to the paper, 80 percent of the local workforce was still employed (HDE, 21 April 1922, 29 September 1922). Production rose 80 percent, as local operators attempted to profit from labor troubles in other fields (Titler n.d., 12–13). This expansion added to the industry's endemic oversupply problem, which set Harlan up for a harder fall later, in 1931. Harlan miners took two additional wage cuts and worked intermittently throughout the 1920s.

During this period, the Norton brothers, Jess and Will, had done well for themselves. After years of moving from camp to camp, the "boys" finally settled at Brookside, a coal camp on the Clover Fork of the Cumberland River. Most people would not be able to detect anything special about the camp or the company that owned it. Its accommodations were not as lavish as those at U.S. Coal & Coke's model coal town of Lynch. There was a company store but no houses with indoor plumbing, no paved streets, hospital, hotel, or clubhouse. However, Brookside had something that was more remarkable to Jess Norton than the vaudeville shows and Gloria

Swanson films which were available in Lynch; it had Janie Mae Brown, daughter of Clarence and Cora Brown.

After a few weeks of the two "eyeing each other" at the commissary and the post office, Jess appeared on the front porch of the Browns' house, seeking their permission to court Janie Mae. Her parents did not agree right away, because they did not know anything about him. His history of wandering from camp to camp did not set well with them. Furthermore, they had never met his parents. In spite of their misgivings, they permitted him to visit Janie Mae. The courtship took place under the watchful eyes of Janie Mae's parents for eight months until, in February 1928, Jess and Janie Mae asked the Browns if they could marry. Janie Mae made it clear that she was bound to marry Jess, even if she had to "run off." The Browns consented, after Jess agreed that he would not move his young bride away from Brookside-Ages. They were married in a simple ceremony at the Pentecostal church on 6 April 1928.

Janie Mae and Jess set up housekeeping in the camp house where Jess and Will had been living. As the oldest daughter of six children, Janie Mae was accustomed to doing housework. Cooking and cleaning up after just two men seemed like a "break" to her. In addition, Janie Mae liked her brother-in-law, Will. Still, she longed for more privacy with her new husband and wished their life together could be more romantic. A year later she got her wish. Will moved back to his parents' house, after a period of layoffs and wage cuts made finances tight.

The layoffs at Harlan Collieries had been precipitated by a 1929 ruling by the Interstate Commerce Commission that ordered the L&N to stop charging other freight customers higher freight rates to subsidize their low Harlan rates. Until 1929, the L&N had been subsidizing Harlan coal in an effort to make it competitive with coal from markets served by other railroads. After the 1929 order, freight rates rose and increased the cost of production for local operators. They, in turn, cut their miners' wages. In October, Janie Mae told Jess the good news: he was going to be a father. The honeymoon was over for the Nortons, and for the Harlan coal industry.

Two years of irregular employment and wagecuts drove Jess and Janie Mae out of their home in the winter of 1930. They moved in with her parents, Clarence and Cora Brown, to cut expenses. By the following year, things had gone from bad to worse for Harlan's miners. Mild weather reduced coal demand further. A seasonal hiatus in the Lake Erie transportation routes disrupted shipment of coal, which prompted local coal operators to propose an additional 10 percent pay cut. This was more than most miners could bear. The Brown-Norton household lived off Jess's and Clarence's intermittent wages and produce from the garden plot that Clarence tended on the Holmes' Mill home place. The women and children gathered coal that had fallen by the train tracks to use as heating and cooking fuel.

On 1 March 1931, after several weeks of clandestine organizational meetings, the United Mine Workers of America (UMW) kicked off their drive to unionize the Harlan field with a massive rally in Pineville, the county seat of neighboring Bell County. Approximately two thousand Bell and Harlan County miners attended, and several hundred joined the union. Local coal operators, coordinating their efforts through the Harlan County Coal Operators' Association (HCCOA), responded to this incipient labor movement by firing and evicting union sympathizers. By the following month, approximately seven Harlan firms had discharged several hundred pro-union miners (Hevener 1978, 34).

An additional several hundred miners, including Jess Norton, walked off their jobs in support of their locked out co-workers. In addition to seeking union representation, the strikers hoped to end wage cuts, elect a checkweighman, and abolish the cleanup system. Jess Norton circulated UMW literature and membership cards and attended weekly union meetings, rallies, and marches in spite of the harassment he received at the hands of company guards and pro-company law officers. He was not alone. The testimonies, oral histories, and memoirs of Harlan union activists abound with tales of pistol whippings, midnight abductions, dynamitings, drive-by shootings, torture, murder, and false arrest, all suffered at the hands of the local law enforcement agents and company-hired guards (Dreiser 1932; Hevener 1978; Jones 1985; Portelli 1991; Titler n.d.).

Jess's father-in-law saw this persecution as reason enough to refuse to participate, even though he sympathized with his fellow miners' desire to improve living and working conditions in Harlan's coal camps. He just could not risk his life and job in such hard times; his family depended upon him. In fact, Clarence condemned Jess for putting his daughter and grandson at risk with all his union activity. On several occasions the two almost came to blows over the union issue. And relations between the two men remained strained until Mr. Brown's death in 1943.

By mid-April, Clarence Brown had lost his job and moved his family back to the old home place in Holmes' Mill. Although the old house had deteriorated, it provided adequate shelter for the family. With the help of their cousins, the free use of land for a vegetable garden, and the willingness to hunt, fish, and do odd jobs, Clarence was confident that he could see his children and grandchild through these hard times. Janie Mae, convinced by his arguments, packed up her son, Ernie, and went along. Jess refused to go. Instead, he joined the other jobless miners who had moved to Evarts, the largest town on the Clover Fork.

Evarts townspeople, most of them sympathetic to the union cause, offered shelter in their homes and barns. The population of Evarts swelled from about 1,500 to over 5,000 that year. Some local businesses donated food, clothing, and supplies to hungry families and extended credit to unemployed workers. Relief committees solicited contributions locally to assist the miners and their families. Unfortunately, there was not enough surplus and charity to go around, and, after several weeks, hunger and disease attacked the families of the jobless miners. The weakest—children and the elderly—were particularly hard hit. Molly Jackson, a local nurse and a miner's wife, reported that her community lost from four to seven children per week to malnutrition and related diseases (Dreiser 1932, 279). The UMW, itself bankrupt, would not provide strike relief for an unauthorized job action. And the Red Cross refused to help the families of striking and locked-out miners, arguing that they were not the victims of a natural disaster and could, theoretically at least, return to work (Hevener 1978, 37). In April, miners began to rob and loot local grocery stores in search of food.

Coal operators and local law officers denounced the growing violence of Harlan's unemployed miners. They urged respect for private property and condemned communist sympathizers as traitors and criminals. Jobless, hungry, and homeless, workers retaliated by setting fire to the company houses. They dynamited mine openings, tipples, and railroad bridges to prevent production. Snipers from both sides shot at one another from the hillsides.

The county's elite—politicians, professionals, and business-men—found themselves in a difficult position during this conflict. The striking and unemployed miners were their cousins and neighbors, people to whom they had always felt a kinship. They sympathized with the miners' cause. However, they depended on the coal operators for much of their business and, to some extent, for their political position. Some of the county elite owned stock in the coal companies and held managerial positions. Their economic and political interests allied them with the coal operators. By and large, the Harlan town elite—Sheriffs Fleenor, Middleton, and Blair, and the judges, county attorneys, and deputies—supported the coal operators. One politician explained, "The coal operators have a hell of a lot of influence in the elections. If they are not for you, it is too bad. . . . The labor question is the only touchy point" (Dotson 1943, 35). County Sheriff J. H. Blair made an even stronger case for coal operator interference in local government when he publicly stated, "I did all in my power to aid the coal operators" (Hayes-Bablitz Commission, 1932, as quoted in Hevener 1978, 16). During this period, he swore in 170 deputies—86 more than usual—to maintain order among the striking miners. All but 6 deputies were on the payrolls of coal companies.

County Attorney Elmon Middleton provided the exception to the rule; miners and organizers regarded him as a fair man. Middleton's career lasted only until 1935 when a bomb, placed in his car exploded and killed him. He had apparently been murdered in retaliation for his attempts to eradicate corruption and racketeering in Harlan County. In 1937 his widow, Ruby Kelly Middleton, became the first woman to hold the position of county court clerk in Harlan.

On 5 May 1931, the turning point for this first unionization flare-up occurred. Since dubbed the "Battle of Evarts," this series of events started when an angry and armed band of miners congregated at the railroad depot in Evarts to prevent a strikebreaker from moving into the Black Mountain coal camp, an anti-union coal operation located a few miles up the Clover Fork. The railroad agent phoned a warning to Black Mountain Superintendent E. B. Childers, who then solicited the aid of Sheriff Blair in Harlan. The sheriff dispatched an escort of fifteen deputies. The chief mine guard at Black Mountain, Jim Daniels, organized a ten-man posse as well. Miners ambushed Daniels's motorcade and killed three mine guards, including Daniels. One miner died in the incident.

The governor sent National Guard troops to restore order in the county, a move welcomed by striking miners who hoped to be delivered from persecution by local authorities. Their hopes were ill-founded. Four days later, officers arrested the UMW's district leaders and several sympathetic Evarts businessmen, some of whom had not even been in the county during the shootings. They were charged with conspiracy to commit murder. The trial, held in Mount Sterling, Kentucky, attracted attention, not all of it sympathetic. A newspaper commented: "It is useless to send men and women of the stripe of the Harlan agitators to the penitentiary. They would be safer in a pine box six-feet under ground" (Bubka 1970, 188). The initial unionization movement failed. By 23 July 1932, with the UMW leadership jailed and local relief funds exhausted, all but 800 of the 6,800 striking miners had returned to work. Among them was a weary and lonely Jess Norton, who, after several weeks of courtship, managed to convince Janie Mae to return to him so that they could raise their baby, Ernie, together.

Local coal companies circulated a "blacklist" of several hundred union activists whom they refused to rehire. Cut off from employment and strike funds, these miners had no dependable source of livelihood for their families. When organizers from the National Miners' Union (NMU), a Communist group, offered support for their cause, hundreds of local miners joined them. By July, ten NMU locals had been organized. The NMU set up soup kitchens and organized miners' wives to solicit and distribute food, medicine, and money (see figure 1.5). The NMU, unlike the UMW, involved women directly in their organizing operations (Dreiser 1932, 292). The presence of women and children at NMU functions did not deter violence, as company guards engaged in drive-by shootings at soup lines and dynamited NMU soup kitchens. Eventually, a nineteen-year-old labor organizer, Harry Sims, lost his life in the NMU organizing effort. Relief supplies were diverted from striking miners, and representatives of the press, the American Civil Liberties Union, and the NMU were either denied entry into Harlan County or threatened and harassed while they were there; many were coerced into leaving the area. Company officials prohibited the circulation of liberal or pro-union newspapers, such as the *Knoxville News-Sentinel,* while the local press advocated the use of "an iron heel" to "stamp out the foul growth" of Communism (Hevener 1978, 58–9; see also figure 1.6).

To combat such censorship and to publicize the cause of the

The Communist Party and the Miners Struggle

in Kentucky. The Struggle against the Wall Street-Hoover Hunger Program

(A Reply to the Lies of Billionaire Coal Owners and Their Press)

The Communist Party of the United States, through its District 17—Alabama, Tennessee, and Kentucky—calls upon all workers to aid in every possible way the heroic fight of the coal miners in Harlan and Bell Counties, Kentucky, against starvation and slave conditions forced upon them by the coal mine owners and their city, county, state and national governments. It calls upon workers everywhere to give food, clothes and money for relief of the miners and their families. We call on workers to demand the release of all arrested strikers and organizers.

BILLIONAIRE MINE OWNERS—HUNGRY MEN, WOMEN AND CHILDREN

These mines are owned by Insull, the International Harvester Company, the Steel Trust, the Detroit Edison Company, etc.—the biggest billionaires and the biggest and richest corporations in America. The most important mines are owned by the same billionaires who have thrown 12,000,000 workers out of mines and factories to beg, steal or starve, in the richest country in the world.

The miners and their wives are always hungry. Their wages are the lowest in the United States for miners. They are robbed at the company stores. They are not paid even their miserable wages in money—but in company scrip. There are thousands of unemployed. Thousands more are blacklisted.

BETRAYED BY LABOR FAKERS

The miners, after having been sold out by the officials of the United Mine Workers, by leaders like John L. Lewis, Turnblazer, Green and Woll of the American Federation of Labor and others who get $12,000 per year salaries, who have been betraying workers for years, then organized in the National Miners Union—a union controlled by the rank and file of its members and affiliated to the Trade Union Unity League—and went on strike again.

JAIL ORGANIZERS—GUN THUG RULE

Almost every organizer of the union in Kentucky has been arrested and charged with "criminal syndicalism." The organizers for strike relief have been arrested. Organizers of the Workers International Relief, the International Labor Defense, and its lawyers have been arrested. Eleven organizers are now in jail in Pineville held for the grand jury under $5000 "peace bond" and $10,000 bail.

Meetings of miners are broken up. Miners have been murdered by company gun thugs. The roads are patrolled by armed mine gun thugs and special deputies paid by the coal companies. Miners and organizers are stopped and searched. Organizers are kidnapped and beaten—as were Weber and Duncan. Meetings are made crimes and the miners and organizers, the strikers and their families, are forced to live under gun rule.

THE ISSUES

Every strike of workers against wage-cuts and starvation today in America sees these same methods used by the bosses, their local, state and national governments—like in Gastonia, N. C., Danville, Va. Elizabethton, Tenn., New Orleans, Lawrence, Mass., in Pennsylvania, Ohio, and West Virginia.

The fight of the Kentucky miners is a fight for the right to live and for basic rights and liberties.

The detailed demands of the National Miners Union and the Central Strike Committee for better wages and working conditions have been widely published since they were adopted by the elected delegates of the miners. They were endorsed by the miners and sent to the coal operators before the strike began January 1st.

These are the things the miners are fighting for, and for which they have not only the right but the duty to fight—for better wages, for the right to organize, for free speech, the right to meet, to be paid in U. S. Currency, etc.

WHAT THE COMMUNIST PARTY DOES

The Communist Party organizes and helps the miners and all other workers in the struggle for better conditions. Its members are active in the National Miners Union as well as in many other unions. The Communist Party shows, by the works of its members in the front ranks of every struggle of the working class, that its deeds are the same as its words. It collects relief for strikers and their families. It organizes defence for arrested strikers and organizers. It is the only party that fights for Workers Unemployment Insurance at the expense of the bosses. This is the way it plays a leading part in the strike of the Kentucky miners. This is the duty of a workers' revolutionary Party. Only the Communist Party aids workers by deeds as well as words. The Republican, Democrat and Socialist Parties are bosses' parties.

WHY THE BOSSES DON'T LIKE REDS

The mine owners and their agents know that the Communist Party is the most experienced, most disciplined and most courageous section of the American working class, that by uniting and fighting for the Communist program, the workers will beat the bosses. That is why the bosses send members of the Party to jail for long terms. That is why their papers and the organizations they control lie about the workers. That is why they want to "outlaw the Reds."

THE RELIGIOUS ISSUE

The coal miner owners and their papers, bodies of business men like Chambers of Commerce who support the billionaires who rob the miners and force them to the starvation level, try to make religion an issue in the strike. The Communist Party knows that prayers and hymns have never kept bosses from cutting wages, raising prices in the company stores, or kept billionaire companies from hiring gunthugs to shoot hungry striking miners.

The Communist Party knows that churches are weapons of the bosses against the workers. In the Kentucky strike, in the textile strike in Gastonia, N. C., in Elizabethton, Tenn., in 1929, most of the churches and preachers were for the bosses and against the workers. In the present strike the leading preachers are already cooperating with the scab-herding U. M. W. A. to break the strike. "Heaven after death, but hell here on earth for workers and more profit for us," is the motto of Rockefeller (a very good Baptist), Insull, Ford, Schwab, Morgan (a good Jew) and Farrell of the Steel Trust (a good Catholic), and other capitalists who own Harlan and Bell Counties, as well as the government of the United States now headed by Herbert Hoover—another millionaire. They give big sums to churches from the profits made from the toil of the workers. But they cut wages and fight against unemployment insurance. The need of the workers is not more religion, but to organize into powerful unions and force the billionaires to pay decent wages.

THE ISSUE OF "WHITE SUPREMACY"

The bosses' papers and their leaflets say that the issue in the Kentucky strike is "white supremacy." They urge miners and other workers to unite with them against Communists and against the strike itself. This means against the interests of the working class. Is "white supremacy" an issue of more importance than the fact there is mass starvation in mining camps, than the fact that there are today 12,000,000 unemployed and hungry workers in America. Negro and white, who with their families, make up a majority of the American people? What cruel fooling of workers! Feeding starving and ragged white workers with "white supremacy"! What they mean is white boss class supremacy—the power to rule and rob millions of both white and black workers of the fruit of their labor.

THE COLOR LINE

The bosses have divided workers on the color line. They lynch Negroes, they force them into worse living conditions than the white workers (but not much worse than those of the white miners today), and then they say to the white workers: "Why do you complain? See, the Negroes are much worse off than you are!" Then the bosses and their papers and their government use every method to make the conditions of both white and Negro workers worse than they were before. They cut the wages of both. They try to get Negroes to break strikes of white workers as in the 1922 Kentucky mine strike, they try to get white workers to scab on Negroes, as in the New Orleans dock strike. They cut the wages of whites and Negroes. They kill and jail both Negro and white organizers.

Race hatred is one of the best weapons of the billionaire bosses. Unity of both white and Negro workers on the basis of equality against the attacks upon both the Negro and white workers and their families will take this weapon away from the bosses.

FIGURE 1.5

A 1932 Communist Party advertisement concerning the National Miners' Union's attempt to organize coal miners in Harlan and Bell Counties. Photograph courtesy of the University of Kentucky Photo Archives, the Herndon J. Evans Collection (82M1; box 3, folder 2).

FOR UNITY OF ALL WORKERS

The Communist Party works for full equality of all races and nationalities.

The only way in which steel workers, textile workers, building trade workers, the whole working class, can fight successfully against wage cuts and hunger, is for white and Negro workers to organize and fight together. It is necessary that white workers protect their Negro fellow workers from lynching, from being jim-crowed, from being framed up and jailed as in Scottsboro and murdered as in Camp Hill, because it is by such means the bosses divide our ranks and drive all of us—Negro and white—lower and lower.

The Communist Party of the United States calls upon the working class to put a stop to lynching of Negroes and other forms of terrorism. In this way all workers can present a solid fighting front to the bosses and better their condition and free themselves from mass unemployment and wage slavery.

WHOSE COUNTRY?

The bosses and their papers say that the Communists are against "our country." Communists are not against the country. We are for the people to whom the country should belong—the working class and toiling farmers. But we are against the capitalist class which has stolen everything in the country worth having and which uses its power to rob the workers and farmers more and more.

The government of the United States is a government of, for and by the billionaire bosses. It is a class government—the government of the boss class. We say to the workers that we must take the country away from the capitalist class and run it by a Workers and Farmers Government—for the benefit of the workers and farmers. Boss government creates ever more suffering for the workers and farmers.

POLITICS AND POWER

The Communist Party of the United States is the only revolutionary political party of the working class. It is composed of workers and working farmers. It knows that the billionaire boss class and its hangers-on will never give up willingly the loot they have robbed from the toilers. They must be forced to give up the country they have stolen. All history teaches this. That is why revolution is the only way out for workers.

The Communist Party organizes the working class for this revolutionary struggle for government power. At the same time it calls upon workers to fight in the most stubborn way against every cut in their wages, for government unemployment insurance at the expense of the bosses, for every legal right they have won by years of struggle and suffering. If workers do not do this they will be, as Marx, the founder of Communism, said, "an army of broken wretches."

THE QUESTION OF REVOLUTION

The Communist Party is not calling on workers to "make a revolution now. We are not that foolish. Such tactics would only play into the hands of the bosses and their government. Communists are responsible to the working class. They do not play at revolution. When we call for revolution the decisive batalions of workers will be behind our Party and its program, and ready to answer the call, because they will no longer be able to bear the ever heavier burden of mass unemployment, hunger wages and starvation placed upon them.

"RUSSIAN REDS"

The bosses and their papers and their agents in the ranks of the working class do a lot of talking about "Russian Reds." This is to make the workers believe that the Communist Party has no business in this country and that no American worker is or should be a Communist. But thousands of American workers are Communists. This worries the bosses. Let's see what this means—

WHAT IS THE SOVIET UNION?

The Communist Party calls upon all workers to support and defend the Soviet Union, the government set up by the Russian workers after the Revolution of 1917, which was led by the Communist Party, because it is a Workers and Farmers Government. There is no capitalism or capitalists in the Soviet Union. There are no millionaire bosses. The workers are not mobbed and beaten down. The government is their government.

THE CONDITIONS OF SOVIET WORKERS

There is no unemployment in the Soviet Union. The wages and conditions of the whole working and farming population get better every day. Miners get an average of $4.00 for a 6-hour day. They do not have to pay rent. Farming, industry, mining, etc., are organized for the good of the workers and farmers.

Since the revolution the working class of the Soviet Union has built an industry that is second only to that of the United States. It is the only country in the whole world where there is no "depression," where there is no crisis. It is the only country in the world, where 160,000,000 people of a hundred different nationalities, where the black, yellow and white races, live together in peace, free from wage slavery and oppression.

WHY CAPITALISTS ARE AGAINST THE SOVIET UNION

That is why the capitalists want to destroy the Soviet Union by war—because it is a living example to the working class of the whole world of the Communist Program put into practice.

The Russian Revolution was not something "foreign." It was a powerful beacon blazing the way which the working class of every country must travel in order to be free from this rotten capitalism with its millions of hungry and starving unemployed; its miserable living conditions; its bloody wars for big bankers and bosses (like the World War and the new war that has already begun in the Far East); its jails for militant workers.

WHO ARE THE COMMUNISTS?

The Communist Party of the United States is the political Party of the American working class. It is composed of native born workers, foreign born, Negro and white, men and women—it is a cross section of the American working class. Conditions in America, not conditions in Russia, laid the base for the Communist Party.

THE COMMUNIST PARTY AND THE ELECTIONS

The Communist Party runs candidates in all elections where it can get on the ballot. It will have candidates in every Southern state in the coming local elections and presidential campaign. It calls upon workers and farmers in the Southern states to rally to its program and candidates.

During the campaign our Party will make extra efforts to expose to the working class, the Hunger Program of the Wall Street Government. Our party bases itself upon the working class and depends, not upon the fraud of boss class "democracy," but upon the organized power of the working class. It has no interests separate and apart from those of the working class.

It organizes the working class to fight against the dictatorship of capital at every point, every day in the year. The election campaign is an important part of this general struggle.

Support the struggle of the Kentucky Miners!

WIN THE STRIKE! SPREAD THE STRIKE!

Support the National Miners Union!

Collect Food, Clothing and Money for the Miners!

Hold Mass Meetings on February Fourth, National Day of Struggle for Unemployment Insurance! Defeat the Wall Street Hoover Hunger Program! Organize Unemployed Councils in every city!

Organize and strike against all wage-cuts! Demand and fight for workers' unemployment insurance at full wages! Expose the treacherous A. F. of L. and U. M. W. A. leaders before the whole working class!

Demand the unconditional release of all arrested strikers and organizers! Fight for the repeal of the strike-breaking criminal syndicalism law!

No Discrimination against Negroes! Fight against lynching! Free the framed Scottsboro boys! Unite the ranks of the working class against the Wall Street Hunger Slavery Drive!

Defend the Soviet Union against attack by Capitalist governments!

Defeat the Wall Street program of Hunger and Imperialist War!

JOIN THE COMMUNIST PARTY—the revolutionary Party of the American working class. Read the Daily Worker—Read the Southern Worker.

(It is not possible to explain in detail in this leaflet the program of our Party on all points. Here we reply briefly to some questions raised by the bosses and their agents to confuse the miners and other workers in connection with the Kentucky Miners Strike. Other leaflets will be issued. Buy and read the pamphlet "Why Every Worker Should Join the Communist Party.")

For more information address P. O. Box 1813, Birmingham, Ala. or Box 528, Knoxville, Tenn.

COMMUNIST PARTY OF THE UNITED STATES,

DISTRICT 17,

Birmingham - Alabama

FIGURE 1.5 Continued

NMU, renowned author Theodore Dreiser organized a committee of left-wing journalists and authors to document the "cruelties" committed against Harlan and Bell County miners. They published their observations of the "class war in Kentucky" interspersed with numerous testimonies collected from local NMU

RESOLUTIONS

WHEREAS, there is a growing tendency among some of our citizens to depreciate the ideals for which we fought, and

WHEREAS, there exists in the United States at this time a great many persons who would see our national ideals destroyed and who would look with favor upon the substitution of another form of government similar to that established in Russia, and

WHEREAS, the communist party of America through its various branches and subsidiaries is seeking to destroy all the principles for which the American Legion stands, and

WHEREAS, there seem to be no laws whereby these communists or radicals who openly seek to destroy our government and all constituted authority, can be prosecuted or punished, and

WHEREAS, the insidious propaganda which is being spread by the American branch of the communist party of Soviet Russia is costing the American people millions of dollars through lost earnings, sabotage, etc., and is causing untold suffering and privation, and

WHEREAS, this propaganda is of a seditious nature and has for its ultimate goal the overthrow of the United States government by revolution, the destruction of all religious beliefs and respect for God and the substitution of the soviet form of government for the present form of government in this country,

THEREFORE, Be IT Resolved: That the assembled members of the American Legion, representing the cities of Southeastern Kentucky, deplore the things which have brought to pass the present situation and urge our national and state leaders to address themselves earnestly to the problem and frame such legislation as will drive these communists and revolutionary agitators from our country.

Be It Further Resolved: That copies of this resolution be sent to our state representatives at Frankfort and our national representatives at Washington, and to the state and national commanders of the American Legion.

Passed unanimously by members of Pineville, Middlesboro, Barbourville and Harlan Posts, American Legion, in session at Pineville, Ky., January 6, 1932.

FIGURE 1.6
The American Legion's reaction to the Communist organizing efforts in Harlan and Bell Counties. Photograph courtesy of the University of Kentucky Photo Archives, Herndon J. Evans Collection (82M1; box 3, folder 2).

miners and law enforcement officials, in a book called *Harlan County Miners Speak* (Dreiser 1932). The committee's effort accomplished little for the miners' movement, particularly after two of its members were discredited by a sex scandal. After only a few months in the Harlan field, the NMU—as bankrupt, bloodied, and battered as the UMW had been a few months earlier—abandoned Harlan County. Many notable local NMU miner-organizers, such as Jim Garland and Aunt Molly Jackson, had fled Harlan County in fear for their lives. Their songs, however, lived on—for a while as leftist labor songs, and later as material for the folk song revival of the '60s and '70s. The songs present not only eloquent descriptions of the horror of the Harlan "mine wars," but also the most clear-cut examples of working-class consciousness and labor militance that Harlan has to offer (see Green 1972 and Greenway 1953 for illuminating discussions of miners' songs).

There is nothing subtle about Sara Ogan's lyrics proclaiming her hatred for the capitalist system and condemning wealthy capitalists for the deaths of her friends and child (Greenway 1953, 258, 274). Her sister, Molly Jackson, recalled, "I still hear my hungry children cry. I saw my own sister's little 14-month-old baby girl starve to death for milk while the coal operators was [*sic*] riding around in fine cars with their wives and children all dressed up in diamonds and silks, paid for by the blood and sweat of the coal miners" (Greenway 1953, 258, 274). These events provide the context for some of the most militant and radical song lyrics of the era, in which Jim Garland urged his fellow miners, "Let's sink this rotten system/to the deepest pits of hell" (as quoted in Portelli 1991, 222) and Florence Reese proclaimed that there could be no neutrals in Harlan County's mine wars.

Still, not everyone joined the NMU, espoused antipathy toward capitalism, or wrote militant labor songs. Only a relatively small minority did. And when the NMU left Harlan County, many of its most notable supporters left with it. By 1985, it appeared that the NMU had accomplished nothing more than the temporary radicalization of a very small minority of Harlan Countians. None of the miners interviewed for this project had much to say about the NMU or Communism. Most claimed they had little knowledge of the movement, never supported it, and were not well acquainted with anyone who had. Pro-UMW miners were particularly uncomfortable with the topic and many took great pains to distance themselves and their union from the NMU. The UMW was not radical, did not advocate the overthrow of the U.S. government, and worked within the framework of the free-enterprise economy, they explained. As God-fearing family men and patriotic Americans, they obviously had little in common with Communists. They noted that, in the past, coal operators and law enforcement officials had falsely accused the UMW of being an un-American, Communist organization in order to discredit pro-UMW miners and to justify violence against them. So, communism was a painful, politically charged topic for Harlan's miners. It was not something they talked about with their children. As journalist Bill Bishop (1976) observed, "Most of those who joined the NMU in 1931 now bow their heads or avert their eyes when asked about the Communists. . . . Some even look away and say no group called the National Miners Union ever entered Kentucky."

With a few exceptions, the events surrounding the NMU in Harlan County seem to have faded out of local memory—apparently too painful for some to discuss and too irrelevant for most others. Only a few of the more politically conservative, anti-union businessmen and coal operators seemed comfortable with the topic of Communism in Harlan. Unlike miners, these people often eagerly introduced the NMU into our conversations. The Depression brought desperate times, they explained, and the miners were not blameless victims in the mine wars. Their reckless radicalism threatened not only the industry but the community and the country. From this perspective, the actions of the Sheriff Blair and his deputies were understandable, if not justified. The recognition of a *real—* if only a minimal—local Communist presence allowed some of Harlan's coal operators and political leaders to explain away the dark side of their own past.

There are also a few Harlan natives who, in writing local histories and their own memoirs, have recorded and reflected upon these events as well. Books on the Depression mine wars include *Welcome the Traveller Home* (1983), by NMU miner-organizer-songwriter Jim Garland; *Growin' Up Hard in Harlan County* (1985), by retired UMW miner G. C. "Red" Jones; and *Harlan County: The Turbulent Thirties* (1986), by William D. Forester, a former schoolteacher and Harlan businessman. As a group, these books run the gamut from complete silence about the NMU (Jones 1985) to condemnation and ridicule of it (Forester 1986), with Garland's (1983) sympathetic insider's consideration of the movement's strengths and weaknesses occupying a middle ground. In short, Harlan County remains deeply divided about these events and their significance.

Consequently, Alessandro Portelli (1991, 238) warns against generalizing about this movement and its subsequent, ever-changing political ramifications for Harlan County's miners. Nevertheless, he and fellow historian John Hevener (1978) have suggested several factors that might account for the NMU's aborted organizing drive in Harlan County as well as its subsequent rejection and virtual elimination from the memories of most local mining families. These include a lack of widespread local commitment, violent repression by local law enforcement officials, funding shortfalls and disorganization in the NMU, cultural differences and ethnic hostility between NMU organizers and local miners, and ideological conflicts between local miners and NMU leaders. Portelli (1991) aptly analyzes this class-based conflict as a struggle over cultural symbolism (see also Corbin 1981; Gerstle 1989). His observations will be explored in some detail in chapter 5, as will the verdict of Harlan teacher-businessman William D. Forester: "It is very likely," he explains, "that [the miners'] bellies were with the [NMU], but their hearts were not" (Forester 1986, 33).

≈♣

After the collapse of these two union organizing drives in 1932, social activist Myles Horton visited Harlan County where he was so struck by hunger and despair that he cried in bed at night. These "gaunt-faced," "lifeless" miners, he observed, exhibited "the kind of despair that you have when there's no hope. People with no hope will not do anything. And they weren't doing anything" (quoted in Portelli 1991, 237–38). It is little wonder that the rekindling of the local labor movement required a significant "jump-start" from extralocal sources.

One such extralocal source was the National Industrial Recovery Act, passed by Congress in June 1933 in an attempt to come to grips with the deepening Depression. Included in this act was a provision guaranteeing employees the right to join a union of their choice and to bargain collectively. UMW President John L. Lewis was one of a handful of national labor leaders who managed to capitalize on this shift of political current, in part by breaking away from the more conservative, craft-based American Federation of

Labor (AFL) and beginning an industry-based coalition of labor unions called the Congress of Industrial Organizations (CIO). By September, the UMW and the Bituminous Coal Operators' Association (BCOA) had agreed on a code that set sales prices, minimum wages, and maximum hours and established district labor boards to enforce these provisions. Subsequently, the UMW and BCOA successfully negotiated two labor contracts. They did so without the cooperation of Central Appalachian coal operators, including Harlan's, who largely refused to follow these agreements. When the U.S. Supreme Court invalidated the National Industrial Recovery Act, it looked as if their gambit had succeeded.

A series of strikes and intense negotiations resulted in a third agreement in September 1935, however. Central Appalachian operators signed this contract, which increased the southern daily wage from $4.60 to $5.10 and retained the previously established thirty-five-hour work week. In the meantime, the federal government passed the National Labor Relations Act of 1935 (the Wagner Act) and the Guffey Coal Stabilization Act, but Harlan County still remained outside the union fold. The UMW, having established itself firmly in the eastern coalfields, renewed its efforts to organize Harlan County during the summer of 1933, hoping to take advantage of political infighting between Sheriff J. H. Blair and the coal operators' association. Although weakened by partisan politics, Harlan operators still maintained a significant army of privately hired guards and deputies to enforce their anti-union stance. After some initial success in organizing the Harlan field, UMW activists once again were arrested, beaten, shot at, dynamited, and otherwise harassed. Even Reverend C. V. Vogel, a minister at Harlan's town elite Methodist church, was forced to leave town after he criticized law enforcement officials' use of violence against pro-union miners. In 1934, union organizers once again fled Harlan County.

The UMW next tried a series of political and legal maneuvers to secure access to Harlan County, supporting candidates for state office, petitioning the governor, and attracting the attention a federal commission charged with investigating corporate America's anti-union backlash against the Wagner Act. Headed by Wisconsin Senator Robert LaFollette, this commission's hearings on Harlan County's labor environment revealed to the state and nation a pattern of unrivaled corruption and repression. The tide had final-

ly turned in Harlan County. By 1938, local law enforcement officers had been indicted, the mine guard system was abolished, the
state police offered protection to participants at UMW rallies, several operators withdrew their membership from the HCCOA, and
all received considerable pressure to negotiate with the UMW.

Still, local coal operators resisted signing UMW contracts even
when the majority of their employees had joined this union.
They fired UMW workers and attempted to organize their employees into company unions. The UMW filed charges against
twenty-seven Harlan firms in July 1937, kicking off a nine-
month National Labor Relations Board investigation, which culminated in ordering these firms to pay back wages to employees
who had been unfairly dismissed due to their union activities.
The final move in the drive to make Harlan County safe for labor unionism came in Frankfort, Kentucky, in September 1937,
when a federal grand jury indicted 22 coal companies, 24 operators, Sheriff Theodore Middleton, and 22 of his deputies for
conspiring to deprive Harlan miners of the civil rights accorded
to them by the Wagner Act. Although the government failed to
win its case, the eleven-week trial cost Harlan operators a great
deal, both financially and politically. For the first time, the HC-
COA and UMW signed a contract. This contract represented a
compromise on issues that had previously divided them: dues
checkoffs and weighing methods.

Two years later, Harlan labor-management relations suffered
from another stumbling block to tranquility as they bargained for
a new contract. Rival unions, such as the AFL Progressive Miners'
Union, had established themselves in Harlan County and posed a
local and national threat to the dominance of the UMW. John L.
Lewis failed in his attempt to obtain jurisdictional protection during the contract negotiations, resulting in a national strike that, for
the first time, shut down all of Harlan County's mining operations.
With UMW strike relief and provisions provided by the federal
government's Works Projects Adminstration, Harlan miners sustained the strike for over a hundred days. The strike persisted, even
after the governor sent National Guard troops to assist the coal
owners in reopening their operations. When, on 12 July, National
Guard troops fired on UMW pickets, killing two miners and seriously injuring three, federal pressure and public outrage forced the
operators to the negotiating table, where a compromise once again

was worked out. The operators avoided a closed shop while John L. Lewis and the UMW were given the means to combat rival unions. This agreement applied to 4,800 employees at twenty-four HCCOA mines. Even during the peak of Harlan County union strength, several nonunion mines remained in operation. Some successfully resisted unionization, while others acquiesced in the following months.

≥●

Among these latecomers was Jess Norton's and Clarence Brown's employer, Harlan Collieries. Jess considered the eight-year, on-again/off-again struggle for union representation to be a victory for local miners and a great step forward for their children and grand-children. He was happy to have escaped serious injury and proud of the role he played in bring the UMW to Harlan County. Conse-quently, and in spite of his father-in-law's intermittent oppositional grumbling, Jess raised his three children on tales of coal operators' greed, government-sponsored repression, miner heroism, and the benevolence of John L. Lewis and the United Mine Workers. They, in turn, carried these stories with them as they went to work in the coal mines of Harlan and the factories of the Midwest. Stories from this period—retold, revised, and revived—informed the subsequent generation of Harlan Countians as they embarked their careers, interacted with their bosses, chose political candidates, evaluated public policy, and advised their children. This complex, divisive history forms a central part of a collective experience that the entire community—not just miners—can draw upon, elaborate, modify, or reject. Much of this research centers upon how Harlan Countians made sense of these events and reconsidered them in light of their subsequent experiences.

CHAPTER 2

Living through Experience

In an introspective moment, retired miner Ernie Norton told me, "Living through experience, I guess, is what makes a union man out of you." His observation bears a remarkable similarity to the historical materialist line of reasoning, as does the remark of a coal operator's daughter: "I'm very anti-union; but, then, I was raised that way. I don't know if I was raised a different way if I'd feel differently than I do" (Sue Bassham Cudd by James B. Goode, SECC-OHP, 8 March 1984). While there may be a kernel of truth to our shared perspective, neither of us gains much analytical mileage by simply making this observation. Certainly, living through experience makes one into a union man, but it might also make one's co-worker into an anti-union man or one's boss into an authoritarian coal operator. Therefore, we must be willing to pursue this issue one step further and inquire: What experiences are remembered, by the individual and the community; and what meaning is attributed to them? Is there agreement as to their meaning? Is that meaning shifting or static? How have experiences been shaped by history and social position (class, race, gender, region, generation)? In sum, how have our ideologies been shaped through our interaction with material and social reality, and vice versa?

This chapter seeks to answer these questions by reference to the life stories of Ernie and Daniel Norton, retired Harlan miners who intermittently worked as underground coal miners from 1950 through 1980. In addition to recounting the experiences emphasized by these men as formative or central to their sense of individual and collective identity, I have also included my own observations of additional contextual factors or events that either did not appear salient to them or, like the issue of Communism, were too painful, risky, or apparently irrelevant to discuss.

⁊

Jess and Janie Mae Norton raised three children in Ages: Ernest, Daniel, and Edith. Most of Janie Mae's kinfolk, her family's oldest friends, and her husband's co-workers lived in Ages or the adjoining coal camp of Brookside, so Janie Mae felt at home there. Jess felt at home there, too. Everyone, especially Janie Mae's father, Clarence, was pleased that the "labor troubles" were over. Both of Janie Mae's parents were pleased that Jess had finally turned into a steady worker who could support Janie Mae and the grandchildren. And Janie Mae enjoyed her life as a housewife and mother. With her mother, sisters, and childhood friends living in the community, she had plenty of company and help with the chores and children.

During World War II, the demand for coal was high. Jess was not drafted to fight because his job as a miner was considered central to the war effort. However, some of his neighbors served overseas, and several local families moved to cities where they could work in defense industries. Harlan's coal operations, like the entire industry, enjoyed the prosperity brought by wartime demand and by the stabilization of prices and labor relations that had been put into place by federal regulation and legislation during the previous decade. From 1935 to 1950, the hourly wage of UMW miners rose from 75¢ to $1.94 (Seltzer 1985, 56). And local nonunion companies tried to keep their wages in line, lest they risk the unionization of their own employees.

Nationally, the unprecedented strength of the UMW and its president John L. Lewis was beginning to erode, although Jess and his son Ernie apparently failed to recognize it. Once mentioned as a possible running mate for Franklin D. Roosevelt, Lewis had by then alienated himself from the Democratic Party leadership by endorsing the candidacy of Wendell Wilkie. His bargaining tactics and attempts to forestall even "one backward step" for miners, during the war, prompted both Roosevelt and his successor, Harry Truman, to take control of the mine industry. Many saw the UMW's wartime work stoppages as selfish and an unpatriotic affront to soldiers who depended upon coal to fight the war (Coleman 1943, 199–206).

Ernie recalled that the World War II labor conflicts renewed some of the hostility between his father and grandfather, who already had an ongoing disagreement about the necessity and benefit of union membership. Ernie sided with his father in this debate even though he saw that his grandfather had a point. But one way you could look at it, Ernie noted, was that miners were fighting to protect American freedoms and rights at home, just as the soldiers were doing overseas. He further pointed out that coal operators eagerly exploited the war as an excuse for overworking their employees, ignoring their responsibilities, and making excessive profits. It was during this period the UMW stepped up its long-standing effort to secure health benefits.

After several wartime negotiation attempts failed, UMW miners walked off work in 1946, thus threatening to cripple postwar economic expansion. The federal government, once again, took over management of the coal industry. Lewis initially secured the UMW demand through negotiations with Secretary of the Interior Julius A. Krug, but he lost ground by attempting to reopen the negotiations with the government in subsequent months. Restraining orders and Supreme Court rulings not only prevented the miners from striking, but resulted in costly fines for the union and its president. The following year, Lewis and the coal operators finally set up a medical and pension plan, financed by a ten-cent tonnage tax and administered by a three-member board composed of one industry, one union, and one neutral representative (Seltzer 1985, 56–60). Although financial mismanagement ultimately handicapped this effort, this health-care and pension plan won John L. Lewis the deep gratitude and respect of Harlan's elder miners, who to this day cite it as a primary factor promoting the health and well-being of themselves, their families, and their communities.

Ernie's uncle Will returned to Ages in 1939, just before the war. His years of riding the rails were exciting, he said, but he was glad to be home and soon returned to working in the mines alongside his brother Jess. He finally "settled down" in 1949, marrying a Jones' Creek widow who had two children of her own. Unfortunately, she died in 1952, leaving him to raise two stepchildren alone. Will's lack of parenting experience made it difficult for him to cope. Janie Mae could see that he needed a woman's help, so she invited him, once again, to take up residence with her and Jess. They shared a home for four years, until his stepchildren reached their teenage years.

All of Jess Norton's children and grandchildren attended school at Ages and then went on to Evarts High School about eight miles up the creek. All but Ernie graduated. Ernie did not like school. In debates with his parents over the matter, he pointed out that they did not have a high school diploma and had done just fine. Besides, he had finished the tenth grade, which was two grades farther than anyone else in the family had gone. He wanted to get on with his life. So, at age sixteen, he found a job in one of the many un-mechanized, locally owned, nonunion mines that had opened in the post–World War II era. These mines were referred to as "pony mines," because they still used mules and horses to haul coal.

Ernie earned seven dollars a day when he started there. After three years, he was ready to strike out on his own. Soon he found the "girl of his dreams": fifteen-year-old Virginia Henderson. She had been "under his nose the whole time," he later laughed. Like Ernie, Ginny had spent all her life around Ages. She lived "up the creek," not too far from the church where Jess and Janie Mae had their first date. Her father had worked with Ernie's father as a miner at Harlan Collieries, or "old man Whitfield's mine," as it was more commonly called. She and Ernie had gone to Ages School at the same time, but as children they were not particularly friendly. The four-year age difference, they say, accounted for that. "You know how children are: girls hate boys and boys hate girls!" they observed. Their courtship began at a restaurant by Highway 38 where Ginny used to go with two or three girlfriends to gossip and watch the boys "run the roads." When he felt like squandering a little of his own paycheck, Ernie would walk down to the restaurant for a burger and fries. It was there that he and Ginny fell in love, sitting at a booth, sipping a shared cherry Coke through straws.

In 1950, Ginny dropped out of school to marry Ernie. He picked her up on the highway bridge and they eloped to Virginia, where there was no waiting period to get married. When they returned, they moved in with Ginny's parents until Ernie could find them a nearby house to rent. It was not unusual for young couples to live with their parents right after they married, although most got a place of their own when they could afford it. Ginny's parents, unfortunately, were upset by the elopement. They treated Ernie coldly and tried "to come between" Ginny and her new husband. After about three weeks, Ernie and Ginny moved into their own place. In six months' time, however, Ernie was laid off at work and the young couple moved back in with Ginny's parents.

Throughout the 1950s, Ernie worked intermittently. When they could afford it, Ernie and Ginny rented a house in Ages Bottom or up Ages Creek. If they fell behind in the rent, they would get loans from either set of parents. A few times, they had to move back in with the Hendersons. When that happened, Ernie got depressed and started drinking to excess. This would go on for months. After a while, Ginny started to wonder why she had ever married Ernie. Her parents always pointed out that they were a bad match and that she was too young to be married.

In 1954, she asked Ernie to leave her parents' house. Her mother forbade him to visit Ginny at all, a move to which Ginny agreed even though she was visibly pregnant with their first baby. It was not that Ernie ever hit her, she explained, but he was mean when he was drinking. She just could not stand to have her child raised by a mean, drunken, out-of-work father. No matter how much she loved Ernie, she was not convinced he had ever really grown up. Even though her parents thought she was too young to be married, it was really Ernie who was too young. Back then, she recalled, he was just an "overgrown baby"—always "talking big" with the boys, getting in fistfights and "blowing his top," but when it came down to it, he always needed Ginny, her parents, or her in-laws to "bail him out of trouble." "Just like man, ain't it?" daughter Cindy would later quip in discussing this period of her parents' lives.

After being banished from the Henderson household, Ernie moved in with his parents, who had set aside a corner of their own lot for him and Ginny. "Build you a house," his father counseled. "A young couple needs a place of their own, if they ever hope to make it." Jess knew that from his own experience with his in-laws. Ernie followed his father's advice. When Jess finally got Ernie a job at Brookside's Harlan Collieries the following year, things began to "look up" for Ernie and Ginny. Ernie sobered up and vowed never to drink "hard liquor" again. When Ginny was convinced he actually meant to follow through on his promises, she returned to him with their bouncing baby girl, Cindy, in tow. Their separation had lasted eight months. Ernie always regretted missing Cindy's birth; but he was there three years later when Ginny gave birth to a boy, whom they named Ernest, Jr. "I don't hold with all that natural childbirth and stuff," Ernie later explained. "I'd have just been in the way at the delivery. But, still, it would have been a comfort to Ginny if I'd have been around. And I should have been able to visit Cindy right after she was born. The father's face is the second one a baby should see, right after the mother's." Ernie did not blame Ginny or her parents for banishing him from the household. It was good for him, he said. It was just the jolt he needed to "straighten up" his life. To this day, Ernie has lived up to his vow never to drink again.

Meanwhile, Jess and Janie Mae's other children followed paths somewhat different from Ernie's. Daniel, the Nortons' second son, did not want to be a miner. When he graduated from high school in 1950, he went to work as a car mechanic at a nearby gas station. Ernie's sister, Edith, married her high school sweetheart at the Harlan County Court House, just after her graduation. Two weeks later, they moved to Detroit, Michigan, where her husband's uncle had gotten him a job in the Ford automobile plant. Janie Mae cried for three weeks after "losing her little girl." But by the time Daniel left to join his sister and brother-in-law in Detroit in 1958, Janie Mae had reconciled herself to the fact that the young folks just had to move away if they ever hoped to make anything of themselves. Everyone was doing it (table 1.1; Garkovitch 1982; White 1987). Janie Mae's grandbabies were a comfort to her when Daniel left home. They also helped fill the void of Will's departure from the Norton household. Of course, Will had not gone too far—just to a home up on Ages Creek across the road from the bottom where Jess and Janie Mae lived. Even with Ernie, Ginny, and the grand-kids living in a small "honeymoon" cottage in the yard, the house seemed awfully empty to Janie Mae in 1958. It "took some getting used to," she remembered.

The Nortons were not the only family who watched their children leave home during the 1950s and 1960s. The local economy, which was dominated by coal, could not support new generations of miners. Harlan County lost 36 percent of its population during the 1950s (see table 1.1). Those who remained had trouble making a living. By 1960, 58.4 percent of the households in eastern Kentucky fell below the poverty level (Census of Population 1960). A 1954 internal memo of the Harlan County Coal Operators' Association kept local operators informed of local economic conditions. It reported that thirteen mines in Harlan County had closed in the previous three years, and "with the closing, 1,708 men were thrown out of jobs; furthermore we estimate an additional 800 men have been cut off at 'going' mines due to economic conditions, or a total of 2,308 men [have been laid off]. In 1953, the average running time of commercial mines was 68 percent. Since October 1, 1953, we have averaged 3.2 days [of work] per week."

At the national level, coal-mining employment declined by 61 percent during the 1950s, with 300,000 coal miners laid off nationwide (Seltzer 1985, 83). The UMW, which had been relatively active and strong during the previous decade, called no strikes in protest of mine layoffs. To the contrary, UMW President John L. Lewis viewed increased mechanization as an essential step to insure the survival and stability of the coal industry. He and the large companies who belonged to the Bituminous Coal Operators Association (BCOA) saw eye-to-eye on this issue. In the long run, he argued, mechanization would benefit both the coal industry and those miners who remained in it. Lewis targeted small "pony mines," like the one that employed Ernie Norton, for extinction. Lewis was correct in his assessment that such companies contributed to the industry's oversupply problem, drove wages down, and frequently endangered workers' health and safety. So, during contract negotiations, the UMW attempted to ban union companies from transporting or processing nonunion coal. And, during apparently bogus organizing drives, UMW members harassed nonunion employees and destroyed mine and rail equipment. Small operators, in turn, saw themselves as victims of a powerful BCOA-UMW coalition and, after almost a decade of legal actions, they were vindicated. The Supreme Court let stand a ruling that, under the terms of the Sherman Anti-Trust Act, declared the UMW and Tennessee Consolidated Coal Company (of the BCOA) guilty of conspiring to drive small coal operators out of business (Seltzer 1985, 78). With the exception of the health and pension plan, there were few bright spots for UMW coal miners during the 1950s. Their president had grown so chummy with the BCOA that he had become, in effect, an aide to the operators. Indeed, he had become a coal operator, having purchased and invested in coal mines, banks, and railroads with union funds.

Meanwhile back in Harlan, George S. Ward, president of the

Harlan County Coal Operators' Association, analyzed the local coal industry's problems in the 1950s in the following address to the Harlan County Kiwanis Club (3 June 1954):

> The cost of production and transportation is too high for us to meet competition! Our companies are now mining in comparatively thin seams, a majority of which are on a hand-loading basis. The thickness of our coal and inside conditions are not conducive to modern mechanical equipment. You must get a high ton per average per man to make a profit. . . . Mines which have to depend on hand loading do not get an average of more than six tons per man whereas in mechanical mines it is three or four times this much. . . . [Other factors include] the piping of natural gas and oil into the southern states (which at one time was one of our principle markets) as a substitute for coal. . . . Then, there is the fact that railroads are displacing coal burning engines with diesel engines. . . .
>
> Another alarming factor is the importation of foreign residual oil. . . . To summarize: high cost of production, high transportation costs, fringe benefits, welfare payments, strip mines, non-union mines, our geographical location and other general conditions make it next to impossible to successfully compete under the prevailing circumstances.

Clearly, Harlan coal operators faced formidable obstacles. Ultimately they did not win their battle against "foreign" oil, the railroad monopoly, coal competitors, overproduction, and geography. Their war against "fringe benefits, welfare payments, and non-union mines"—in other words, the UMW—met with more-predictable success. The UMW had been playing into coal operators' hands throughout the 1950s.

෧

Ernie worked at Harlan Collieries with his dad from 1955 until 1964. Until 1964, things had gone well for the young family. The children went to school in Ages, where their parents had gone. They were good students—much better than their parents had been. Ernie and Ginny took the children to Sunday school and started going to church themselves. And in 1958 Ernie bought some land and began dreaming of building his own house. He did most of the work on the house after work and on weekends. His father helped. By 1963, Ernie had completed construction on a beautiful three-bedroom bungalow-style house. He and Ginny were thrilled to move their children there.

The trouble at work started just after Ernie had started construction on the house, in 1959 just a year before the United Mine Workers national contract expired. During contract negotiations, Whitfield persuaded Brookside miners that he could not pay them the $24-per-day wage rate, to which the BCOA and UMW had agreed. He had to extend operations to a new area, so there would be expensive, unproductive preparatory work to do. As a temporary cost-saving measure, Brookside miners agreed to prepare the area for $16 per day. They understood that, once production resumed, they would be paid the contract wage of $24 per day. Miners would draw their paychecks from a nonunion subsidiary of Harlan Collieries during that period.

After four years, the miners concluded that their employer had abused the agreement. Senior workers were kept on low-wage jobs and, even after switching to productive work, many employees still received the lower wage rate. Ernie found it both unfair and personally degrading. He complained about it years later:

> [The company] kept some of [the employees] for years, like *three years* under that other coal company! And, if we went to them and said, "Hey, this man's got to be signed up [under a union contract]. He is doing the same kind of work we do, producing coal, union coal; but he's still working for [the other company]." They'd say, "Well, now, we don't need him. We'll just let him go. We're just letting him work 'cos, you know, he's old and not ready for retirement yet; but he can't do nothing." Now that's what the comeback was. They didn't respect that man. He worked his life for them but they were taking advantage of him. That last three years, they'd let him work for $16 a day and doing the same work that I did for $24.

By the time the United Mine Workers contract expired again in 1964, Ernie was angry about the situation. His father had retired from the company by then, but both he and Ernie played an active role in this ill-fated strike. A slow coal market, high local unemployment, out-migration, inadequate strike benefits, court injunctions against picketing strikers, and lack of public interest contributed to the strike's failure locally. As the strike wore on, violence erupted. Ernie got in a fistfight with Ginny's cousin because he was "scabbing" at the Brookside mines. Later that night, someone threw dynamite at the cousin's house, and rumors circulated that Ernie was involved in the incident. Ernie and Ginny recalled that they were at home watching TV when the explosion occurred. When her cousin expressed skepticism about Ernie's alibi, Ginny swore she would never speak to her cousin again. Eight years passed before, at Ernie's urging, she and her cousin reconciled their differences over the matter.

One evening during the strike, a car drove by and fired shots into Ernie and Ginny's living room while they were sitting on the couch watching TV. They dove off the couch, to avoid the flying bullets, and scrambled back to the bedroom to check on the children. Tucked safely in bed at the back of the house, the children were in little danger. Still, Ginny recalled never having been so scared in her life. Over twenty years later, she still attributed her "nervousness" to that incident. Ginny continued to be so "nervous," in fact, that she could not drive a car. Ernie sent Ginny and the children to stay with another cousins in Harlan the next night. He and two friends hid outside in the toolshed with shotguns, waiting for the return of the drive-by shooters. No one came and they never found out who did it. "I'm glad I never found out who did that," Ernie said in 1986. "That kind of thing is impossible to forgive. There'd still be hard feelings over it yet, that is, if I hadn't have killed them at the time. Yeah, it's better this way."

As time passed, many Brookside miners did as they had seen others do in the previous decade: they packed their bags and left. Ernie stuck it out for eighteen months, which was longer than most. In the end, he too was forced to leave Harlan County, "owing everybody from the junk yard to Sears & Roebuck." He and Ginny lost their car, their land, and their new house. Not long after that, the strike collapsed, and for the first time since 1939 there was no union contract at Brookside. The Brookside operations, suffering from the lengthy strike and poor market conditions, closed shortly thereafter and remained idle until 1970, when Eastover Mining Company, a subsidiary of Duke Power, bought it from the Whitfield family.

ۮ

In 1964, Ernie moved his family up to Columbus, Ohio, where his brother Daniel had settled down and taken a job as a welder. Daniel had married Lucy Simpson from Bell County, Kentucky.

Ernie and Ginny thought it remarkable that, after all his travels, Daniel married "a girl from home." Daniel joked that he knew more Kentuckians than Ohioans in Columbus. Although they were happy and made a good living, Ernie and Ginny wanted to raise their children in Kentucky. They stayed with Daniel and his wife until Ernie got a job manufacturing stereo speakers. Within three months, Ernie moved his family to a small apartment in the same subdivision where Daniel and his wife owned a two-bedroom ranch-style house.

Ernie and Ginny's children, Cindy and Ernest, Jr., had a hard time adjusting to city life. They had always been A and B students at Ages, but their grades suffered in Columbus. The children at school made fun of their accents and called them ignorant hill-billies and briar hoppers.[1] Their second hand clothing made them the butt of jokes. Junior cried every day and feigned illness in an effort to be excused from school. Cindy hated school and spent all of her recesses and lunch periods alone.

Ginny had similar difficulties. She had no friends in Columbus, even though she had been considered outgoing and popular at home. She recalled: "I thought it was awful and I was so depressed. I was real depressed. I hated it. I just couldn't get used to it. . . . I didn't like where we lived, it wasn't a real good. Well, it wasn't the worst neighborhood there; but it wasn't the best either. Oh, and the roaches, Oh God, they were awful; and roaches are something that make my skin crawl. I couldn't eat. I couldn't do anything on account of those roaches, even though they had it [the apartment] sprayed once a month; but, still, there were so many! I never did like it. I was always unhappy there."

People up there were hostile, she said. She illustrated her point with the following anecdote: "Dad [Clarence Brown], he was driv-ing this pickup truck. He was real proud of that truck. He loved that truck; and he accidentally bumped this other guy. He didn't hurt the car; he just bumped it a little. And that guy got out and he cussed him all to pieces. And he reached in [the truck] and he was going to try to grab him [Clarence], you know, and I was rolling that window up as fast as I could. And I thought, 'God, these people are wild. We got to get out of here!'" Even when she was shopping, she could not get along with the city people. "They were really rude, in the stores even. They'd just jerk something right out of your hand, even if you were looking at something. . . . The only ones that was really nice, I thought, was the ones from Kentucky. . . . I was surprised at how many [people from Kentucky and Tennessee] there were."

After eight months, the dissatisfied Nortons moved back to Harlan County. "There's about 35,000 people in Harlan County," Ernie said. "And I haven't heard of any of them starving to death. We're going back to Harlan County and we're going to make it just like 35,000 other people makes it." Like many return migrants, they told and retold stories, emphasizing the negative aspects of city life and complaining about discrimination they suffered (see also Batteau 1982b, 454; McCoy and Watkins 1981, 20–35; Philliber and McCoy 1981; Schwarzweller and Brown 1967; Schwarzweller, Brown, and Mangalam 1971; White 1987, 38–52; Wooley and Reid 1974, 53–54; Doris Kilbourne by Teresa Kilbourne, SECC-OHP, 23 March 1979). Not all Appalachian out-migrants hated city life, of course. Some preferred it and many have remained in a variety of midwestern cities and suburbs with no regrets (Brown 1971; McCoy and Watkins 1981; Wooley and Reid 1974, 54).

When the Nortons returned to Harlan County, the children went back to school in Ages, where, ironically, their classmates teased them about their "northern" accents. Ernie and Ginny found jobs in Harlan. Ginny waited the lunch counter at the drug store and Ernie drove a grocery delivery truck. They rented a house near Ginny's parents, who watched the children after school until Ginny returned from work.

There were many changes in Harlan County during the period from 1960 through 1972. By then, most companies had either demolished their camps or sold their camp houses to the families who lived in them. Brookside was one of the few company-owned camps left in Harlan County. With mechanization and increased competition from alternative fuel sources, the coal industry's workforce had declined 70 percent (Seltzer 1986, 9). Likewise, the membership of the UMW had declined dramatically, both locally and nationally. John L. Lewis retired from the presidency in 1960, leaving behind an even more corrupt and authoritarian successor to his position, Anthony Boyle. Boyle, like Lewis, preferred to run the UMW from the top down, with a tight control over district leaders whom he or his predecessor had appointed.

After a decade of mine mechanization, layoffs, high unemployment, management-union collusion, poverty, and out-migration, the 1960s did not hold much promise for Harlan County or the coal industry upon which it relied. The health and pension plan, which so many mine families had counted on, was mismanaged and inadequately funded. Throughout the 1960s, more and more miners and their dependents were declared ineligible to receive benefits: disabled miners, widows, and the marginalized miners who could not find work at unionized mines or continue paying their union dues. Boyle followed in his mentor's more-recent footsteps: he called no strikes and persisted in negotiating weak, sweetheart contracts with the BCOA. This no-strike period stood in stark contrast to the previous period when, from 1935 to 1952, UMW miners walked off their jobs eleven times in strikes lasting from seven to fifty-nine days. From 1952 to 1971 the UMW leaders authorized no strikes against the BCOA. Throughout the 1960s and 1970s, however, rank-and-file miners disregarded the wishes of their leadership and launched "wildcat" (unauthorized) strikes, even after the Supreme Court ruled, in 1970, that wildcat strikers could be fined and sued (Seltzer 1985, 89). Miners also mobilized around the issues of black lung disease, mine safety, and union democracy. Increasingly, they formed coalitions with other community groups as they addressed industry-related issues, such as strip mining, taxation, land ownership, pollution, road damage from coal trucks, and public safety (Seltzer 1985, 89).

Although he was no longer employed as a miner and did not participate in these internal UMW struggles, Ernie Norton had a special interest in the black lung issue. His father, Jess, had died in 1969 from respiratory complications. Ernie worried about developing black lung from his fourteen years as a miner, although he took some comfort in the fact that his Uncle Will had apparently not suffered any ill effects from the job. "You'd like to say that you ain't got it," Ernie explained. "But, now, you'll feel the effects of it when you get to climbing mountains. Or, maybe, when you go off to sleep at night, you hear a little wheeze that ain't supposed to be there." Concerned that disability or death from black lung would undercut the financial support for his children, Ernie cheered silently from the sidelines for the black lung movement. His prayers for black lung compensation were eventually answered by the federal government.

In 1969, in a break with fellow UMW leaders, Joseph A. "Jock"

Yablonski decided to challenge Boyle for the presidency of the UMW. "I have been a part of this leadership . . . but with increasingly troubled conscience," he explained. "I can no longer tolerate the low state to which our union has fallen" (as quoted in Selzer 1985, 110). Boyle fired Yablonski from his position as the director of the union's political action division, denied him access to the *UMWA Journal,* and sent loyalists to disrupt Yablonski rallies. With the support and advice of Ralph Nader and Joseph Rauh, Yablonski successfully raised funds, formulated a platform, and took his message to the increasingly disgruntled union members. So significant was his challenge that a threatened Anthony Boyle ultimately ordered Yablonski's murder. On New Year's Eve 1969, gunmen entered the Yablonski home and killed him, his wife, and his daughter as they slept. This shocking act of violence delivered a staggering blow to the UMW membership, even in Harlan's District 19, where support for Lewis and Boyle had been strong. As we shall see, Harlan miners disagree as to the meaning and importance of these events. They nevertheless played an important role in the next generation's disillusionment with labor unions generally.

❧

Another important factor in the decline of local UMW solidarity during the 1960s and 1970s was the increase of small, locally owned mine operations. Small operators, such as Ernie Norton's first employer, leased mineral rights from land and energy companies who no longer found it profitable to produce in the slack times. The increasing availability of relatively inexpensive strip and auger mining technology, during the 1950s and 1960s, made it possible for such small operators to mine coal for open sale on the "spot market"—that is, without a supply contract. Small operators recruited employees through kinship and community ties. In spite of the difficult and unsafe working conditions in these marginally profitable operations, the union made few inroads organizing there. "If you go to a mine and everybody at that mine—let's say, a 25-man mine, he's some kin to the owner; he's a nephew, son, brother, uncle, in-law. Well, you can whistle at the wind at that mine because you're not going to get those folks [in the union]," noted former UMW district president Joe Phipps. ". . . It's a family affair."

After fifteen years of industry turmoil and decline, things finally seemed to be turning around for Harlan County, the coal industry, and the UMW by the mid-1970s. The OPEC oil embargo had temporarily shifted the balance back in favor of coal, as the federal government promised to subsidize coal liquification and gassification programs and set the nation on a coal-fueled journey toward energy independence. Coal prices rose from $7.01 per ton to $15.75, from 1971 to 1974. Small operators, who had previously had to scratch out a living from their puny, capital-starved operations, enjoyed windfall profits. Large energy companies reopened their operations, and utility companies signed long-term supply contracts. Employment in Harlan's mines rose 58 percent, from 2,416 employees in 1970 to 4,103 in 1980. And, industry-wide, employment rose 67 percent, from 144,000 in 1970 to about 241,000 in 1978. Boyle and his followers had been convicted in the Yablonski murders. The Miners for Democracy movement had finally succeeded in installing a reform-oriented, rank-and-file president, in one Arnold Miller.

When Norman Yarborough, president of Eastover Coal Company, bought the Brookside and Highsplint operations from Bryan Whitfield in 1970, Ernie pushed all of his reservations and health concerns "to the back of his mind" and applied for a job. He needed those higher wages to pay for Cindy's college expenses in the next few years. Then, of course, Junior had to go to school, too. Besides, Ernie always enjoyed the challenge of coal mining more than any other work he had ever done. "It kind of gets in your blood, you know?" he explained. Ernie's brother, Daniel, moved his family down just in time for his oldest child to start school at Ages Grade School. Daniel observed, "Out of all the places I went, I never went nowhere to stay!" He was happy to be home. He explained, "I'm sure it's because I was born here and so many of my relatives live here; and you just know a lot of people. It's a small town. It's a slower pace. . . . I never did want to stay away. I left because I had to, to get jobs. . . . I always looked forward to coming back" (see also Garkovitch 1982; White 1987). Harlan County's population increased 11 percent from 1970 to 1980 (see table 1.1).

The first order of business at the long-idled Brookside mines was to restore and repair the facilities. Eastover handpicked a skeletal crew and immediately took a vote on union representation. The employees selected the Southern Labor Union (SLU), locally regarded as a "company union." Ernie said that this had been a shrewd management maneuver. "The company came in and they had just a handful of people, like eight or ten. They voted to have Southern Labor [Union] represent them; and they done that real quick and got it settled. And, of course, once you get a union in, you've got to wait 'til the contract expires before another union can come in," he explained. Later, Eastover "really boomed and got up to 150 or 160 men."

The new workers questioned the SLU'S ability to represent their interests. They were satisfied with the wages. Eastover had raised them twice in three years, from $18 per day to $28 per day and, finally, to $45 per day. They were, however, dissatisfied with their medical benefits, pension plan, job security, and working conditions. The company had pushed them hard to get the operations started. Employees were afraid to complain about safety and overwork without the protection of a legitimate labor union. John Campbell, Ernie Norton's best friend, was one of those who was afraid to complain. As a repairman, he got only eight days off during the first year he worked for Eastover. He frequently worked ten-hour shifts and always worked on the weekend. "They [the management] don't really threaten you that much, it was just understood that you're expected to do what you're told. . . . My average work week was 70 hours, 70 hours a week. . . . They'd come in fifteen minutes before quitting time on Friday and say, 'We're going to work tomorrow.' They didn't say, 'Do you *want* to come in and work tomorrow?' They said, 'You're *going* to work tomorrow,'" he complained. "If I had come in and said, 'I ain't working Saturday,' . . . they'd have had somebody else in my place. Because the company did have the right to hire and fire."

The miners interest in UMW representation was reciprocated by a reform union leadership devoted to reestablishing its prominence in this eastern coal field. Local pro-union activists advised the leadership against sending any organizers who had been associated with the previous regimes of Lewis and Boyle. District 19, of which Harlan was a part, had been a hotbed of Lewis-Boyle support. It had even supplied the gunmen in the Yablonski murders. Still, this organizing effort could not be tarnished by the corruption and murder that had characterized their administration. Therefore, rank-and-file miners and relatively inexperienced organizers were sent to Brookside. One of them was Joe Phipps, a Lynch miner who, one decade later, became president of District 19. The UMW devoted $2 million to the Brookside campaign and strike (Seltzer 1985, 131).

In June 1973, the Brookside miners elected the UMW as their bargaining representative, by a vote of 113 to 55. In contract negotiations, they demanded (1) portal-to-portal pay, that is, having pay periods include travel time from the mine face to the area of production; (2) a safety clause to protect miners who reported unsafe conditions; (3) participation in the UMW medical plan; (4) a pension plan; and (5) a safeguard against de facto wage cuts through subcontracting arrangements.

When contract negotiations broke down at Brookside in July 1973, the miners walked out. The company obtained a court injunction to limit Brookside pickets and hired nonunion workers to take their places. It also expanded production at the SLU Highsplint operations nearby. After traveling to Harlan County, filmmaker Barbara Koppel, who had been filming a documentary on the UMW's democratization efforts, decided to shift the focus of her project to the Brookside strike. The result was an Academy Award winning documentary of the strike, *Harlan County, U.S.A.* During the next year, as the company and pickets struggled over the issue of replacement workers at Brookside, Koppel filmed the events. Company foremen and nonunion workers armed themselves before coming to work, where they confronted pickets, many of whom were women. The pickets taunted the "scabs" with sticks, bottles, and rocks. Soon, pickets began carrying weapons as well. Mine foreman Basil Collins threatened them with a gun, and one night there was a drive-by shooting. All of this was captured on film.

People on both sides of the conflict became anxious and frightened. Ernie's brother, Daniel, recalled:

> We had really faced situations where there could've been lots of people killed during that strike. It's scary. I mean, you think you'd never get yourself in a position that you would hurt somebody, seriously, maybe kill 'em or something like that; but you can get on a picket line and you can get so worked up that you would do that. You definitely would. And I'm sure that some of the people who were working as scabs at Highsplint felt the same

way. . . . They got worked up. It's not a good thing. I'd say [we were] very lucky not to [have] no more violence than there was. . . . There was some potentially dangerous days and nights there; and I wouldn't want to go through it again.

A local storekeeper, John Deaton, Jr., added, "This place was tense, just about everybody who came in here had a pistol sticking in his hip pocket. And, you know, where there's guns, there's trouble liable to break out any time. Especially when people's on strike. There's nothing to do really. They're cranky and, possibly, drinking. And a drinking man with a gun is not hardly responsible."

For its part, the company was successful in securing court injunctions, which restricted picket numbers and sites, and in petitioning the Kentucky State Police to escort workers past the pickets and to protect company property. The miners, on the other hand, succeeded in taking their case to the American public. They gave interviews to the national newspapers and television reporters, protested at Duke Power's board meetings, gave handbills to Carolina consumers paying their utility bills, and promoted their cause at fund-raising parties where they showed hair-raising film clips from *Harlan County, U.S.A.*

The Norton brothers steered clear of the limelight. But their friend and neighbor John Campbell stepped to the forefront. He came to think of himself as an expert on public relations. In a 1986 interview, he reflected on the company's failure to do what the strikers did so well: deal with the media. "We were looking for help. We wanted the public on our side. . . . We met with the National Council of Churches and asked them to take their pension funds out of Duke Power stock, which some of them did. . . . There was several newspapers that came in here. The company, for some reason or another, was rude to the media. They never *did* learn. Why would Yarborough talk straight or talk mean?" he asked. "He did not know how to play the game. He lost out on a lot of opportunities, I'm sure, by not using common sense. The media can absolutely make you look good or bad."

The Brookside miners, on the other hand, cooperated with the media, in particular the makers of *Harlan County, U.S.A.* Daniel observed:

[*Harlan County, U.S.A.*] probably made [the county] look bad and, of course, we don't *need* to look bad now, 'cos the strike's over; but, really and truly, you don't want to think of things being bad in Harlan County. But now there were at that time, and there *still are,* people just like the movie showed. There's houses that way. There's plenty of people that lives without bathrooms here; and plenty of people that lives without water [indoor plumbing]. . . . At the time, we wanted to look as bad as we could. We wanted to make Eastover look bad. We wanted publicity and that type of thing gets publicity. If you'd have showed somebody's houses up on . . . Ivy Hill [a middle class area of town], you weren't going to get publicity; but, if you show a little shack sitting up here at the head of Bailey's Creek with some kids out there with no shoes on in the snow, you're going to get sympathy. You're going to get people on your side. This is the way we live. And, for some people, that is the way they *still* live. They still live that way. But we did take advantage of things like that. But that's the name of the game. I never did feel that Eastover was as bad as I tried to make them appear to be. In my own heart, I didn't feel that way. But it was necessary to make Eastover look bad for us to gain.

The national public relations campaign seemed to work. Public support grew, and eventually federal mediators interceded in the negotiations. Ernie was surprised at Yarborough's anti-union hostility and unwillingness to compromise with the UMW workers, at first. But later he arrived at the following conclusion, based upon his own assessment of Yarborough:

> We really expected the company to sign that contract. We didn't anticipate a fourteen-month strike. This was strictly Yarborough's decision. Even though Duke Power was in a non-union area and they don't like unions, . . . they gave Yarborough a free hand. Of course, he rejected it. . . . His dad was a coal miner for a while and he wasn't in the union long enough to draw a pension and get the benefits. . . . They got rules and his dad didn't qualify. So, he didn't like the union personally, for that reason, and probably for other reasons, too. Naturally, him being the president of a company, he would have had a much freer hand to do anything he wanted to without the union to help him on his way; and I'm sure he didn't like that and *especially* because he had personal feelings against the union. I would say that Yarborough was just strictly non-union. He don't like union. Now, Bryan Whitfield, the owner before him, didn't like unions; but he wasn't *possessed* with it.

In a separate interview, Yarborough offered the same explanation for his anti-UMW attitude. The union had not provided his father with a pension and medical benefits. At great personal and financial cost to himself, Norman Yarborough supported his father but allowed him to believe that the money had come from the union he had admired.

Like the Whitfields, the Yarboroughs came to Harlan's expanding coalfields from Alabama. They were not, however, a family of wealthy planters, entrepreneurs, and engineers, as the Whitfields had been. The Yarboroughs were coal miners who moved to Harlan in 1933. Norman Yarborough's took his first job at age 14, hand-loading coal for thirty-six cents per ton at Harlan Fuel Company. From there, he worked his "way up the hard way," from coal miner to president of Eastover Coal. The "closest thing to a handout" he ever took was a GI bill loan to fund his college education. As a "self-made man," Yarborough did not favor labor unions, government "handouts," such as welfare or food stamps, or Affirmative Action hiring programs. Yarborough advocated hard work and maintained that problems could be solved on a personal basis, without the interference of a union. The union's failure to provide for his father in his old age proved to him that the organization was corrupt and hypocritical. In the end, Yarborough had to set his personal feelings aside. After striking miner Lawrence Jones was shot and killed in August 1974, the federal government put pressure on the company to sign the contract. Two days after Jones's murder, Eastover and UMW negotiators reached agreement. The men who killed Jones were never prosecuted.

Brookside women, primarily miners' wives, played an important role in the strike and maintained a high profile on the picket lines (Maggard 1988, 1990). State police arrested and jailed them for blocking the entrance to Brookside. The women, explaining that they had no babysitters, took their children to jail with them. Pictures of women and children who had been incarcerated in Harlan County scored another point for strikers in the media war (see figure 2.1). In addition, some miners thought that women prevented violence on the picket line. Daniel Norton praised the Brookside women, although his own wife refused to participate. "There's no doubt in my mind . . . that the women won that strike. They prevented violence and they got results. They got publicity. Of course, some of them got roughed up a little bit. . . . It was kind of tough on them women; but the courts can tie a union's hands,

FIGURE 2.1
Brookside picketers photographed in the Harlan jail by Earl Dotter.
Photograph courtesy of the University of Kentucky Photo Archives,
UMWA Collection. © Earl Dotter.

through fines and things; and, when the women came into it, the company had to deal with just private citizens," Daniel noted. The entry of women reenergized the strike, according to Daniel, who said," "They [the company] just about had us [striking workers] beat down. It would have led to violence, I'm certain, because there was no way we were going to watch somebody [strikebreakers] go to work. . . . I'd say, after the first little bit of violence, the company would have gained the upper hand. . . . When somebody [on the company side] is killed, you start losing ground." Joe Phipps agreed with Daniel's assessment: "[Those women] had a very, very, very, very large part [in the strike]. If it had not been for those wives, it's very likely that they could've broke that strike down. And, if it hadn't been for those wives, probably there would've been a great number of people killed" (see figure 2.2).

The Brookside strike was a central event in the lives of local miners' wives, most of whom were housewives without high school

FIGURE 2.2
Brookside women on the picket line. Photographed by Earl Dotter,
courtesy of the University of Kentucky Photo Archives, UMWA
Collection. © Earl Dotter.

diplomas. For many, it was a life-changing experience. They came
out of the strike with stronger political commitments, higher self-
esteem, a sense of solidarity with others in the community, and a
"take charge" attitude. Those who went on to get their GEDs, go
to college, find jobs, and start their own businesses cited the strike
as an important lesson or a turning point in their lives (Maggard
1988, 148–79). Nevertheless, even as the Brookside strike undermined patriarchal gender dynamics among some mining families,
it also mobilized traditional gender ideology in support of class
solidarity, thus reinforcing patriarchal structures of action and
thought even as they were eroding. For example, strikers assumed
that men, both strikers and strikebreakers, would be less likely to
attack women physically, so that the presence of women on the
picket line would necessarily make it a safer place for all. The
women, for their part, carried signs that impugned the masculinity
of strikebreakers (see figure 2.2, second sign on the left in the front
row). This was not a new rhetorical strategy, either. Back in 1932,

Florence Reese's song "Which Side Are You On?" referred to miners as "gentlemen" and posed the following alternative: "Will you be a gun thug? Or will you be a man?" Class and gender often became discursively intertwined in the discourses of Harlan's mining families, where "real" men mined coal, financially supported their families, and "stood up" for their fellow miners. (This agenda is a somewhat contradictory one, as will be discussed later.)

The Nortons, Campbells, Deatons, and other United Mine Workers families thought that the unionization of Brookside would eventually pave the way for organization of the rest of the county. No doubt, Arnold Miller and the rest of the UMW leadership hoped this would occur as well. This, however, was not to be. The Brookside strike caused hard feelings between workers, friends, and relatives in the county. The Highsplint miners, in particular, resented having been picketed by their co-workers. John Campbell had predicted this particular outcome. He explained:

> Mainly, it was a strike against Brookside but, from time to time, we would pick on Highsplint [the nearby Southern Labor Union operation run by Eastover] and Arjay [in Bell County] just to harass the company some. That kind of hurt us in a way. When we brought Highsplint out and kept them out for a couple of weeks, we had a lot of trouble. That was a mistake on our part, I'd say. But it come from the chief organizer of the UMW at that time.
>
> I called him myself and told him it was a mistake, that we couldn't gain nothing. If we kept these people out for a week, if we kept them out for two weeks, that wasn't enough coal to where Duke Power could possibly miss it; and it wasn't going to hurt them, cost-wise. But it's going to make enemies. It's going to make enemies between employees at the Highsplint mines and us. . . . He said, "You're wrong. . . . We've got to show them that we can shut them down." I said, "I think you're making a mistake."
>
> It turns out that organizer was wrong. It turned out exactly like I thought it would. Eventually, we got that contract at Brookside. And Highsplint, all they had to do was accept the union. No strike. Continue working without any loss of pay. They could have signed a union contract; but where we made so many enemies, more or less out of spite, they voted for the Southern Labor Union.

Young miners from Highsplint would later admit that the company bribes for their loyalty had indeed forestalled further unionization. While Daniel did not talk about this factor explicitly, his brother Ernie thought that it was important. As he put it, "In this county in the late 1970s, the nonunion mines were paying high wages. In some cases exceeding UMW wages. They did that to hold off the UMW. . . . There was just enough UMW in this county to hold a threat over the local industry."

After the strike, Eastover demolished its dilapidated camp houses. Mining families moved to houses, trailers, and apartments wherever they could find them. With the destruction of Brookside, Ages lost some of its vitality. The school closed down and the community lost two of its three stores. When the company put a baseball field on the former Brookside house sites, local residents recognized this as a point of no return for their community. Although some young families remained in Brookside-Ages, they all worked and attended school outside the community. Neighborly intimacy decreased among this segment of the local population, although the "old-timers" remained relatively close. Still, things just were not the same, Ginny lamented. Theirs was becoming a community of "old folks." The empty school building and playground saddened her most of all. She almost hated to go to the building to cast her vote on election day—it was so cold and barren these days.

The demolition of the Brookside camp was not an unprecedented move. In fact, the company abandoned Brookside long after most other Harlan coal town and camp houses were sold to residents or left to stand empty. It was no longer profitable or prudent to maintain homes for the company employees. The poor maintenance and living conditions at Brookside had become a national symbol of corporate neglect and exploitation and a rallying point for miners during the 1973 strike. By 1985, these houses were a dim memory to young folks. Equally important, Eastover employees and their families no longer had a convenient place to congregate and discuss their grievances against the company. They were dispersed throughout the county to live a splintered, commuting existence. This was to have a dampening affect upon class solidarity (see also Kerr and Siegal 1954; Lipset 1963, 104).

The company learned another lesson from the Brookside strike: the importance of public relations. One of the company's most successful community relations efforts came during the flood of 1977, when it donated labor and heavy machinery to the clean-up and salvage efforts. Acts such as these helped redeem the company's tarnished image, as this poem by a committed union man attests (Deaton 1978):

Three years ago we fought you a battle,
We kept your name in the news;
We'll never forget the night it was over,
When we all were singing the blues.

It's been a struggle to prove our point,
Both parties have been to blame;
Cooperation in the last few months,
Has changed the name of the game.

It's not our intention to apologize,
For the difference in our views;
But what you've done for us this month,
We want you back in the news.

. . . .

There'll be remarks as to why you cared,
Such as the trouble we had before;
But the kindness you've shown during our disaster,
You'll never want a Seventy-four.

May the good Lord bless the responsible parties,
For supplying us with your labor;

There's one good friend we won't forget
Duke Power, "Our Friendly Neighbor."

Daniel Norton expressed a more cynical view about Eastover's flood relief effort:

Now, there's a few good things you could say that Yarborough done; but he done it, in a sense, to get even for when we gave them such a bad name in the news media. When this flood came along [1977], they did a lot of work. They did more than all the other companies in the whole county put together. They did a tremendous amount of work. Of course, that's all tax deductible; it didn't *cost* Eastover to do this. They got it back on taxes. And, of course, they had numbers that they charged this work to and a lot of work that wasn't supposed to be charged to it, was [meaning that they claimed production costs as tax-deductible donations]. Even though they did do a good deed by helping to clean up the county, it turned out to be profitable for them. . . . and it gave them a chance to look good after looking so bad during the strike.

ﾟ▲

Eastover Mining Company operated at Brookside from 1974 until 1982, when the Carolina public utility commissions stopped the company from passing the higher costs of their coal on to their consumers. In Harlan County, there were two schools of thought about why Eastover could not produce its coal as cheaply as competitors could. Yarborough blamed the UMW. The UMW protected inefficient workers, decreased management flexibility, and increased the financial burden upon the company, who had to pay high wages, make burdensome contributions to miners' pensions, and provide other costly benefits to employees. Ernie and Daniel blamed management inefficiency and incompetence for the problems at Eastover. "Why, they had so many managers, they had to fight over who was going to make the coffee in the morning. They didn't have any work to do," Daniel chortled. Management never instituted a maintenance plan, he further observed. And so production was constantly being slowed by costly breakdowns. Bad investments and misallocations of funds contributed to the loss of profit. "Just look at tipple over there [at Brookside]! They built it all wrong and it never has seen a bit of use," Ernie complained. Others, who preferred to remain anonymous, intimated that Norman Yarborough was in the business for his own personal profit, not to provide affordable coal for Duke Power and ensure their financial well-being. He hired his friends and skimmed money out of the corporate till, they said. Of course, these were only rumors. Yarborough was never fired or prosecuted for his financial or management dealings. And many in the county, including Dr. Vivian Blevins, former president of Southeast Community College, expressed admiration for Yarborough and his "innovative" management techniques.

The final straw for the company came in December 1981, when one of their coal refuse dumps unleashed an avalanche of sludge onto the houses along Ages Creek. That was, in Daniel's words, "the beginning of the end." The company paid millions of dollars to victims of the disaster. They then faced the formidable and costly task of cleaning up the mess. All of this contributed to the cost of Eastover-mined coal. Duke Power, in fact, was paying more to mine its own coal than it would have cost to buy coal on the market. When the public utilities commission ruled that Duke could not pass the higher cost of its coal on to Carolina electricity consumers, Duke shut down its Brookside operations. In July 1983, Harlan coal operator Pat Abbott bought Eastover's holdings in Harlan County; he closed the Brookside mine and took its equipment up to Highsplint. He continued to operate the SLU mines at Highsplint.

Soon thereafter, he refused to sign even the SLU contract. He preferred to run his business without the interference of any union. Ernie Norton, out of mining work again, decided to go into the service station business with his brother Daniel. They ran a service station in Coxton, about four miles down the road, for two years. Daniel "did the mechanic work" and Ernie "did the books." In 1985, they sold the business to a neighbor and retired.

ॐ

In its own way, the period from 1950 to 1980 was just as dramatic and important to Harlan County miners as the Depression "mine wars" had been. True, there was no publicly recognized Communist movement, and there were fewer local murders, false arrests, and election riggings. The local pro-labor folksongs and poems from the period have not as of yet emerged as nationally recognized classics. Local writers have felt less compelled to produce histories and memoirs on the period, perhaps because they are still relatively young or the events are too fresh on their memories. But the lack of local historical revision might also stem from the relative lack of state and national media attention to these years. Except for the 1973–74 Brookside strike, which produced two books (Ewen 1979; Wooley and Reid 1974) and a film, there was little to report about labor activism in Harlan during this 30-year period. The big national stories had focused elsewhere: the corruption and mismanagement of the UMW, the Miners for Democracy struggle (centered outside the District 19 Boyle stronghold), the decline of the regional coal industry and economy, and endemic Appalachian poverty.

As far as the miners' union was concerned, according to Ernie

Norton, these years were a regrettable period of decline and loss. "[My father's generation] had it rough. When union was hard to get, they had to get it," he noted. "But now, it turns out, [the union] hasn't been held." Ernie's shift from active to passive voice in this passage may denote an unwillingess to shoulder the entire burden of blame for this loss. His father might have won the union, but Ernie, by himself, did not lose it. The following chapter examines additional factors at work during the 1970s and 1980s that influenced Harlan's decline in union strength. These factors helped to set in motion yet another round of union-related Norton family tension. This time, Ernie was cast in the awkward role of playing father-in-law to a nonunion miner.

CHAPTER 3

It's Good Not to Worry about Bills and Stuff

"It's good not to worry about bills and stuff," Linda Taylor said as she recalled the 1970s coal boom. One of several returning women students enrolled in my evening community college course, she had come back to school in 1984 in the hopes of regaining a measure of economic security. Unlike her pro-union miner father, Linda did not pin her financial hopes upon the UMW or any labor union. And, unlike her mother, she did not pin her hopes upon a breadwinner husband. Through a combination of choice and circumstance, she faced the shifting economic tides of the 1980s as an individual economic free-agent. She was not alone. Many of her friends, relatives, neighbors, and former co-workers, including Cindy and Bobby Carson (Ernie Norton's daughter and son-in-law), had arrived at a similar position.

This chapter explores the lives and experiences of the contemporary generation of Harlan mining families, those for whom the union "was not held." Like the preceding chapters, this one intersperses description with analysis, the informants' words with my own. This chapter departs from previous ones, however, inasmuch as it offers more detailed, ethnographic description and shorter, more conversational quotes in place of life-history interview material. This is because the subjects of this chapter were, more or less, my contemporaries. Our lives were connected as friends, fellow club members and bowlers, and teacher-students. We socialized and spent our spare time together. In many ways, we shared similar experiences and memories of growing up in the 1960s and 1970s.

On the other hand, several factors differentiated and distanced us as well. As before, occupation, class, status, power, and, in some cases, gender differences separated us. There was still an age and life-cycle barrier. I was 25. They ranged in age from 32 to 45. I had never been married and had no children. They had all been married and had children. And, perhaps equally as important, I shared the pro-union sentiments of their parents. At UC, I had been one of the founding members of the Association of Graduate Student Employees, a union for research and teaching assistants. After I left Harlan, I would serve on the union's executive board for the maximum number of terms. None of my friends shared my faith in collective bargaining. This did not appear to cause tension between us, as I rarely volunteered information on this topic and never attempted to persuade them to change their position. When asked, I explained my viewpoints as briefly and honestly as possible. I think that they appreciated my candor. And I know that we all, at least, shared the position that "it's good not to worry about bills and stuff."

ॐ

In 1973, during the heat of the Brookside strike, Ernie's daughter left home to attend Eastern Kentucky University in Richmond, Kentucky, about two and a half hours from Harlan. She had gotten good grades in high school and was chosen salutatorian of her class. She went to school to become a nurse because she liked helping people. The night before she left, she was so excited that she could not fall asleep. Among other things, Cindy was worried that her father would not be able to afford college while he was on strike. But Ernie dismissed her objections. He did not think that the strike would last long. And, besides, the financial aid and student loans would take care of things until he was working again. On the drive back from EKU that August day when they had delivered Cindy to her dorm, Ernie and Ginny discussed Cindy's future with excitement. They were proud to send the first Norton to college.

Unfortunately, things did not work out as Cindy and her parents had planned. Cindy found her studies difficult, especially chemistry, which she ultimately failed. About two weeks into the semester, Cindy started to feel ill. She could not breathe, particularly when she lay down at night. The doctors at the infirmary could never pinpoint the trouble, but Cindy was convinced it was a respiratory disorder or an allergy. She studied every evening until one or two in the morning and then could not sleep at night. She was too tired to enjoy the football games, beer blasts, dances, and night clubs around campus. She slept best at home, so she returned to Ages every weekend.

At the end of her first semester, Cindy dropped out of college. She was unhappy there and her grade point average was a disappointing 2.2. Her father was still on strike at Brookside, and Cindy felt guilty asking him for spending money. She decided to postpone college until after the strike. She got a job as a bookkeeping clerk to assist with the family finances. Her job enabled her to help buy groceries and pay some bills. She was particularly proud that she could rent her brother a tuxedo to wear to the senior prom. "You know, it may seem little now," she reminded me, in retrospect. "But, when you're in high school, that's a big deal!"

Two years passed. The strike had ended successfully and her father was working steadily. Ernie Jr. graduated among the top 10 percent of his class at Evarts High School but, unlike Cindy, he had no interest in going to college. This greatly disappointed Ernie and Ginny, but at least they could be grateful that Ernie Jr. did not choose to become a miner. He had the sense to get a "desk job" for the Social Security office. It did not pay very much, but it was a relatively safe and stable job.

In the meantime, Cindy fell in love with Bobby Carson. Bobby drove a milk truck in Harlan and had grown up in nearby Loyall, the same railroad town to which Ernie's paternal grandparents had initially immigrated in the 1920s. In 1975, Cindy and Bobby married in a simple ceremony at the Baptist church in Ages, with family and close friends in attendance. They had a modest reception at her parents' house but did not go on a honeymoon. They started saving money for a house immediately.

When Bobby was growing up, his parents owned a small drive-in restaurant near Harlan. Bobby's father died of a heart attack in 1963 and his mother had to sell the business. She could not manage it, with three boys to raise. After that, Mrs. Carson got a job in medical records department at the Harlan Appalachian Regional Hospital. Money was tight around the Carson household, but Mrs. Carson was a good financial manager. Her boys all ate well, had nice clothes, and graduated high school. Bobby was a high school football star. He was the only one of Mrs. Carson's boys who remained in Harlan after he grew up. The eldest, Corbin, found construction work in Florida, and the youngest, Leslie, was a Marine stationed in San Diego. Bobby and Cindy rented a dark, cramped apartment in Loyall, just six blocks from Mrs. Carson's house. They wanted to be near her since they were her only family in town. They alternated between Mrs. Carson's and the Nortons' houses for Sunday dinner. Bobby stopped by his mom's house on his way home from work, when he was not running late. They talked on the phone at least once a week.

About a year after Cindy and Bobby married, Bobby quit his job at the dairy and took a job mining coal for Duke Power up at Highsplint. "I never in the world dreamed he would become a miner," Cindy complained later. "When I first met him, he looked so trim and clean in his white uniform. That's one of the things I liked about him. He was so clean, neat, and sweet-smelling; but, now, look at this! [She pointed to the pile of gray underwear she had just folded, and sighed.] You can't get these clothes clean. I set aside a few pairs of underwear for his days off and when we travel. His work underwear is just as black as can be! And he's done ruined my bathroom, where he comes in after work to take his clothes off and shower."

White underwear was not important to Bobby Carson. He rolled his eyes and shook his head in disbelief when Cindy complained about the laundry or the mess Bobby made when he returned home from work. "Oh, she's got it real bad," he teased her. "What with having to throw my clothes in a Kenmore washer. Why, wonder what she'd say if she had to scrub them on a washboard like her granny did?" Bobby wanted to have a few things in life and he figured the mining provided the swiftest route to success. When Bobby started working underground in 1977, he made a little over $100 a day. He had a group health-insurance plan and was working steadily. He could get overtime pay when he wanted it. He liked his boss and the guys at work, too. Some of them became his closest friends. After a few years on the job, he had saved enough to buy a nice car, an old Jeep to take four-wheeling and camping, photography equipment, and a new guitar. In 1978, he and Cindy moved to a comfortable home in Lawnvale, a middle-class residential zone between Harlan and Loyall. Their new house was twice as big as their childhood homes. And, as Bobby was fond of reminding everyone, it had appliances their parents had never even imagined (see also Yarrow 1982, 330).

Ernie was disappointed that his son-in-law felt no compunction about working at a nonunion mine, especially the one at High-splint, where Ernie and his co-workers had picketed in 1973. Ginny had convinced him, however, not to cause trouble over the matter. Family harmony and love was important, she said. Bobby was a good provider for Cindy and Julie, and "the girls" loved him very much. Ernie, who remembered his own father's and grand-father's disputes over the union, did not want his grandchild to suffer and "feel torn" in the same way as he had. So he did not criticize Bobby. Instead, he just tried to remind Bobby of the many ways in which he had benefited from the labor movement. Bobby did not disagree with his father-in-law's point, but he thought the UMW had served its purpose, its time had passed. Ernie, in turn, disagreed on this claim but recognized that Bobby's views were as much a reflection of 1980s conservative political ideology and his generational upbringing as anything else. Perhaps, Ernie thought, the pro-union pendulum would swing back in his granddaughter's lifetime.

My colleague Michael Yarrow links the eighties' decline in per-ceived power among UMW miners in central Appalachia with a reassessment of the union's history of militance as well as a shift in the the definition of manliness among the region's miners. As the wildcat strikes of the 1970s are being reinterpreted as "foolish and ignoble" rather than valiant attempts to establish union power and democracy, masculinity is increasingly defined less by the ability to "face down" one's employer than by the dedication to providing a living for one's family and loyalty to one's workmates (Yarrow 1990, 49). The tension between the demands of masculinity—the ability to exert power in the workplace and political arena, or the obligation to provide a living for one's family—can be discerned in the relations of the last four generations of "Norton" men. Clarence and Bobby placed priority in their obligations to their family over anything else and, so, have been unwilling to partici-pate in union actions. Jess and Ernie, on the other hand, can justify their union militance by appeal to the same logic: They are making a better life for their families. With Ginny's assistance, Ernie devel-oped sympathy for his son-in-law's dilemma and an appreciation of Bobby's commitment to and support of Cindy and Julie. This paved the way for a more congenial relationship between these two men than the one shared by Ernie's father Jess and his grandfather Clarence.

≥≥

Bobby had entered coal mining, along with a lot of other new-comers, on the heels of a temporary coal boom. Of course, at the time not many people realized it was only temporary. Coal demand had risen, coal prices surged upward, profits were up, out-migrants had returned home, and jobs seemed relatively plentiful. Under reform leadership, the UMW had negotiated a strong national contract in 1974 and completed a successful organizing drive at Brookside. Although the UMW represented only two Harlan County operations—Eastover Mining Company at Brookside and U.S. Coal & Coke at Lynch, most local companies tried to keep pace with UMW wages and benefits in order to avoid having their own workers unionize.

While demand and coal prices were up from 1973 to 1976, the industry had become increasingly inefficient. Established com-panies mined even the poor seams of coal, and small, under-capitalized operations invaded the market. Increased activity re-quired new numbers of workers and managers, many of whom lacked the necessary training or experience to do an adequate job. By 1977, over half the national coal mine workforce was, like Bobby Carson, under the age of thirty-five (Seltzer 1986, 15). Labor-management relations, during this transitional period, were marred by confrontations, absenteeism, wildcat strikes, and lack of teamwork (15). All of these factors contributed to an overall de-cline in coal mine productivity from nineteen to fourteen tons per worker per shift (17). It would not be long until the industry would suffer, once again, the ill effects of overproduction, compounded, this time, by production inefficiency.

≥≥

In 1977, Bobby was earning a good living in coal, so Cindy quit her bookkeeping job to focus her attention on their new baby, Julie. Julie was Cindy and Bobby's only child. Childbirth was so hard for Cindy that she vowed she would never have another child. At first, she and her mother argued about whether it was best to have one child or two. Her mother thought one child would grow up lonely and become selfish and spoiled. In the old days, she pointed out, you had lots of children so they could help you with your work, be a comfort in your old age, and take care of you. Besides, there was always the possibility of losing a child. In that event, any mother would be inconsolable; she would have no other children to love and raise.

Over the years, Cindy's mother had changed her mind. When I returned for a visit in 1991 with my own two-year-old daughter in tow, she conceded that Cindy had made a wise decision. These days, she warned me, a family could only afford to raise one child. Even then, it was a struggle. When we asked Bobby his opinion on the matter, he shrugged and said that, since the woman had to carry the babies and go through labor, their opinions were more important than men's. Cindy and her mother were pleased by Bobby's understanding and easygoing attitude. But sometimes Cindy wondered if Bobby secretly longed for a son. He never said he did.

Bobby and Cindy's primary concern was that Julie get a good education and prepare for a career with some stability and security. They complained bitterly about the politics in the school system but knew that Harlan had many talented and dedicated teachers. They thought that, with their diligence and participation, Julie would get a decent education in the local schools. Cindy and Bobby were not the only Harlan Countians, or Kentuckians, who expressed concern their local public educational system. Education-related news items made the front page of the local newspaper quite often in the mid-1980s, as rural Harlan parents blockaded the roads to protest local school closings and busing, children boycotted school to draw attention to inadequate facilities, and community leaders and activists sponsored adult literacy programs and formed organizations to promote educational advancement and reform.

After I left Harlan County in 1986, the state legislature passed a comprehensive school reform package in response to a Kentucky Supreme Court ruling that declared the state's method of funding education to be unconstitutional. Using local property taxes as a funding base for schools meant, of course, that more money was spent on students from wealthy districts than was spent on those from poor districts, such as students in Harlan County. The Kentucky Educational Reform Act (KERA) aims to equalize funding among state school districts, place more control over schools in the hands of the local community, teachers, and principals, and eliminate nepotism, corruption, and overpoliticization of local school boards. Since this reform measure passed, Harlan County's school officials have become embroiled in several conflicts with state education officials. The county superintendent, a principal, and three school board members were ousted for misconduct and incompetence. In 1992, the state took over management of the Harlan County school system.

≥≥

On a typical day, Bobby and Cindy got up at 6 A.M. They "slept in" until 9 or 9:30 on the weekends. While Bobby got ready for work, Cindy fixed breakfast and packed his lunch pail. At 6:30, she woke up Julie, and the Carson family sat down to breakfast. Bobby usually left for work around 7 A.M. He and his buddy Frank Johnson took turns driving to work at Highsplint. Their commute to work took about thirty-five minutes, even though it was only an eighteen-mile drive. Highway 38 was a curvy little two-lane road then. As I was leaving Harlan in 1986, the state highway department had just begun work on upgrading the road. Each return visit finds a new tunnel or an old curve eliminated.

On weekdays, while Bobby was winding his way to work, Cindy was back home getting Julie ready for school. She drove her there every morning and returned home to wash the breakfast dishes and do the daily chores. Cindy tried her best to keep the house clean, but, like most coalfield housewives, she fought an "uphill battle." She had to dust the house twice a week; but laundry was her most time-consuming chore. She shook each item of Bobby's work clothes, including the underwear and socks, on the porch before putting them in the washing machine. Then, she washed them twice in a heavy-duty detergent and ran bleach through a rinse cycle to clean the machine before washing the regular laundry. She had thought of using bleach to restore Bobby's underwear to its original white. But a friend of hers had done that and caused her husband to break out in an uncomfortable rash. She decided not to risk it. Instead, she maintained two sets of underwear for Bobby: a work set and a weekend set. On the weekend when it was warm, Cindy and Bobby usually did the gardening and lawn work. But some weeks, when Bobby had to work on the cars or they were planning an out-of-town trip, Cindy did the outdoor work by herself. She did not mind running the lawn mower. It gave her another chance to work on her suntan, which she maintained throughout the winter with weekly trips to a "tanning bed."

In the afternoon, Cindy ran errands and dropped by her folks' house before Julie got out of school at 3 P.M. Her usual errands included going to the post office and the grocery store. In the summer, she drove up to Ages to take care of the garden. She picked Julie up from school every day at 3 P.M. She was an active participant in the community, a member of the local parent-teacher organization and the homemakers' club. She and Bobby both belonged to the Harlan Jaycees, club which had only recently begun to accept women as members.

Bobby usually got home from work around 6 P.M. and liked to have supper after he got cleaned up, around 6:30. He was always starved when he came home from work. If Cindy did not feel like cooking, she had Bobby pick up a pizza or some chicken. Sometimes, they just went out to eat. But Bobby never cooked himself, and, like most Harlan County men, he did not help out with the housecleaning. He was too tired after his day at work. And, although Bobby had a close relationship with his daughter Julie and took an active role in raising her, he left the day-to-day caretaking responsibilities to Cindy. Dirty diapers, runny noses, tears, and discipline largely remained "mother's work," at least among the working-class families I knew.

The Carson family attended the Baptist church at Ages, where Cindy had gone since she was a child. She wanted to go to church more often, but Bobby objected to "running up and down the roads" at night. They had considered going to church somewhere closer. There were Baptist churches in Loyall and Harlan that would have been more convenient for them. But Cindy enjoyed the fellowship at the church in which she was raised.

Bobby and Cindy were best friends with Bobby's co-worker Frank Johnson and his wife, Jeannie. They went out for dinner at Western Sizzler Steak House or Pizza Hut. Once or twice a week, they went to the bowling alley, where Bobby and Frank bowl in a league. At first, Cindy and Jeannie watched Bobby and Frank bowl and visited with the other onlookers. Later on, they joined a league themselves. When they had an opening on their team, they convinced me to join them, a decision they probably still regret. I joined the team, not because I was a particularly talented bowler, but because the bowling alley was an important place for recreation and socializing in Harlan. Next to church, it was the best place to meet and talk with people.

On league nights, Julie usually stayed with Bobby's mother but, sometimes, she went along with her parents. Julie spent Saturday nights with her other grandparents, the Nortons. Cindy and Bobby usually met Julie and her grandparents at church the next day. Like most Harlan women, Cindy relied on her parents and her mother-in-law for childcare. Cooperation among women—kin, friends, and neighbors—compensated, in some part, for the lack of professional day-care facilities in the county.

Bobby and Cindy spent a good deal of time together, as a couple, certainly more than many of their contemporaries. The sex-segregated lives of Harlan Countians had struck me almost immediately after my arrival there. During the day, men who had jobs went to work. Most women worked at home, and even those growing numbers of women in the workforce usually held positions in female-dominated occupations, such as schoolteacher, secretary, cashier, and waitress. Most of the jobs for men were in fields with low female representation, like truck driving, mining, and construction work.

At family gatherings or at parties, adults clustered in same-sex groups: Women went to the kitchen to prepare refreshments and look after children; the men headed to the porch or living room to talk. As far as I could tell, men and women discussed many of the same topics: work, local politics, the latest gossip (about such topics as love affairs, drug addiction, alcohol abuse, impending divorces), and their relationships with spouses, family members, and friends. In addition to these topics, men also talked about sports, cars, and hunting.

Cindy and Bobby did choose to spend some time apart, however, especially in the fall when Bobby attended high school football games with Frank or some of his other buddies. Cindy did not enjoy sitting out in the cold for these games, since she neither cared about football nor understood it. And Bobby, a former high school football player, preferred to talk about the intricacies of the game with his male friends. So, during football season, Friday nights were the "girls' nights" at home. Cindy helped Julie with her homework, played board games, or rented a video. When basketball season started, however, Cindy went along with Bobby to some of the big games, particularly the ones between local rivals. She like basketball better than football because it was a faster-paced game, she understood the rules, and the gyms were heated. Bobby and Cindy, like many Kentuckians, were fans of the University of Kentucky basketball team. They drove to Lexington for games when Bobby's boss gave them tickets.

I myself had grown up in a small eastern Kentucky town with a widely recognized tradition of strong athletic programs and had often contemplated the importance of sports in promoting community identity and solidarity. But participant-observation in Harlan County gave me an additional opportunity to reflect upon the function and meaning of games in this context. First, it was obvious that high school games provided individuals with entertainment and an opportunity to socialize with neighbors. Identity with, and support of, a local team was one of the ways in which people reaffirmed their community identity and solidarity. The hometown team symbolized the community's talent and worthiness. Such a close identity between team and community was facilitated by the residential clustering of kin groups in rural neighborhoods and towns in the county. Most of the fans at high schools games were alumni of the school and the neighbors and relatives of team members. Some, like Bobby, were former team players. Local rivalries were particularly significant and sometimes became bitter, as teams competed to prove their superiority—athletic, social, cultural, and personal—and to earn "bragging rights" for the year. However, local rivals generally supported one another in contests with teams from outside the county.

In many ways, the playing field provided a model for how society should operate, particularly to Harlan County's men. Men, or their surrogates—sons, nephews, cousins, and neighbors—competed freely in a manner viewed as healthful and wholesome. Rules governed and contained the struggles so that men could exercise their "natural" competitiveness without harming the community. This stood in contrast to other forms of competition among males, like the competition for jobs or profits, which were potentially devastating and divisive. Team sports also enabled the individual to excel and simultaneously contain his selfishness. Teams depended upon and rewarded individual talent. When players exalted their own goals over team goals, they were censured. No one liked a "ball hog." Sports heroes still had to be "team players." The playing field reinforced local themes of cooperation, mutual dependence, and community loyalty—themes that figured prominently in the political ideology of Harlan's miners as well.

＆

By 1985, Harlan's coal industry and its laborers were, once again, deadlocked in a competition with other coalfields, energy sources, and themselves. And the local team, particularly the labor component, was losing. As the price of oil fell and the threat to national energy security decreased, down went the demand for coal. The federal government had accomplished little toward coal conversion or industry stabilization and regulation. If anything, the government's actions had only made things worse for the eastern and Appalachian coal industries. The National Clean Air Act of 1970, designed to combat air pollution, sent utilities in search of the cleaner-burning, low-sulfur coal that could be found in the western coal fields of North Dakota and Montana. Harlan County and eastern Appalachian coalfields suffered in the shift. Long-needed reforms and legislation, brought about through community and miner activism during the 1970s, forced companies foot their bills on the environment, occupational health and safety, and the quality of community life, expenses that companies historically had transferred to the taxpayers. Deregulation of the railroads had increased the transport costs for remote coal producers, such as those in Harlan. Many of the highest, most productive coal seams were depleted, so companies increasingly mined in less attractive areas. In short, the cost of mining coal had risen throughout the 1970s.

In the late 1970s and early 1980s, coal management began to turn the tide in its favor, raising productivity through a variety of mechanization and restructuring programs that helped them reduce labor demand and replace union with nonunion employees. Coal's ability to turn a profit and compete in the global energy market attracted the interest of oil corporations. They expanded their efforts to acquire all sorts of coal-mining operations—union and nonunion, eastern and western, deep mines and strip mines. The changing structure of coal corporate ownership introduced new negotiating challenges to a struggling, inexperienced UMW leadership. Oil-owned companies could afford to "wait out" a long strike, could conceal their assets and profits from union negotiators, and, freed from the obligation to pay into the 1950 UMW pension plan, could afford to pay relatively high wages and benefits to forestall unionization of their nonunion holdings (Seltzer 1985, 187–209).

During the 1970s, the UMW could not meet these new challenges. Arnold Miller's inexperience in leadership and his nonconfrontational interpersonal style served him poorly, both in his negotiations with management and in his power struggles with his opponents within the UMW. In 1978, after the relatively successful 1974 contract had expired, Miller presented his constituency with a series of contracts that failed to satisfy his constituency. On several occasions they rejected the contracts recommended by Miller, and as they became increasingly disillusioned, miners launched several wildcat strikes. Attacked from opponents within and without the union, Miller found his health beginning to suffer. In November 1979, after a lengthy and contentious strike, Miller resigned from the presidency of the UMW. He was succeeded by Sam Church, a Boyle loyalist and antireformer (see Clark 1981 for a more complete analysis of the Miller regime; also Yarrow 1979 for an ethnographic description of mine workplace relations during this period).

From 1979 through 1982, Church attempted to usher in the return of a previous era of labor-management cooperation while he enriched his own coffers through questionable financial dealings with UMW funds. He was operating, however, in a historical era and an industrial context that differed from those of his hero, John L. Lewis. In Lewis's heyday, the BCOA was the dominant force among coal operators. The UMW-BCOA alliance stabilized the coal industry without federal intervention and enabled coal operators to enhance productivity through mechanization. Even though this program eliminated hundreds of thousands of miners' jobs, Lewis did not call a single strike during the decade. The establishment of an industry-wide health and pension plan, funded by the coal operators, lent credence to Lewis's argument that the industry and its workers would be better off after the painful transition of mechanization and the elimination of inefficient producers was accomplished.

But when the UMW contract expired in 1981, the old BCOA members did not dominate the industry as clearly as did the more diversified multinational oil corporations, whose interests were not so closely tied with coal or the regions that produced it. The 1978 coal recession had driven more small operators out of business and even further enhanced the position of oil-dominated multinationals. These corporations continued to boost productivity through new mechanization programs, massive layoffs, and a combination of bonuses and intimidation designed to enhance production from the remaining workers (Seltzer 1985, 187). And they continued their efforts to reduce labor costs by eluding UMW contract obligations: restructuring and subcontracting to increase their proportion of nonunion employees and seeking to reduce their contributions to and, ultimately, abandon the pension and health plans of 1950 and 1974.

This was the context in which Sam Church had pledged a strike-free contract negotiation in 1981. He and his BCOA allies negotiated a contract that, while it offered an attractive wage and benefit package, did not address health and safety issues, and enabled operators to chip away at their UMW employee base (Seltzer 1985, 194–95). Once again, the membership recognized the concessions and rejected the contract, a move that surprised Sam Church and undermined his bargaining position with the BCOA. He responded by complaining that his constituency was apparently too interested in "fishing" and enjoying their vacation from work to concede now. His remarks only lent credence to the increasingly popular, media-fed opinion that coal miners had become fat, lazy, and spoiled during the 1970s (Maggard 1983). Nevertheless, the nine-week strike resulted in a contract that offered additional benefits and, more importantly, a few more protections against subleasing and subcontracting arrangements. On 9 November 1982, Sam Church's ungrateful constituency replaced him with Richard Trumka, a liberal candidate who had pledged a more militant leadership and had been critical of Church for his alliances with coal operators and his inability to halt the decline in UMW membership and union coal operations.

The mid-1980s found both the UMW and Harlan's coal industry struggling. Increased competition from nonunionized strip-mining operations (in the western United States and throughout the world), the decline of the BCOA and rise of oil-dominated multinational corporations, new forms of mechanization (such as long-wall mining), subcontracting and leasing arrangements, excess capacity, increased costs of production (due to rail deregulation and environmental, safety, and health legislation), and a decrease in the demand for metallurgical coal were among the many factors that dampened the prospects of coal operators and union workers in the 1980s. The increasingly conservative political tenor and anti-union sentiment of the 1980s—represented by the policies of the Reagan administration and, in particular, its outright destruction of the Professional Air Traffic Controllers Organization (PATCO) in 1981—informed and constrained Harlan miners' visions of the future. To most, the future seemed quite bleak.

ᘒ

In 1985, Bobby Carson's job was to retrieve coal from a forty-two-inch high seam at Pat Abbott's nonunion Highsplint mine. To operate his continuous mining machine in such low coal, Bobby had to lie in a reclining position. As he dislodged the coal from the seam, shuttle cars picked up the coal and carried it to the conveyor belt, which transported the coal outside the mine and to the processing plant. Bobby did not talk about his work much.[1] When he did, he used vigorous hand motions to indicate where the action took place. As I listened to the following description of his place in the production process, I was impressed by how frenetic and risky this job was (see figure 3.1).

"You can't just fool around. When a [continuous] miner's digging coal, you got a shuttle car coming up here," he said, motioning behind him. "And, while I'm digging, he's loading. The heads turning, digging the coal down; the arms are gathering it on a conveyor, dumping it in his car. He's gotta take this, . . . run down through yonder to the belt and dump it on the belt. Then, another [car] comes in here; he'll go this way [motioning to the right] and the other one coming the other way [motioning to the left]. You can't go the same way. You're supposed to advance the belt [which carries coal from underground] so the cars don't have to run too far; but lots of times you're way behind. You're behind on everything!" Bobby spoke hurriedly about his work, just as hurriedly as he seemed to do it.

Bobby and the rest of the crew relied heavily on his buddy, Frank, the roof bolter. Roof bolts and the more traditional supports, timbers, kept the mountaintop over the workers from coming down and crushing them (see figure 3.2). Frank talked about

FIGURE 3.1

A continuous mining machine in operation, circa 1982. Photograph courtesy of the Kentucky Coal Association.

FIGURE 3.2
A dual roof bolting machine in operation, circa 1982. Photograph
courtesy of the Kentucky Coal Association.

his job differently than Bobby did. He took a methodical, studious
approach to his explanation. No waving arms or frantic gestures.
He rubbed his chin as he told me what he did:

> You got your roof that you can't predict. Well, just so-so. You can
> sound the top with tools, you know, with a hammer or some-
> thing; and you have a roof control plan. You bolt the top. Usu-
> ally, above the coal you have what we call slate and maybe some
> thin layers of rock and, then, maybe some solid rock to where
> you can drill into that [solid rock] and it'll support the roof that
> is between it and that rock; and that's what your bolts hold up.
> After you mine the coal out of it, the bolter puts temporary jacks
> in there, bolts his top and keeps on moving. And, of course the
> miner (Bobby) sits way back on the end of the [continuous]
> miner; he don't have to go no farther than his bolts. He just cuts
> so many feet, then he stops and backs out; and the bolter, that's
> me, sets temporary supports and, then, bolts; and you keep ad-
> vancing different ways.
>   There's faults in these mountains. Experience teaches you

things about it; but, before you get there, you don't know. You have to learn from experience. . . . You're supposed to mine kind of like a checkerboard: you take a square and leave a square. And that keeps your roof supported, unless there's fault in it, ... Some kind of faults, you can't control. You don't know they're there.

Frank's job required him to go in new sections of the mine, where there were no roof supports. It was dangerous work, so he could not rush it. Roof falls and rock slides worried miners the most. They troubled Frank, particularly, because he was most at risk and he felt responsible for his co-workers. He thought about roof falls often and talked about them, too. In contrast, Bobby rarely talked about the roof or other potential hazards. When I asked him if the danger of his work bothered him, he shrugged it off, saying, "You learn to live with it and you do quite well." One night, however, Bobby came home from work complaining. This was unusual for him. Interestingly, he confined his remarks to the work domain under his control. He did not complain about the attitudes, carelessness, or incompetence of his boss, the mining engineers, or other miners. He never placed blame, either on individuals or on general market forces: the pressure to work quickly, to maximize profit or production. He started off with a simple statement about his job.

It's the worst job in the world. It's the dirtiest. It's the most unhealthy and most dangerous; but, still, when you live in it for a while, you don't notice it. You're not aware of it. . . .

I don't like it. I don't like the filth and mud. It's always muddy and nasty and you wade in it and you lay down in it and you can't stand up till you come back out. It's just miserable. . . .

While you're working in a mine, you're so close. Your equipment is so big. If you're working in a forty-two-inch coal seam, your machinery is touching the bottom and top. There is very little clearance; and it is so wide and so big! And this is *mobile* equipment that runs by electricity. You've got very high voltage there; you're always cutting cable with equipment. . . . That's reckless but you *have* to do that.

By 1986, Bobby felt the strain of a decade of mining, but he could see no alternatives. Market competition, for coal and jobs, formed the context through which he interpreted his situation. His boss was struggling for his company's survival in bad times and was doing the best he could, Bobby thought. In the five-year period, from 1981 to 1986, the number of coal jobs in Harlan County declined by almost one-third, from 4,441 to 2,955 (BEA 1991). In 1985–86, the official unemployment rate hovered around 15 percent (Appalachian Center [AC-UK] 1992). Per capita income was around $8,000, which was 45 percent below the national rate (AC-UK 1992). Bobby knew that if he could not keep up, there were plenty of young men who would be happy to take his job. Heck, he joked with his usual dry wit, there might not be any job to take, if they go to long-wall mining! "Long-wall" mining is an even more mechanized technique of removing coal, requiring less labor than the continuous mining system under which Bobby worked in 1985–86.

Bobby's wages had dropped some since 1982, when he earned a career-high $110 per day. In 1985, he regular pay was $80 per day, about $4 below what he originally earned when he started in 1977. His boss instituted new cost-cutting measures in 1985. Workers with less seniority took temporary layoffs for six to eight weeks, during the summer. Anyone who failed to bring a written doctor's excuse for an absence had to give up three days' work. Workers with minor illnesses had to chose between either paying $20 and spending half the day in a doctor's waiting room or resting at home unnecessarily and losing three day's wages. When Bobby had a cold, backache, toothache, or flu bug, he went to work.

Bobby did not complain much about the new rule, but his friend Frank did. One evening when we were picking beans in the garden at Ages, we talked about the rule and other changes at work. Frank reminisced about the "good ole days" of the 1970s, when coal was booming and bosses were eager to keep production going. Even nonunion miners, like Bobby and Frank, had some clout. "Back when coal was booming," Frank recalled, "we could pretty much tell them what to do, but now there's a million guys who would take your job. Now they can do whatever they want to us." I looked at Bobby to see his reaction. He tossed a weed he had just pulled and threw his hands up with a look of resignation.

Of course, there were aspects of his job that Bobby still enjoyed. One of the most important, to Bobby, was the friendship of his co-workers. They got along well and enjoyed pulling pranks on one another. Bobby liked to "roughhouse." Frank preferred "mind games," like stealing a tool, swiping a lunch box, or hiding from co-workers. Bobby also found his job to be a challenge, both mentally and physically. Even on days when he was tired and tense, he was proud to be able to do such a tough job. The same went for Frank. The switch to mechanized production had not completely eliminated the solidarity and craft identity among Harlan's miners.

In 1986, Bobby's continuous miner broke down frequently. The boss postponed servicing and repairing equipment, sometimes until it was too late. When the miner broke down, Bobby helped out with other jobs around the site. He liked to get off the miner for a change of pace and scenery. Sometimes he loafed around or pulled pranks on the other men. Most of the time, he was a diligent worker. He fetched tools for the repairman, straightened the work area, and tended to the details that often get ignored in the rush of production, like rehanging the plastic sheets that channeled the air circulation. Bobby did not mind hauling the fifty-pound bags of rock dust for the night shift; but he hated to "muck the track" (clearing the rail track of coal and debris) and hand-load the fallen coal onto the belt line.

When the boss needed an extra hand on the next shift, Bobby was among the first to volunteer to stay. This bothered Cindy because she did not want Bobby to "wear himself out." He could get hurt if he got too tired, she reminded him. But Bobby wanted to earn all the money he could while there was work. Bobby got along well with Pat Abbott, the coal operator for whom he worked. They sometimes bowled together. The boss even lent him and Cindy his Gatlinburg condominium for weekend trips. Once a year, the boss flew his employees in his private plane up to Cincinnati to see the Reds play. Wives were not included in these out-of-town excursions, though. When they ran into each other around town, the boss always stopped to "chew the fat" with Bobby and to wink at Cindy, whom he called Bobby's "better half."

&

When coal boomed in the 1970s, it brought prosperity to the local economy. New businesses sprang up along the bypass around Harlan, financed directly or indirectly by coal profits. With the bowling alley, movie theater, shopping mall, and fast-food restaurants came jobs, many of them jobs for women. There were also increased opportunities for women to attend community college or vocational school to train for jobs in health and business services. The new local economy offered women employment opportunities as never before. The women responded (U.S. Department of Commerce 1970, 1986; U.S. Department of Labor 1985). Between 1970 and 1980, the number of women active in the workforce rose by 66 percent, from 2,661 to 4,030 (Census of Population 1980). That was double the rate at which men's workforce participation increased in the 1970s, even when mining jobs were plentiful. Of course, women were starting from almost "ground zero" (see also Tickamyer & Tickamyer 1991).

Not all of those women took jobs in traditionally female-identified fields, either. During the 1970s, women entered the male domain of mining. In Kentucky, the number of women miners increased from zero, in 1970, to 464 in 1978 (Coal Employment Project 1990). One of these was Linda Taylor, a college classmate of Cindy's. Linda, a widow, started working at Highsplint in 1979. Back then, Duke Power owned the mine. Her husband worked there before he died in a car accident, leaving her with four children to support. Sheb Wilson, her husband's former boss at Highsplint, got her a position as housekeeper for his sister-in-law. The pay was low, however. Her brother-in-law worked at Highsplint, and he told her that women were being hired up there. So she decided to give it a try. When she started working, she earned $7.50 per hour, and when she was laid off in 1981, she was making $14 per hour. "I just couldn't believe it! To me, I was rich," she said.

She started out working the third shift, from midnight until 8 A.M. This worked out well for her and her children, who were big enough to stay by themselves. A close neighbor was "on call" for the kids in case something happened while she was at work. She slept while they were in school, then fixed supper and got them ready for school during the evening. At work, she was responsible for rock dusting and laying out supplies for the morning shift. She found these tasks boring but wound up hating her second job, "mucking the belt," even more. Mucking meant shoveling fallen coal onto the conveyor belt so that it could be transported out of the mine. Because she felt she had to prove herself to the others, she said, she worked very hard at this strenuous job. When she started mucking, she wore a size-five blouse and, by the time she got another assignment, she wore a size ten. Like many women miners, Linda felt her bosses used this job to discourage her from staying on (Yarrow 1985; Yount 1986).

Another friend of Cindy's, Beth Walker, agreed with Linda's assessment. Beth worked at Brookside after it was unionized in 1974. Under the UMW contract, Beth could bid onto better-paying, more satisfying jobs as they became available. Beth eventually became a roof bolter under this system. Linda, on the other hand, had to move from job to job. She never got to train on the bolter or continuous miner, but she finally got a job that she enjoyed. She "serviced" mining equipment, that is, oiled and greased machine parts in a preventative maintenance program. After she took this position, Linda found that her co-workers were more of a hindrance than a help. For instance, when she arrived at work, the grease gun had always disappeared. It usually took her over half an hour to find it, hidden in a remote section of the mine. Then she had to drag the forty-pound tool, as she crawled through the low coal seam, back to the machine. After that, she had to rush through her work to make up for lost time.

Linda was a "quiet-turned" woman. She did not confront the men about hiding her grease gun. Their boisterous pranks and rough language intimidated her. She rarely spoke to them at all, fearing that they would get the wrong impression if she acted friendly toward them. "People don't have a good opinion of women that work in the mines. . . . I know that," she explained. "The men get the wrong idea a lot of the times. If you're just a little bit friendly, you know, they can take it the wrong way. . . . If you just say 'hello' to them, they think, 'Oh, she likes me.' You have to be real careful with that, you know, around here."

Linda used two strategies to avoid confrontations and sexual harassment. First, she interacted with her co-workers in a reserved, professional manner. She never complained, disagreed, or "chit-chatted." Second, she made it clear that she was a Christian widow woman, uninterested in romance. "I didn't have a lot of bad luck with them talking, you know, what you would call sexual harassment. . . . I think that has a lot to do with the way you act," she told me. Her attitude was, "You don't have to change because I'm here. I'm just trying to make a living." She added that her co-workers acted differently in groups than when she was alone with one of them. "The men there are just big 'put-ons,'" she observed. "They try to act macho in front of each other, but when they're alone, they're like different people. They'll apologize [for the way they treat women]."

Beth was not as charitable in her characterization of male miners as Linda had been. Beth started working at the Brookside mine as a childless divorcee in her early twenties. On her first night there, her boss asked her out on a date, which she declined. He did not ask her out again, which was a relief to her. However, she continued to have trouble with her co-workers. They cussed her, "propositioned" her, and discussed sex graphically in front of her. "There's something about a mine that makes men act like animals," she said. "I don't know what it is, but down there the regular rules don't apply." After three years underground, she had concluded that men around Harlan were "sexist, ignorant, and close-minded."

Beth Walker was no Linda Taylor! She was neither quiet nor meek, but outspoken and strong-willed. So she adopted a different strategy for dealing with the men at work. She acted like "one of the guys," laughing at their jokes, tolerating their pranks, and making light of their sexual overtures. She tried to downplay her femininity by acting like a "tomboy." Nevertheless, while she worked there she became romantically involved with two fellow employees. She was engaged to the first when he was killed in a mining accident. She married the second. After that, she quit her job, had a baby, and began to study nursing at the county community college.

Making the transition from her status as single career woman to a housewife-mother and full-time student was difficult for Beth. She missed having her own income and space. "I was independent when I worked in the mines. I had my own money and my own place; and I liked that," she reminisced. "It's hard to be dependent." More than that, she resented her husband's lack of involvement in household tasks and child rearing. She had to do the cooking, shopping, and household chores, take care of the baby, and go to school full-time. Her husband, she said, only had to work at a single job. "I worked the same job that my husband works now; and I *know* what it's like. And I *know* that, when I worked it, I didn't just come home and collapse," she recalled. She resented the fact that she never had enough time to study and do her best work at school.

In an introductory sociology class, Beth complained about the double standards by which Harlan Countians judged men and women. We expect one kind of behavior from men and another from women, she told the class. In Harlan, men are allowed to cuss, to drink, to flirt, and to be promiscuous. Women are not. What really angered Beth was that men could be independent, earn their own living, and excel in a career. Yet when she tried to do that, she was ridiculed, harassed, and ostracized. In a private conversation later, she apologized for her comments, saying that "working in the mines has given me some problems in relating to men." However, she said, what she learned in sociology class had further strengthened her conviction that a woman should have a career and her own money. The problem in Harlan, she said, was that there had never been job opportunities for women. As long as women depended on men for financial security, men had the "upper hand." Local women allowed men "to dictate to them and to run around on them."

Beth and Linda both had conflicts with miners' wives when they worked underground. Many miners' wives gossiped about them and accused them of trying to steal their husbands. Women should not be crawling around in dark, cramped, isolated places with men, they proclaimed. When Beth went on a date, she was "cheap." When Linda ran into a married co-worker in the grocery store parking lot and stopped to talk with him, she was accused of "home-wrecking." Men and women, alike, complained that women miners took jobs from men with families to support (see also Yarrow in progress). No one seemed to notice that Linda had a family to support. She guessed they expected her to remarry immediately after her husband's death. She did not think she would ever love a man like that again, she explained. Women like Linda and Beth posed a double threat to miners' wives: They could either steal their husbands' jobs or steal their husbands.

The strength of public opinion against women miners impressed Beth so much that, five years after she quit mining, she selected this as the topic for her research project in my introductory sociology class. Her survey concentrated on two areas: women's job performance in mining and society's reaction to women in nontraditional occupations. In her paper she expressed disappointment that women would oppose women's employment as miners. Notice how she equated a belief in equality with "approval of women miners." Her survey analysis revealed many of her underlying assumptions: that women should agree on major political matters; that sexual equality entailed equal access to jobs and equal pay for women; that local gender ideology defined women as weak, incompetent, and emotional; and, finally, that the local community used ridicule and "stigmatization" as social control mechanisms. The following excerpt best illustrates her thoughts on the matter:

> Since our leading industrial [*sic*] is coal, I thought everyone would have a close personal opinion on the woman coal miner. I surveyed forty people between the ages of seventeen and sixty-one. All forty were white. Thirty-one were women, nine were men. Twenty-one were single, nineteen were married. I thought I would find that all women believed in equality. Although the majority of people surveyed did think women were equal to men, there were a surprising number who didn't.
>
> Question #1 stated, "Do you think women should be allowed to work in the coal mines?" Although thirty of the forty people surveyed answered yes, . . . seven of the ten that answered no were women.
>
> Question two stated, "Are women physically capable of the work?" Thirty-seven answered yes, thirteen answered no. However the people that did comment on the question said that some men were not capable of the work either.
>
> The third question stated, "Do you believe in the superstition that women are bad luck in the mines?" Wording it as I did may have had some effect on the answer. Most people do not admit to being superstitious. Three answered yes and thirty-seven answered no.
>
> Question four said, "Do you think women deserve the same pay as men?" Thirty-six answered yes while four answered no. Three of the four were women theirselves [*sic*].
>
> Question number five asked, "Do you think a man would risk his safety more for a woman than a man?" Twenty-five people said yes, that a man would protect a woman over another man. Fifteen answered no, that any person would look out for his fellow worker no matter if it was a man or a woman.
>
> Question six asked, "Do you think a woman would risk her safety for a man?" Twenty-three said yes, seventeen said no. Almost a split opinion on this question. Fifteen of the no answers came from women.
>
> The seventh question stated, "Do you think society stigmatizes the woman coal miner?" Thirty answered yes while ten answered no.
>
> Question eight asked, "Do you think the children of women

who are coal miners are subjected to more than usual ridicule from their peers?" Twenty-four answered yes, sixteen answered no. Children are often caught in the cross-fire of societies [sic] expectations.

Question nine, "Do you think a woman is emotionally capable of handling an emergency situation?" Thirty-one of the forty answered yes and nine answered no. According to this survey, women would react well in an emergency situation.

The tenth question stated, "Would you object to your spouse working in the coal mine?" Although men and woman [sic] answered this question, the nine men that were surveyed said they did object. Two women said they would object to their husbands working in the coal mines. While twenty-nine said they did not object.

Several of her questions reflected her awareness of the ideological linkage between mining and masculinity. Miners, their bosses, and the community have evolved a conception of mining as physically demanding and dangerous work suited only for the strength and characteristics cultivated in men. These beliefs have persisted, even though mechanization has diminished the physical demands of many mining jobs. The definition of mining as men's work has facilitated class solidarity among miners (Yarrow 1985, 40–41). It has also made male miners reluctant to open their ranks to women.

Ernie Norton, like most miners, opposed women's working underground. He did not oppose women's working in general, however. Both his wife and daughter took jobs to support the family during strikes and layoffs. One evening, when he, Cindy, and I were sitting on the front porch chatting, the topic turned to women coal miners. Ernie started out by arguing that mining was men's work and, therefore, unsuitable for women:

> In the first place, that's the worst thing that ever happened to a coal mines was when the requirements, wherever they come from, from the unions and the companies or the government or whatever, Equal Rights or whatever it was that forced 'em to hire women to work in the mines is, to me, the downfall of that operation. From that day on, it will never be the same for so many reasons. They're [women] not built to take care of a man's work. Now, they can drive a truck. They can do men's jobs and do things outside. . . . [But a woman] fears more than a man; and they'll never be beyond that fear in the mines.
>
> But the thing is, they can't produce coal. A woman cannot

do the work of a man. . . . She can't do what's required of her to do, if she's going to be equal. . . . [Women] could run a shuttle car. There's certain things that they could do.

But, really, all they ever turned out to be here [at Brookside] was goof-offs. In Brookside operations here, I don't know many of them that wasn't fooling with men or doping it up.

At this point, Cindy interjected, "Don't men do that, too? Fool around and dope it up?" Like me, Cindy had heard her father dismiss young male miners in the same fashion. Ernie frowned and responded, acknowledging Cindy's point. Then, he switched the tack of his argument:

Nowadays, [miners] do [have illicit sex and abuse drugs], yes; but, really, [women] don't do that *because* they're a woman but that's the *kind* of woman that's working in the mines: them that *has* to have a job. There's some that don't have a man. Maybe their man is killed or something and they can't get no other thing, except Welfare. They get them a job and they do well with that money; but they can't produce. I don't care who says they could. . . .

But you know the kids are bound to be embarrassed by the fact that their mother is working in the mines. Or even sorry for their mother, to see her get up and go there; and she can't possibly take care of [her children]. Fathers cannot be mothers, I don't care under what circumstances. A mother is 75 or 80 percent of the family, to the children. . . .

Of course, it's bad to see that woman working and a good, available, strong man walking down the road [unemployed]. She could be at home, maybe; there's a lot of cases where the man and wife is working in the mines. She could be at home taking care of her kids while this other man is making money for his family, to raise his family; and he can't get a job.

Before Cindy could respond, her father cut off the argument with the following pronouncement: "There's so many ways you can get in arguments over women working in the mines; but, now, women are *not* for the mines and the mines are *not* for the women. There's no doubt about that." Cindy rolled her eyes and left the matter there.

Opposition to women's working underground united miners, like Ernie, with Harlan Countians from a variety of backgrounds. A nineteen-year-old male classmate of Beth's who also wrote about women coal miners shared Ernie's position on the issue. "It is true that women's roles are changing but I do not think that people in mining towns will ever be in favor of women working in the coal mines," he wrote. This young man, hower, did not think that women were incapable of the work. He just saw it as culturally inappropriate. He explained, "I do not think it is because people think women are not able to do the things required to work in the mines. Women are thought of . . . as a thing of beauty." He recognized that tough economic times might force women to work in the mines but, nevertheless, he noted that "things would have to be extremely bad for me to let my wife work in the mines. That is, if I were married." He predicted, however, that women coal miners would become "a thing of the past" because of a greater local emphasis on education and alternate careers as well as a general fear of the risks associated with underground mining.

The debate over women coal miners even found Ernie siding with local coal operators. His former archenemy, Eastover Mine Company president Norman Yarborough, visited my Appalachian Studies class and told the students that women's menstrual periods made them too emotional and untrustworthy for jobs that might endanger the safety of others. Reporting on local operator Pat Abbott, Linda Taylor said that, on the first day at work, he had marched up to her and yelled in her face, "What are you doing here? Don't you know that I'm prejudiced against women?" Later she regretted that she had not fired back a witty remark. Instead, she stood there silently as her face turned red.

One might wonder why coal operators continued to promote the ideology of mining as *men's* work when it might, in fact, be against their best interests. After all, the creation of a brotherhood of miners has strengthened their class solidarity and increased their power and self-esteem in such a way as to make resistance and rebellion possible. So why not follow the lead of other industries and replace male labor with relatively inexpensive and allegedly more compliant female labor? With increased mechanization, women are able to perform well at most mining jobs. Even Ernie admitted that. Yet foremen placed women on hand-loading jobs, precisely those which required the most upper body strength. And they also seemed to condone male employees who harassed women and sabotaged their work, presumably decreasing productivity. This certainly poses a paradox.

Michael Yarrow (1985, 41–42) has identified and explored

this paradox. He explains operator antipathy toward women miners as a result of their socialization into dominant patriarchal culture and their ideological investment in masculinity as a labor control device. For instance, the patriarchal association of masculinity with the "breadwinner" role can be used to discourage strikes or high rates of labor turnover. After all, a man with a family to feed should hesitate before walking off his job. Generally speaking, early coal operators preferred to hire "family men" because of their higher degree of stability (Corbin 1981; Trotter 1990). Second, masculinity's association with strength, competence, and competition provided foremen with the means to motivate higher production levels, either through production contests or by ridiculing poor performers for being lazy, weak, or fearful (Yarrow 1985, 41–42).

When Beth Walker worked as roof bolter, one of the more dangerous jobs in underground mining, she ran into this motivational tactic several times. Foremen appealed to masculinity and courage to keep miners working, even when they were at risk. She related an incident:

> One time, I heard the roof ripping and, usually when it does that, oh, it falls really big! And I went and told the boss, "It sounds like it's going to all come in." Well, the guy I was working with [my assistant roof bolter], he said he wasn't going in there either; and the boss told us to go get the bolting machine out. . . .
>
> Well, [the boss] stood around there and talked to the guy I was working with long enough to talk him into going [back in there to work]; and I was still refusing. "I'm not going. I'm not going to risk my life". . . . and it caused a lot of bad feelings.
>
> I guess that it could be blamed on being a woman; but I wasn't going to risk *my life*. If I'd have been a *man,* I wouldn't risk my life. Me knowing that it might fall any minute!

Although Beth did not think her gender influenced her in this situation, other women miners I interviewed, including Linda, did. They thought that their gender was an asset on the job. Many noted that men valued bravery and often took unnecessary risks that endangered themselves and others. Women, in contrast to men, enhanced mine safety because they did not take unnecessary risks and were, like good mothers, always looking out for the welfare of others.

By 1985, there was only a handful of women miners. Most had

been laid off and had found other jobs, gone back to school, or moved away. Mining remained a male-dominated profession, and most people agreed that it was inappropriate for women to work underground. Nonetheless, for many Harlan women the experience of working in the mines was empowering and liberating. Some, like Beth Walker, could not return to the status quo ante when she quit working in the mines. She challenged her husband's shirking of housework; she remembered her financial independence; and she knew she could do "a man's job" (see also Anglin 1993; Maggard 1988).

ò▲

Bobby Carson and Linda Taylor worked in small, locally owned, nonunion mines. Their relationship with the owner was personal, Bobby's in particular. He liked Pat Abbott, socialized with him, bowled with him, used his condominium, talked sports with him, and so forth. He did not characterize his relationship with Abbott as an adversarial one but approached him more as a surrogate father (Portelli 1990; Yarrow 1985). Bobby's own father had died when he was young, and perhaps that contributed to their close relationship. He saw Abbott has a businessman who was trying to make a profit, provide a decent living for his family and his employees, and contribute to the community in trying economic times. He trusted him to provide the best wages, benefits, and working conditions that he could afford.

Abbott cultivated this sort of relationship with his employees by dressing in work clothes, going underground to talk with them and oversee their work, sharing his plane and condominium with them, and generally being friendly and approachable at work and in the community. This paternalistic style of labor management was a persistent feature of local coal mines (Portelli 1990) as it has been elsewhere (Edwards 1979; Yarrow 1985). It articulated well with local conceptions of kinship and community identity, a point that will be discussed further in the next chapter.

Linda's reaction to Abbott's management style was somewhat different from Bobby's, largely because, as a woman, she was never considered part of the mining "brotherhood." After a rocky start, when Abbott screamed in her face that he was prejudiced against women, their relationship improved. Linda remained intimidated by his gruff manner and did not talk with him much. However, she went to church with the woman who cooked for Abbott, Joy Perry. Joy invited Linda to come to the Abbotts' Clover Fork home for the employee breakfasts that Abbott sponsored before each morning shift. Through Joy, whose relationship with Abbott was more traditional—he was the boss and she cooked for him—Linda came to enjoy some of the same perks that Bobby did. She offered a more critical analysis of why Abbott provided these benefits. She explained:

> He must do these things to make [miners] do better in the job or something. Or work harder. . . .
>
> A lot of men wouldn't go [to employee breakfasts]. Just certain ones would go. On my section, I tried to talk 'em into it. Because I wouldn't have gone if it hadn't have been for Joy. Because I was so backward and everything. . . . She talked me into coming at a prayer meeting. . . . and so I went. And it was real good. They had this big long table and all the men, you know. . . . Most of our section did go and they enjoyed it. They loved her cooking.
>
> But Pat [Abbott] would be hurt if they didn't show up. Once he had a fish fry up here at [the Evarts] Multi-purpose Center and all the men didn't come. And he was real hurt; and he let them know he didn't like it because they didn't come. You know, he has this for them and they should come and take advantage of it. That's what he thinks.
>
> Then, a lot of them say, "He's just trying to butter us up" and all that. You know how some men are. They wouldn't take it no matter how much he meant good. They figured he was up to no good but I think he meant well. I don't know. I tend to look at the good side of everybody. I don't see the bad.
>
> We [Linda and her children] got to go to his condo in Gatlinburg. My friend, Joy: her and her daughter went and we got to go with 'em. She asked him if we could go and he said, "Sure!" It was real nice.

Linda oscillated between suspicion and trust, when she talked about Abbott. She thought that he might be offering these services to get his employees to work harder, but, on the other hand, she preferred to "look at the good side." The breakfasts offered her an opportunity to socialize with her co-workers above ground, where they did not harass and threaten her. In addition, she got to take her four children on a vacation she might never have been able to afford otherwise. These were important benefits to Linda.

Linda had equally mixed opinions about the UMW. Her father had been a union supporter; but neither she nor her husband had belonged to the miners' union. "You know, there's two sides to everything; and I try to look at both sides, because my mom and dad was UMW. They're strong union people," she said. When Linda married as a teenager in 1965, she and her young husband could not find work. Neither had graduated high school. They sold moonshine at one point. Then they moved to Indiana, where Linda was miserable. She had two babies, a full-time job, and no car, and she had to carry her laundry to the laundromat. They moved four times in six years in search of work and a better home. When they came back in 1971, they were still poor. "[My husband and I] had a hard time for *so long,* you know? Our kids were young and never had nothing [during the late 1960s]; and I just was glad that John had a job. I didn't care if it was union or not. I wanted him to work!" she said.

She was not against the union in principle, however, only in practice. The UMW's internal conflicts and the rash of wildcat strikes that occurred in the 1970s had discredited the union in her eyes. "I believe in a union standing together; but I don't think they [UMW] were fair on some things," she complained. "They'd have a strike over every little thing!" She was the first to point out, however, that she had benefited from the union's existence. The UMW presence in Harlan County, she thought, raised the standards for working conditions and wages. Her bosses "tried to keep ahead of the union to try to make them look good, I guess. [Eastover Mining Company] paid the men more here [who were not in the UMW] more than they paid the men down there [who were in the UMW]. . . . They paid 'em good; and they give 'em good raises. Ah, we just thought we was in heaven! It was so different than what we had been used to. It was good to not worry about bills and stuff, like we had before, just to live. It was going good."

Beth, although she had belonged to the UMW, had mixed feelings about the union as well. She credited the union for the job-bidding system that enabled her to get a rewarding, higher-paying job. On the other hand, she complained that it remained a sexist organization. It could have done more to prevent sexual discrimination and harassment at work. She also disapproved of her Brookside co-workers who interpreted the contract inflexibly and used some provisions to take unfair advantage of the company. She cited a 1981 incident when workers protested against management doing cleanup work after a mine sludge slide in Ages. According to Beth, they could "file time," if management did miners' work, and then collect the pay for the job done by the management person. This was ostensibly to protect miners' jobs. However, in a community disaster such as this, Beth thought, everyone should pitch in together. She complained about the legalistic approach that some miners took. "Here was all these union people filing time and collecting a bunch more wages in a disaster situation. That wasn't right. . . . If they laid off somebody and the boss started doing their job, that wouldn't have been fair. Maybe I would've seen it in a circumstance like that," she noted. But they nitpicked down there. . . . A boss couldn't pick up a shovel to shovel. They'd be filing time on it. I said, 'Well, that's ridiculous. If I'm working with that man, I'd rather see him work, too, than have him sit there and watch me.'"

In short, Beth (the most pro-union of my young miner friends) expressed many of the same reservations about the UMW that her anti-union peers had recounted. Like them, she thought that the union miners of the 1970s had gone overboard to protect jobs and workers' rights, particularly through "wild cat" strikes (see also Seltzer 1985, 247). She regretted the bureaucratization of labor-management relations and, instead, suggested that there should be more flexibility in abiding by contractural agreements, particularly during emergency situations like the Ages mudslide. She and all of the Harlan miners that I interviewed, both young and old, advocated more egalitarian, flexible, and cooperative relations between workers and management. The themes of community, egalitarianism, and anti-bureaucracy will be revisited in subsequent chapters because contradictions and debates over their meanings, and the proper means to achieve them, drives much of the public and private political discourse in Harlan County. For now, let me just note that, Harlan miners did not necessarily disagree over principals or abstract goals but, rather, on the means to achieve them. There was a particularly noticeable generational disagreement among miners as to whether the UMW provided a solution to their workplace woes or simply reproduced and exacerbated problems that were inherited from the past.

ꝭ

In 1986, Cindy joined the increasing numbers of local women looking for a job. For the previous two years, she had been taking night classes through the local community college, where she had met Linda Taylor and Beth Walker. She hoped to be a data processor, bookkeeper, or secretary. She had taken a few math courses and was contemplating a course in computer programming. Cindy also stepped up her efforts to earn extra cash selling her garden produce and crafts at roadside stands and flea markets. Her increased participation in this informal economic activity was not unusual in Harlan County or other parts of eastern Kentucky where jobs and cash were hard to come by (Halperin 1990). The local newspaper, for instance, noted an increase in the gathering of wild ginseng (HDE, 17 October 1984, 7). Also, the illegal sale of alcohol, or "bootlegging," remained a common practice in "dry" areas, and the drug trade appeared to be brisk. Law enforcement officials launched several campaigns to destroy marijuana patches, during 1985 and 1986; and drug arrests, including the arrest of a local businessman for drug dealing, were common.

Meanwhile local leaders struggled to formulate plans to revive an economy that was losing hundreds of jobs per year (Eller et al. 1994, Appendix B, table I), forcing unemployment into double digits (Eller et al. 1994, 19), and increasing the per capita government transfer payments approximately 26.5 percent, from $1,790 in 1980 to $2,435 in 1986 (AC-UK Eller et al. 1994, Appendix B, table XXVIII). Many local miners, including Ernie Norton, remained pessimistic, however, as indicated by the following economic analysis by Ernie:

> It don't look good for coal and we certainly ain't got that much timber left here; and this ain't going be no farming country. There's been right many service jobs come in this area but those are minimum wage, part-time jobs. That's not no great amount of income. . . . We really don't have much room in this area and where it's located and the transportation system [is inferior]. . . . and, even with good highways, it wouldn't be feasible for a factory to set up in Harlan County when they can set up in Rich-

mond or some better, more centrally-located place. I mean, industry is tough to get. I mean, people's begging, just like Martha Layne [Collins, Kentucky's governor in 1986,] did for Toyota [to locate a facility in Georgetown, Kentucky]; that's the name of the game; and I don't think nobody can persuade anything to come to Harlan County. I mean any *major* thing. It's possible that maybe some day there may be some small factories come in here; but it would have to be something pretty small.

For many people, leaving seemed the only solution. "I'd recommend you go to another area. There's nothing here to look forward to. If I was young I would [leave]," said Daniel, who had left the county during the 1950s. "I don't see nothing great happening to Harlan County in the future." One of my teenage sociology students predicted, "As the years go on, I think more young people will leave Harlan for a different style of life." Such forecasts depressed Cindy. She had unhappy memories of the times she moved away from Harlan. Bobby had never lived away from the county and did not share her fear. However, he hated to leave his mother alone as she approached her senior years. They both resolved to do their best to stay. Others, like Linda Taylor and Beth Walker, wrestled with similar issues but reached opposite conclusions. They both wanted to leave Harlan County as soon as they got their degrees. In the period from 1980 until 1990, Harlan County lost 5,315 residents, or 12.7 percent of its population.

In 1987, Bobby was seriously injured in a rock slide. His shoulder and arm were crushed and he lost some use of his right hand. Although he underwent two surgeries to correct his various problems, he could not keep his job operating the continuous miner. His former employer, by then a subsidiary of a multinational energy corporation, opposed Bobby's collection of workers' compensation benefits. The case was settled in Bobby's favor shortly before my 1991 return visit. When I asked Bobby and Cindy about it, they entertained me with humorous anecdotes about the bungling private detectives who trailed Bobby hoping to photograph him in vigorous physical activity. They bore no ill feelings toward Pat Abbott for the legal maneuvering. They were certain that the corporate lawyers had instigated it.

By 1991, Bobby had won his compensation benefits and found a job with the state highway department. Cindy had dropped out of community college so that she could work full-time as a clerk-receptionist at a local law office. She also sold her crafts at booths in area flea markets and craft shows on the weekends to earn extra income. Cindy's parents and Bobby's mother were both generous with their time and money. They took care of Julie, so Cindy that could go to work and sell her crafts. They also helped out the best they could by buying school clothes for Julie and giving the family generous cash gifts for birthdays, anniversaries, and Christmases. Cindy said that, if it had not been for their parents, they might have lost the house. But they were quick to point out that Cindy did her part. Everyone admired her consummate shopping and financial management skills, noting that she could stretch a dollar farther than anyone they knew.

Beth Walker and Linda Taylor had been laid off in the early 1980s. After earning their associate's degrees at the local community college, they got new jobs. By 1991, Linda joined the 12 percent of the local population who opted to leave Harlan County; she moved "downstate" to Lexington with her kids and was working as a dental hygienist. Beth, on the other hand, did not have such good fortune. She left her abusive husband after he was laid off from work. She formed one of a growing number of local female-headed households. (From 1980 to 1990, the number of single-parent households had risen 31 percent in Harlan County [Lousville *Courier-Journal*, 4 August 1992, A1, A19]). In 1991, Beth was working as a cashier at an Evarts grocery store. She supplemented her income with food stamps, and her son received free lunches at school. She wanted to move away from Harlan to get a better job, escape her ex-husband's harassment and abuse, and make a better life for herself and her son. But, temporarily at least, she was stuck in Harlan. She could not raise enough money for a major move. Frank Johnson was the only one of my friends who still worked in the mines.

❧

From the perspective of a research project attuned to the question of Harlan County miners' class consciousness and the resolution of contradictory image of Appalachians as political activists, the family story and county/industry history told here indicates that, since the 1930s, there has been a general trend away from pro-union, labor militance in Harlan County. Ernie Norton and his son-in-law Bobby Carson clearly symbolize a historical-generational shift away from class solidarity and confidence in the labor union movement, particularly in the UMW. However, like all narratives, this one simplifies the reality it seeks to represent. It is true that, in 1985 and 1986, there were no major unionization efforts in Harlan County's mines, no major strikes, and no clear shifts in local public opinion favoring the UMW or labor unions generally. And many of the Harlan workers interviewed for this project expressed pessimism about the future of the local coal industry and economy and, sometimes, seemed depressed and defeated by the global economic shifts that threatened to tear them away from the homes, land, and people they loved. But that is not the whole story.

Harlan Countians otherwise remained politically active, participating not only in mainstream electoral politics and civic projects, but in groups advocating educational reform (Forward in the Fifth, KERA), environmental cleanup and regulation (Kentuckians for the Commonwealth [KFTC] and other community efforts; Silver 1991), repeal of Kentucky's broad form deed (KFTC), tax reform (KFTC), and economic development. Even the apparently innocuous community effort to construct a miners' memorial included an element of political struggle and activism, as chapter 7 shows.

All was not quiet on the labor front either. In June 1985, union workers from the Cas Walker Supermarket in neighboring Pennington Gap, Virginia, set up informational pickets at the local nonunion Cas Walker store in an effort to pressure their employer into negotiating a new contract. Harlan was chosen as a site for informational pickets, not only because its store received supplies from Pennington Gap, but because the food workers' union hoped to "receive a boost from Harlan County's union ties and loyalty to labor organizations" (HDE, 11 June 1986, 12). The following spring, in an unpublicized move, miners walked off their jobs at a nonunion multinational coal corporation for one afternoon. But after settling their dispute with management, they were unwilling to comment upon their action. This event occurred in the midst of a much lengthier job action at the Harlan Appalachian Regional Hospital. From 1 April to 3 June, lab technicians, licensed pratical nurses, and clerks picketed to protest the hospital's demand for a "flexibility clause" that would enable management to decrease employee hours and switch job assignments, moves that were seen as a threat to the accrual of seniority. Harlan County residents assisted the striking workers by donating food and money to the strikers, writing letters to the editor in support of the strike, and refusing to cross the picket lines. Business suffered both at the hospital and at the adjoining health clinic, which was not, at the time, a target of the strike.

In the local coal industry, Arch Minerals employees cooperated with their district and local UMW leaders in an effort to publicize and resist restructuring and subleasing arrangements aimed at replacing union employees with nonunion workers. And two counties away, in Pike County, Kentucky, UMW workers engaged in a lengthy, sometimes violent strike against A. T. Massey, another oil-controlled multinational seeking to avoid union contract negotiations by creating subsidiaries and subleasing coal operations. In 1989, four years after the Massey strike was settled, the hot spot shifted to nearby southwest Virginia, where Pittston employees struck in protest of their multinational corporate employer's move to end payments to the UMW-BCOA benefits and pension plan of 1950 (see Couto 1993 for a comparison of these two job actions).

So, while Harlan's younger generation of miners expressed less confidence in the UMW and labor organizations than their parents had, it is difficult to reach a final conclusion on what this means for resistance, protest, and social change in Harlan. This generational transition might just mark another a temporary local lull in the ebb and flow of Harlan's labor-management history, or, alternatively, it might represent the local death of the UMW, labor organizations, and class-based political action generally. In either case, political activism has not died in Harlan or elsewhere in the mountains. The 1970s and 1980s have seen the formation of community organizations, cross-class coalitions, and alternative forms of political resistance in Harlan County and neighboring coalfield communities (Gaventa, Smith and Willingham 1990; Fisher 1993).

Before more directly exploring questions concerning political ideology and class consciousness among Harlan miners, however, it is necessary to extend this description and analysis beyond work experiences, the history of labor-management conflict, the industry's changing markets and ownership structure, the politics and turmoil of the UMW, and the national political climate. As central as these factors may be in identifying the opportunities for and constraints against working-class solidarity and action in Harlan County, such extralocal, macrolevel forces are not all-determining.

Much of the interactional and symbolic work toward forming a class identity and political ideology occurs at the local level, in the communities, homes, schools, and churches of Harlan County. The next chapter discusses the importance of the domains of household and community, family structure, and kinship ideology in Harlan County.

CHAPTER 4

Knowing Who You Are

A sociologist visiting Harlan in 1949 observed that, years ago, "the family and the local community were the two basic social units" in the county (Cressey 1949, 389). But, he claimed, industrialization had changed all that. "More far-reaching than the disruption of the economic organization was the breakdown of the older community structure," Cressey argued. "The people found themselves living in a 'human wilderness.' The destruction of the older social solidarity was almost complete" (391). This depiction of industrial Harlan County as a place where social solidarity, family, and community have been obliterated gives little credit to the people of Harlan, their ability to adapt, resist, and create. It also fails to recognize the strength and resiliency of local cultural traditions and values. This characterization furthermore stands in sharp contrast to Appalachian stereotypes of a traditionalistic, familistic, and clannish people. And, finally, it is further called into question by the Norton-Brown family history, in chapters 1 through 3, several academic studies which emphasize the structural and symbolic importance of Appalachian kinship and community identity even in the industrial era (Batteau 1982a, 1982b; Beaver 1976, 1986; Brown 1952, 1988; Brown, Schwarzweller, and Mangalam 1963; Bryant 1981; Egerton 1983; Foster 1977; Hicks 1976; Mann 1992; Pearsall 1959; Schwarzweller and Brown 1967; Stephenson 1968; Weller 1965; White 1987), and a more recent revisionist history documenting the positive aspects of coal camp life (Shifflett 1991). This chapter argues contra Cressey (1949) that said life in industrial Harlan County involves a complex interchange between class, kinship, and community and that industrialism did *not* obliterate traditional community life or family solidarity. More specifically, by exploring the ways in which family structure and kinship ideology overlap with and inform—but also contest and contradict—communal harmony and class conflict, this depiction is intended to challenge oversimplified bipolar oppositions between modernity and tradition as well as evolutionary assumptions concerning the direction of history.[1]

&

In chapter 1, I somewhat ironically noted my disappointment in Harlan Countians for their general ignorance about family history, genealogy, and extended kinfolk. I complained, how could they be so much like me?: allowing themselves to remain uninformed about their family's history and genealogy. I also complained, this time only *half*-jokingly, about how much detective work was involved in deciphering genealogical connections and reconstructing family histories. These remarks were intended not only to poke fun at my own naivete, but also to illustrate the fallacy of Appalachian stereotypes: namely, the idea that Appalachians are so clannish and family-oriented that every individual has a perfect recall of eight generations of history and an accurate cognitive mapping of hundreds of kin-mediated social relationships. Obviously, it would be difficult to remember such a large amount of information, assuming a person were even interested in such matters. Few people in Harlan County were really that interested.

In making the point that Harlan Countians are not all clannish, family-bound genealogists, however, I run the risk of trivializing the importance of family and kinship in Harlan County. To do so would be a grave mistake. Harlan Countians value close-knit families and see this as a defining characteristic of the local community—one that sets them apart from people who live elsewhere, particularly non-Appalachians, suburbanites, and city dwellers. My own observations in Harlan County, of both ideology and action, lead me to conclude that kinship functions at a number of different levels: it organizes a broad array of social relations, including those directly concerned with production, reproduction, and decision making; it offers economic, social, and psychological support to individuals; it provides a counterhegemonic resistance to capitalist and bureaucratic modes of organization; and, finally, it serves as a primary source of personal identity. Naturally, I am not the first to make these observations about the cultural, social, and personal significance of kinship in Appalachian communities (see, for instance, Batteau 1982a, 1982b; Beaver 1976, 1986; Billings, Blee, and Swanson 1986; Brown 1988, 1952; Brown, Schwarzweller, and Mangalam 1963; Bryant 1981; Egerton 1983; Foster 1977; Halperin 1990; Hicks 1976; Pearsall 1959; Stephenson 1968; Weller 1965; White 1987).

One of my students shared a story that illustrates the underlying importance of kinship for Harlan Countians' personal identity. One day she was cleaning her house, when a man arrived seeking her assistance in some genealogical research he was doing. He had been adopted as a baby and was trying to locate his biological parents. Somehow, he had traced a kinship connection to her, and since she was an amateur genealogist herself, she was especially eager to help. Much to her surprise, she could not locate any information on his parents. "And so," she sighed sadly, "he left. And he didn't even know who he was!" The implication here is that, in order for a person to "know her- or himself," she or he must also know her or his kinfolk. The linkage between family and self-identity is based on the idea that family members share more in common than genetic material or "blood." They also share common character and personality traits, talents, and dispositions (see also Batteau 1982b; Beaver 1986, 57–58; Bryant 1981, 50–51; Foster 1988, 64).

Regardless of whether individual identity and character were attributed to a family's genetic material or to its socialization practices—there seems to be disagreement and confusion on this point—the fact remains that family background is always relevant in Harlan County. As in other Appalachian communities, the first order of business among new acquaintances centered upon the location of that person within a local array of kin networks. In my case, they might ask if I were related to Lois Scott, a woman who was active in the Brookside strike, featured prominently in *Harlan County, U.S.A.* and is pictured in figure 2.2 (back row, first woman on the left). When I replied that I was not, to my knowledge, related to this woman, they would ask about my hometown, parents' occupations, mother's maiden name, and parents' birthplaces.

Harlan Countians, like Americans generally, trace their ancestry bilaterally—that is, through both the male and the female lines. Also, like in the rest of the United States, surnames pass patrilineally. The conjugal bond between husband and wife formed an important base of family solidarity, although the fundamental and unbreakable family tie occurred between parents and their offspring. This is the cultural, social, and personal bond that was most difficult to break—unlike marriages, which were becoming increasingly fragile during the 1980s. In spite of this relatively recent rise in local divorce and singe-parent household rates, the conjugal family—parents and their unmarried children—remained the ideal unit of kinship and society.

Even though conjugal families were considered as basic, independent social units, they often maintained relatively close ties with some extended kin—parents, grandparents, siblings, and first cousins, primarily. Families frequently lived in close proximity, shared produce from their gardens, borrowed items from one another, and worked and socialized together. Yet, at the same time, they established their economic and social independence by setting up separate households, acquiring their own land, and maintaining separate finances. As Allen Batteau observed, Appalachian kinship reciprocity stood in contrast to the kinship system in inner-city black neighborhoods, where the sharing of material goods and services sometimes posed a hardship to oneself or one's children (Stack 1974; see also Harvey 1993 as another comparative example). In Appalachia, one did not expect to sacrifice the conjugal family's well-being on behalf of extended kin (Batteau 1982a, 31). The aid that Bobby and Cindy Carson received from Cindy's parents, for instance, was deemed remarkable: it was neither expected nor demanded by the children. Long-term persistence of such unequal exchange obviously threatens the independence of Cindy and Bobby's conjugal unit. The strain of this economic dependency could ultimately threaten their marriage, as had happened in the cases of Cindy's grandparents and parents.[2] This generation's current success in negotiating the treacherous waters between dependence and independence could be linked to the following factors: (1) the fact that Cindy and Bobby have been married for about twenty years now; (2) they spend above the local average amount of time together as a couple; (3) they have a child; (4) both of them are working hard to earn money for their family; and (5) they each have close and affectionate relationships with their in-laws (in spite of Ernie and Bobby's disagreement about labor issues).

Loving and sharing behaviors, such as these, constantly demonstrate and reinforce kin ties (see also Schneider 1968, 24; Foster 1977, 108–11). And as long as exchanges between kin remain relatively equal and reciprocal, they provide the social and material basis for recognizing extended kin. Since most Harlan Countians could theoretically claim some type of kin tie to one another, it is only through the social construction of family that one recognizes one's kin (Bryant 1981, 28–29; Batteau 1982b, 450–53). When such sharing and interaction are disrupted, kin networks rupture and gradually disintegrate—that is, for all practical purposes, the family ceases to exist.

A crucial moment in the evolution or reproduction of a kin network comes right after marriage, when a young couple sets up a household. In the agrarian period, such couples often received gifts of land and livestock from either or both of their families. They settled in the community near one of the original homesteads and cooperated with extended kin in agricultural work projects. When both spouses came from the same isolated farm community, they maintained ties with both sides of the family. Sometimes a young couple affiliated with one side or the other. Families with plots of bottom land served as the nucleus for residential clusters. While this system remained egalitarian in nature, its "imbalanced factionalism" gave rise to kin groups that mobilized economic surplus and exercised political dominance (Brown 1988; Batteau 1982a, 36–37).

The economic and political restructuring of kin ties continued during the industrial period. Among local coal operators, merchants, and the political elite, marriage put large amounts of economic surplus and political power at stake. Among working-class families, such as the Browns and Nortons, economic uncertainty periodically required young couples to live in the homes of their in-laws. Such patterns of co-residence and mutual support, while they were sometimes necessary, placed a strain upon the young married couple. As newlyweds, both Janie Mae and Jess, as well as Ernie and Ginny, suffered marital difficulties when they moved in with their in-laws. Just as economic conditions might keep (or force) families together, they can just as readily split families apart. When the coal economy suffered a recession, members or segments of families might launch a migratory search for work, as Jess and Janie Norton's children had already done (see also Schwarzweller, Brown, and Mangalam 1971) and their grandchildren were contemplating. Economic uncertainty and increased poverty probably also introduced stress into marriages. It is no coincidence that Harlan County witnessed a dramatic increase in single-parent households and divorce rates (*Courier-Journal*, 4 August 1991, A1, A19) while undergoing a period of coal recession, out-migration, and economic sectoral transformation favoring female over male labor (Scott 1993, 1994). To sum up, then, changing economic circumstances, geographic dislocation, political disagreements, and personality conflicts provide the context in which relatives may be divorced, disclaimed, rejected, or forgotten.

In most cases, the restructuring of kin relations unfolds gradually over a long period of time. Someone's uncle, for instance, might move across the country in search of work and then marry and settle down in another state. Visits become increasingly infrequent, until they cease altogether. By the next generation, the families have completely lost touch. Sometimes, however, the rupture can occur rather suddenly, dramatically, and consciously. Family members quarrel violently and then verbally disown each other with the phrase, "I don't claim her [or him]." In those cases, conflicting family members may take steps to distance themselves from one another with avoidance tactics: moving away, limiting interactions, or refusing to speak. More subtly, a person or family trims branches of the family tree through indifference, snobbiness, or being too busy to associate with them. Sometimes, the reconstruction of family can be conscious, as in the case of one of my colleagues at the community college. As a family genealogist, she admitted to limiting her research to her father's side of the family because they were distinguished lawyers and judges. She was not particularly interested in her low-status maternal relatives. The construction of family need not be a conscious process, however. In most cases, people honestly did forget—or never knew—many of their distant kinfolk.

ٿٻ

As the observations of my community college colleague suggest, social status clearly affects family reputation and processes of kin group affiliation. After industrialization, this was especially true. It was then that, as Allen Batteau (1982b) put it, kinship became "an expression of *class* codified within an idiom of kinship" (463). In Harlan County, as in most of central Appalachia, elite families formed economic and political alliances with coal operators and businessmen from outside the county. Their least fortunate neighbors and kinsmen became landless coal miners who, for the most part, moved away from Harlan County or into coal camps with laborers imported from outside the region. There they worked, socialized, and intermarried with other mining families, forming new kin networks and family affiliations. Local miners used kinship as an idiom to express class and union solidarity, often referring to their co-workers as "brothers." The elite, on the other hand, lived along "Silk Stocking Row" with the other bosses and managers or, alternatively, kept residences in the independent mercantile centers of Harlan, Cumberland, and Evarts. Residential segregation, patterned by class, kin group, and race, persists in Harlan County today, as it does in most American communities.

Until this point, I have presented a fairly simple depiction of the relationship between class and kinship in industrial Harlan County. I suggested that the structural and ideological contradictions within the local kinship system made it possible for families to restructure themselves according to economic and political interests, changing relationships to the land and each other, and to new opportunities and crises. During the 1910s and 1920s, absentee-sponsored capitalist development, pursued and sponsored by local elites, provided the conditions by which Harlan County's families and communities were restructured along class lines—with members of the working-class residing and intermarrying in coal camps and the capitalist class residing and intermarrying in mercantile town or elite neighborhoods on the hills surrounding coal company towns. Social and geographic distance, conflicting economic interests and political goals, and uneven material exchange, I observed, provided the impetus for people to disclaim, ignore, or forget biological ties.

Although this depiction of the class-kin-community dialectic is more accurate than Cressey's 1949 portrait of a "human wilderness" bereft of meaningful community and kin relationships, it nevertheless remains oversimplified. There are caveats that must be added if one is to understand the complex dynamics at work in Harlan County. First, it is important to note that not all local elite (merchants, professionals, and politicians) worked for, or allied themselves with, outside capitalists. Nor did they all become coal operators. In 1932, for instance, Evarts became a center for striking and unemployed miners, precisely because the leaders and businessmen sympathized with the pro-union miners' cause. Similarly, Elmon Middleton, the county attorney for much of this period, was known for his evenhanded enforcement of the law. He also befriended several miners and union organizers in spite of the fact that many of his elite kinfolk and neighbors were committed anti-unionists.

Interclass alliance was also common in small, locally owned mines where owner-operators worked side by side with employees, who were also sometimes their kinsmen. Though the work was hard, the conditions dangerous, and the relationships conflictual, there seemed to be little hope of unionizing mines. Kinship bonds, which extended across class lines, received top priority. As a union organizer put it, "If you go to a mine and everybody at that mine— let's say, a 25-man mine—he's some kin to the owner; he's a nephew, son, brother, uncle, in-law. Well, you can whistle at the wind at that mine because you're not going to get those folks [in the union] . . . it's a family affair." In mines like these, management-labor relations were both paternalistic and patriarchal. And even in operations where owners and employees were not kinsmen and neighbors, kinship idioms of paternalism and patriarchy have been routinely mobilized to reinforce hierarchical workplace relations and ensure workplace discipline and order (Yarrow 1985; see also Portelli 1990).

And as a final complicating factor, there are also processes of intraclass political and economic competition that are too easily ignored in a Marxian-inspired rush to examine labor-management conflict.[3] In fact, some of Harlan's most bitter political conflicts during the time I was there occurred not between workers and their bosses, but among local elite (capitalist) families. One man, for instance, attempted to murder his own brother in retaliation for his having outbid him for a contract to provide coal for a regional utility company. In 1957, a prominent Harlan man murdered his brother over a financial matter. Thirty years later, his nephew pursued an economic and political vendetta against two brothers-in-law over the disposition of a family will. Convinced that they had cheated him out of the family inheritance, he started directly competing with them in business and local politics—alliance or employment by one of these families made one the automatic enemy of the other. This process, whereby an elite family restructured itself and ultimately drew the rest of the county into their squabble, seemed far more relevant to the operation of local politics and daily life in Harlan than either party affiliation or union membership.

ᚠ

From the very beginning, then, kinship has organized Harlan County social relations and local politics. And it continues to do so today.[4] Indeed, the very definition of community in Harlan County builds upon kinship ideology and ideal models of family life. In Harlan County, community was discursively defined as a place where egalitarian relationships of reciprocity and mutual affection prevailed. Even in the political realm and in government bureaucracy, relationships were supposed to be egalitarian, reciprocal, personalized, and nonbureaucratic. An examination of the political ads for local candidates illustrates how Harlan Countians idealized and defined local community. In 1985 and 1986, it seemed apparent that a candidate running for office had to accomplish two goals: to establish his or her identity as a community insider and to locate him- or herself in the local array of kin networks. The text of a typical political ad ran like this[5]:

> My wife is Betty (Long) Milton, daughter of the late Julia (Jansen) Long and the late Carter Long, of Wallins. Her grandmother is the late Molly Gold Jansen. . . . My family and I are lifelong residents of Harlan County. We attend the First Baptist Church of Loyall. My first concern is for my family and their welfare, and my concern for them is one of the reasons I am interested in serving in political office. . . . Most of you who know me are aware that I try to accommodate people to the best of my ability whenever possible. You know that I am easy to talk to. . . . For your family and mine, Vote and Support Philip Milton.

The following advertisement communicated a similar message. Since the candidate had lived outside the county for much of his adult life, he included a photograph of himself standing behind his grandparents, lifetime residents of the county. The text read:

> I would like to take this opportunity to introduce myself and my Grandparents to the People of Harlan County who may not recognize me. My name is Jebediah Jarvis. I am married to Amanda Jarvis, have three children, Rachel, Jebediah and Daniel. . . . I was born and raised in Harlan County. My parents are

Mr. Paul Jarvis and Mrs. Minnie Smith Jarvis of Harlan. . . . My grandmother has offered to cook for the jail for another four years [she had previously been the cook under another jailor for six years]. . . . Many people I have talked to during this race remember her and would like to have her back. Thank you for your vote and support. . . . "God Bless Harlan County!"

Most candidates neglected to cite any qualifications for the office *beyond* personal reputation, kinship identity, and commitment to the community. "My first concern is for my family, and my concern for them is one of the reasons I am interested in serving;" "I am easy to talk to;" "I was born and raised in Harlan County," they said. They promised to treat constituents like family and to "accommodate" their needs. The second one vowed to hire his grandmother to cook for prisoners in the local jail, a striking illustration power of the "family" model of community relations. In Harlan County, political candidates either implicitly or explicitly promised government services and programs in return for votes and political support. Sometimes, they offered jobs and favors as well (Batteau 1982b, 450–51; Caudill 1962, 334–61; Foster 1967, 229; Ireland 1977, 141–58; Pudup 1988, 24–26). The relationship between officials and constituents was seen as reciprocal: votes were exchanged for favors or jobs.[6]

Of course, as in any "family" relationship, there was always danger of a "squabble" breaking out. The community of Cumberland had several of them in the mid-1980s. After a series of disputes over tax rates, a federal probe of the sewage treatment, and a two-year feud with the city council, the town's mayor Gene Shepherd finally resigned in January 1988 to avoid facing the charge of "excessive salary of a family member and certain political allies" (HDE, 12 September 1988, 3).

Less than a month later Shepherd's successor, Carl Hatfield, threatened to resign as the result of a disagreement over whether he should document his expenses. The following newspaper account illustrates how the "family" model informs the antibureaucratic nature of local government. "When the meeting turned to the last topic on the agenda, the mayor's expense account," the reporter wrote, "a feverish discussion ensued with Hatfield saying he would not be made to look like a crook and therefore would not be made to fill out invoices and keep receipts of his expenditures. 'I was in the military for 21 years and had to keep records of all those things

and I'm not about to do it now,' Hatfield said. 'It was never required of anyone before and if that's what you want, to question
my integrity, then that's it for me' " (HDE, 25 September 1988, 1).

In this case, Hatfield insisted upon being taken at his word.
The contrast between how things worked in the "outside world,"
represented by the military, and how they worked at "home" was
critical. This model of politics and government personalized the
relationship between politicians and constituents; it enabled them
to press moral claims upon one another without regard to proce-
dure. While this humanized and personalized a rigid, alienating
government bureaucracy, it is also invited corruption, nepotism,
and inefficiency (see also Caudill 1962, 354–61; Ireland 1977,
141–59; Pudup 1988, 24–26; see also the Lexington *Herald-
Leader*'s series on county government corruption and nepotism, 30
January 1994 through 12 February 1994).

In no place was nepotism more apparent than in the Harlan
County education system. In 1985–86, everyone complained
about the local schools. The county ranked 101st out of 120 Kentucky counties in per-pupil spending in 1985 and 118th in high
school graduates (Chandler 1987, 176). It had high illiteracy
(HDE 18 October 1986, 1) and high school-dropout rates (HDE, 5
August 1986, 1; 5 September 1986, 1,2; 9 September 1986, 1,10),
and low student achievement scores. For several weeks in 1985, the
county school system became embroiled in a controversy regarding
the school superintendent's contract. Representatives from the op-
posing factions of the Abbott and Potter families effectively para-
lyzed the school board until finally a court order reinstated the
superintendant. Parents protested poor school facilities at Black
Mountain and the closing of several local elementary schools. In
1986, the local newspaper published excerpts from a report by the
Mountain Area Community Economic Development agency that
cited corruption as a common problem in the region's educational
systems (HDE, 5 September 1986, 1,10).

A local businessman put the situation in a political and economic context:

> We all know the problem [with schools] and some of us know the
> solutions; but they won't admit it. It's a tragic thing and it's not
> only in Harlan County but in eastern Kentucky, in general. The
> school systems . . . are so political that they really don't give a
> damn about students, which is tragic. They think about them-

selves and how much power they have and the schools and the children are secondary. . . .

I think it's evolved from many, many years ago. The school superintendent had more jobs to give than any other one person in the county and that's the reason [politics] got so involved [in schools] in the hills. Back in the 1930s, if you could give out 150 to 200 jobs during the Depression, you talk about *power* . . . and it's stayed the same. In this county, at one time, we had 900 teachers. That's a lot of power; and when one man or one group of men or women can control it, it's a strong political "stick" that can be swung in any direction. It makes the state and federal people say, "Boy, I gotta go get [the support of school officials] because I need them in my election." It doesn't only generate power here; it's far-reaching.

His analysis was equally applicable to local and county government.

Social relations, however unequal and conflictual they may have been, were greased by the language of egalitarianism. For the most part, Harlan Countians were unceasingly modest. Even the wealthiest local elite stressed that they were "just plain folks." The Abbotts, for instance, always wore khaki work clothes—not suits and ties. They shopped in local stores, went bowling with their employees, spoke to people on the street, and drank coffee with corporate executives and miners alike. Disclaimers, such as "What do I know? I'm just a hillbilly," "I'm just a plain country boy," or "We're known as an ignorant people and we're just trying to live up to our reputation" prefaced answers to my interview questions. In fact, many people used these disclaimers in an attempt to dissuade me from interviewing them altogether. "You're the expert. What are you asking me for?" they would reply.

Yet there was a tension between egalitarianism and elitism: people liked to think they were "a cut above" the common folk. The socially adept could so skillfully make the claim to superiority that no one took offense. A woman from a local elite family told this story to a number of people at a church dinner: "Some of my kin from Oklahoma came in here to do research on the family tree. They told me that the Hamells were descended from royalty. I said, 'Well, if we are, the blood is pretty thin now!'" Her rhetorical strategy allowed her to assert both her social superiority and her egalitarian ideals simultaneously (see also Batteau 1982a, 38).

The use of humor as a social leveling devise was quite common in Harlan County. During his term as president of the Jaycees, Randy Head appeared in local and state newspapers and on television to publicize and raise funds for a monument to Harlan miners who had died at work. When the memorial was dedicated, he addressed the town from a platform with Kentucky Senator Wendell Ford and other prominent politicians. To keep him from "getting the big head," Head's fellow coal miners and friends "gave him a hard time," mimicking his quotes from the newspaper, referring to him as "Mister President," mockingly deferring to him as if he were royalty and ridiculing everything about him: from his cowboy boots to his awkward public speaking. Randy's experience as "head honcho" did not perceptibly change him; he was still the same shy, personable guy with the same old friends. The ribbing had served its purpose in his case.

I received the same sort of treatment from the Nortons and my other friends, who, upon learning that I was working on my doctorate, referred to me as "Dr. Scott." When faced with a problem, they would jokingly remark, "We'd better ask Shaunna. She's a 'doctor!'" To this, I would usually reply that I had no idea what to do and crack a well-worn joke about how my parents had obviously wasted their money by sending me to school. My education had been useless. Thus, we made our nods to egalitarianism while never explicitly acknowledging the disparity in our educational credentials and social statuses. Bobby's friend Frank was best at "keeping me on my toes" concerning my educational pretensions. He had a large vocabulary and was confident using it. When I unnecessarily used a polysyllabic word, he would substitute a simpler synonym. One hazy summer evening Bobby, Cindy, Frank, and I were picking beans in the garden when I yawned and complained, "I'm so lethargic this evening!" To which, Frank replied, with a grin, "And lazy, too."

Community identity and loyalty dominated public discourse in Harlan County while I was there. In a county that had suffered the negative consequences of profit outflow, capital flight, absentee land ownership, poorly designed and administered government programs, negative stereotypes, and victim blaming, a suspicious attitude toward outsiders should be expected. Nonetheless, to the extent that they blamed their problems exclusively on outsiders, they ignored the conflicts and problems *within* the community. In fact, they tended to scapegoat outsiders for almost everything that went wrong in Harlan County. According to some local reconstructions of history, the Harlan mine wars of the 1930s were caused by foreign agitators and communists. One woman claimed that a mine guard was actually an innocent store clerk caught in the cross fire at the Battle of Evarts. Coal companies from outside the area, not local operators, ruined the environment with strip mining, they implied. The media created negative "hillbilly stereotypes" but local elite neither believed nor repeated them, they asserted. While comforting perhaps, none of these claims are true.

In a similar vein, local businessmen manipulated their employees and potential customers through appeals to community loyalty and demonstrations of communal solidarity. Local operators "stuck by the community through thick and thin." They reinvested their capital locally, created jobs for their neighbors, participated in local churches and civic organizations, and ran for public office. Therefore, the community and their employees owed them something in return. Businesses urged consumers to patronize local businesses. They implied, and sometimes explicitly stated, that their economic problems were caused by disloyal customers. The newspaper (HDE, 24 July 1986, 10) quoted a local restaurateur, "I've always stressed the need of getting people to work and shop at home. I still have faith in Harlan County and I know things are down right now, but I still have enough faith that I went into debt to run a business here in Harlan County. We're a home-owned business. I've got 25 Harlan County employees and Bob Smith has been my manager for 20 years."[7]

Workers and citizens used appeals to social solidarity and egalitarianism, as well. Miners and their families, for example, utilized egalitarian community rhetoric to control local operators and to pursue claims upon them (see also Anglin 1992, 1993). More coercively, they might use humor, ridicule, and gossip as weapons to motivate operators to respond to their concerns. Finally, they could involve the larger community in boycotts of the operators' other businesses or withdrawal of electoral support for their political candidates.

Managers in absentee-owned corporations did not respond to community censure in the same way. They did not depend upon the support of the community for their power and prestige; their orders came from outside the region. The aloofness of corporate managers and rigidity of corporate hierarchies frustrated local miners. They wanted to exert more control over their working conditions and to participate in more congenial, personal relationships with their bosses. As Ernie Norton put it, local miners wanted "to be in a position to negotiate." On a visit to the UMW District 19 office, I overheard a union representative express a similar desire to the labor relations representative from a multinational energy corporation. He complained about bureaucratic procedures and hierarchy in the corporate setting. "I can tell you these things for a fact. What can you tell me?" he asked rhetorically. "Nothing! It's like when the men have some little problem or grievance at work and they would just take it to the foreman to be settled. But what can the foreman do? He has to ask you and you have to call corporate headquarters. You can't take a dump without clearing it with corporate headquarters" (see also Yarrow 1982, 273).

The ideology of community emphasized the experential, historical, and structural common ground between the local elite and the working class. It did not, however, articulate the equally important differences and conflicts between the classes, which was voiced so eloquently in the labor protest songs of the 1930s. The question "Which side are you on?" lurked beneath the surface of much of the public discourse in Harlan County, occasionally emerging to disturb the surface of communal harmony that Harlan Countians labored so arduously to achieve. I was fortunate enough to participate in some local events that allowed me to observe this dialectical discursive battle between harmony and conflict. One of them, the construction and dedication of the Harlan Miners' Memorial, comprises the topic of chapter 7. The other discursive contest occurred at a retraining and testing workshop for "displaced," or laid off, miners in 1986.

At the time I witnessed this exchanged, it struck me as quite remarkable that a challenge to elite hegemony could be launched in this arena. The setting was an all-day affair in which "displaced miners" were subjected to a battery of tests administered by local government employees. The tests, ostensibly designed to gauge the educational level of the local workforce, included sections on writing, vocabulary, and mathematics, reminiscent of school achievement tests and college board exams. During some components of the exam, examiners verbally quizzed miners on a one-to-one basis. To speed up the process, I was asked to assist in the administration of this section of the exam and I acquiesced, in spite of my feelings of role conflict and personal discomfort.

As I administered the exam, however, I became increasingly uncomfortable with the entire process. I found it personally difficult to ask adult men to pronounce, define, and provide synonyms and antonyms for words that did not seem to be a part of anyone's general vocabulary. On the other hand, I felt even worse when they could not read words or solve basic problems that I would expect a sixth-grader to understand. At first, I thought I was just feeling guilty for the educational advantages bestowed upon me by my middle-class status. But that was not the only source of my discomfort. After additional reflection, I realized that I was participating in an exercise that, although it *may* have been designed to assist laid-off miners and further local economic development, was actually functioning to legitimate unemployment and reinforce these workers' feelings of powerlessness and unworthiness. It seemed to me that, for the most part, the exams reminded miners of their lack of formal education. The tests did not even attempt to measure, legitimate, and value skills that might have been useful in mining. Miners' knowledge had historically been devalued and stigmatized by capitalists and middle-class professionals alike, and now, it seemed, such knowledge had become irrelevant and obsolete. I thought that the testing process was as humiliating and demeaning to them as it been for me.

After the exams were completed, the "displaced" miners had coffee and doughnuts together and then sat down to hear a lecture by a local businessman and appointee to Harlan's economic development council. Speaking on the county's future economic prospects, this young, successful, college-educated man was a descendant of the first Euroamerican settler in the county and a member of a prominent local family. His speech included both paternalistic and egalitarian overtones: as a Harlan Countian, he was one of them and his economic prosperity was inextricably connected to theirs; yet, as a college-educated business owner and political leader, he could also claim social superiority over them.

With a certain air of noblesse oblige, the young man explained his plans for revitalizing Harlan's economy and putting them back to work. He proposed to the audience that Harlan's economic future lay with increased tourism. Although this seems to be a debatable proposition at best, tourism has emerged as eastern Kentucky's most viable economic option. Rather than challenge tourist-based economy as a goal, as I was tempted to do, the miners responded with a different set of concerns and questions. Apparently, they had not been humiliated and silenced by the day's events, as I had imagined. In fact, they had the opposite reaction: they were angry about past injustices and committed to building a better Harlan County and a better life for themselves and their families.

They raised two central issues during the discussion period following the presentation. First, they wanted assurances that jobs generated by future economic development would go to local workers, not imported ones. Second, they predicted that coal companies would oppose alternative economic development. The coal industry, they said, monopolized the land and resources and did not want other industries to compete with them for labor. Also, the industry had never paid its fair share of taxes, which was the primary reason that the county could not provide the educational system, utilities, and transportation infrastructure required to attract alternative industries. Instead of making them feel stupid and unworthy, as I had erroneously predicted, the tests appeared to have reminded them of the failure of the county educational system. Their response was not individualistic victim-blaming, but a systemic analysis that laid the blame squarely on coal operators.

The businessman responded to these challenges by focusing his attention on the miners' first point: the anti-outsider argument. However, the miners kept steering the conversation to the second issue: the local class structure and political economy as a barrier to alternative economic development. This discursive maneuver threatened to shatter the communal bonds between the speaker and the miners and, by extension, the local elite and the working class. When one unemployed miner asked point blank, "How are you going to get by the coal operators when they own 85 percent of the land and they ain't wanting no union and no other industries here?" there was no elegant way to escape the issue. Wiping the sweat from his brow, the businessman was forced to admit, "You're getting into an area I don't want to talk about." Others joined in, accusing the coal operators of collusion, tax evasion, and corruption. Again, no comment.

Finally, the businessman's childhood friend (who was not a "displaced" miner) interceded with a less threatening question:

"What pressure, if any, is being put on Kentucky Utilities [head-quartered in Lexington, Kentucky] to buy Harlan coal?" The speaker answered this question promptly, thus shifting the discourse to a safer terrain from which he could launch his own rhetorical attack. Lack of community loyalty, such as this, was the main problem in Harlan County. He advised the laid-off miners to protest the purchase of out-of-state coal, to write their congressmen in support of protectionist legislation, and to patronize local stores such as his own. He did not make the mistake of opening the floor for further questions and, instead, concluded his presentation with a personal narrative designed to remind the miners of their common identity, background, and interests as Harlan Countians. He was born and raised in Harlan County, he said. He got his bachelor's degree from the University of Kentucky. He *could* have gotten a job "working in a bank in Lexington" but his love for Harlan County brought him home. Since he was a native, he wanted to do his part to solve the problems his community faced. Thus, the daylong workshop for displaced miners came to a close.

Examples of the dialectical tension between community harmony and class conflict, egalitarianism and stratification, hegemonic and counterhegemonic discourses abound in Harlan County: in informal conversations, newspaper ads and articles, letters to the editor, government documents and court proceedings, public speeches and ceremonies (see chapter 7), religious sermons, testimonies, and rituals (see chapter 6), local histories (Forester 1986; Jones 1985; see also Scott 1991), oral history narratives, and on and on. Even a cursory examination of these discourses points to some of the contradictory structural and ideological forces at work in Harlan's political economy and to an ongoing, but mostly submerged, tradition of kin- and community-based counterhegemonic resistance to capitalist domination. I will continue to explore this theme in the following chapters, but for now let us pause to reconsider one of the questions that originally inspired this research: "Are Harlan miners class conscious?"

CHAPTER 5

I Don't Know What Makes Them So Greedy

Harlan Countians who have strong political commitments, either for or against labor unions, usually cite experience as their teacher. Instead of attributing their political commitment to an abstract principle or a charismatic leader, they cite the "school of hard knocks" (life) as their source of knowledge. As a Harlan miner's wife put it, "I've been . . . accused of being a Red. I never heard tell of a Communist until after I left Kentucky [1932]—then I had passed 50—but they called me a Red. I got all of my progressive ideas from my hard, tough struggles and nowhere else" (Hevener 1978, 67). Similarly, Ernie Norton explained that his strong commitment to the United Mine Workers comes from a lifetime of struggle and poverty: "I can recall my dad working for awfully small wages because we were unable to have a radio in the house or the type of clothes we ought to have and so on and so forth. And through experience, living through experience, I *guess* is what makes a union man out of you. . . . They [his father's generation] had it rough. When union was hard to get, they had to get it. . . . but now, it turns out, it hasn't been held." Along the same lines, a coal operator's daughter commented, "I'm very anti-union; but, then, I was raised that way. I don't know if I was raised a different way if I'd feel differently than I do" (Sue Bassham Cudd by James B. Goode, SECC-OHP, 8 March 1984; see also Yarrow 1982, 294).

Taken together, these remarks speak to the social embeddedness of knowledge and ideology just as they point to the discursive contingency of class identity and consciousness. Ernie Norton, it appears, would agree with Gramsci's observation that there is no guarantee for ruling-class hegemony: it must continually be produced, reproduced, and defended. Similarly, there is no guarantee for class consciousness. It, too, must be produced, reproduced, and defended, but often in the face of more powerful, organized oppositional forces who control property, the means of production, and the legitimate use of force. Challenging these forces involves an individual risk of life and livelihood. It also requires a collective coordination of activities and interests, and ultimately rests upon the ability to develop a counterhegemonic ideology through which to imagine an alternative political economy, to challenge common, everyday assumptions, and to think in new categories. In Harlan County, like elsewhere, this project can be a difficult, risky, uneven, and contradictory.

This being the case, it seems rather foolhardy and pretentious to continue with the original question of class consciousness. Rather than attempt to overgeneralize about a few Harlan miners and then compare them to a static, imposed definition of class consciousness, I elected to pursue a less universalistic and essentialist goal: to outline a few themes from my interviews of Harlan miners, identify their underlying assumptions, and speak to their political implications. This more limited project is tricky enough. After all, political ideology changes through time and is articulated differently in different settings to different audiences. It is often internally contradictory, and it varies with each individual (Wilentz 1984, 17; Yarrow 1982, 397–405). I have found Bertell Ollman's (1987, 91–92) metaphor of political ideology as a "provisional map" that only approximates the reality it seeks to represent and is constantly being revised and updated (see also Mann 1987, 45–55) to be helpful in my thinking. The following account is my own "provisional map" of the political ideology a few (18) Harlan miners. As a provisional map of others' provisional maps, this description "freezes" a dynamic process in time and is, therefore, necessarily limited and partial.

To be more methodologically specific, this depiction is based upon eighteen months of participant-observation, interviews, conversations, and archival research among genealogical records, court proceedings, census data, newspapers, and oral history collections. Tape-recorded life-history interviews with eighteen retired and active miners form the centerpiece of this research. Among the topics covered in these tapes were their life histories focusing on employment, work experiences, relationships with their bosses and co-workers, mine safety, women miners, and the UMW as well as general topics, such as current events, local community and politics, and their predictions for the future, reflections on the past, and aspirations for their children and grandchildren. Locally authored historical and autobiographical texts (Forester 1986; Garland 1983; Jones 1985; Titler n.d.) also contributed to the local discourse on the community and its past. And, finally, relevant secondary literature about Harlan County (Banks 1983–84; Billings 1990; Corbin 1981; Ewen 1979: Gaventa 1980; Hevener 1978; Maggard 1988; Portelli 1990, 1991; Taylor 1990; Wooley and Reid 1974) informed my reading of primary historical sources. In short, this discussion arises out of a dialogue between primary and secondary historical sources, the academic literature, some Harlan County mining families, and this author, it can only be partial and tentative.

ঽ▰

For the most part, the oral history interviews that I collected, as well as those housed in the archives at Southeast Community College, offered ego-centered autobiographical narratives. An exception to this rule was UMW District President Joe Phipps, who did not limit his narrative construction of the past to events that occurred in his lifetime. Like the sociologist C. Wright Mills, who was cited in chapter 1, Joe Phipps emphasized the connections between biography and history. He recounted his life story in the context of union activity, which, in turn, had to be explained in relation to American industrial development. He said:

> This country hit a revolution near a scale that you would not believe in the 1880s; they call it the Industrial Revolution. . . . and this country was expanding by leaps and bounds and profits were huge, huge, huge, huge! . . . and they were working people under slave labor conditions. . . .
>
> In no time, they became the world's number one producer in just about everything; but they didn't care how they got there. And they exploited the American labor to the point that children, toddlers if you will, were being slaughtered in the mills and the mines and the industries all over this country. . . . In the 1910s, these huge organizations branched out and came into the coalfields [of eastern Kentucky], formed coal camps and they virtually kept those people [miners and their families] prisoners in their own homes, if you could call 'em that. . . . They controlled

those people from cradle to grave. . . . Something had to be done.

In the view of men like Joe Phipps and the Norton brothers, the "something to be done" consisted of organizing a union. It was the union, under the leadership of John L. Lewis, that improved their lives. The union, they said, was the only thing standing between them and starvation wages, dictatorial control of coal operators, and unsafe working conditions. The union promoted safety legislation, offered them a mechanism through which to negotiate with their employers, protected their jobs, secured for them a pension, and provided them with medical care. In return, they offered gratitude and loyalty. This reciprocal relationship between the union and its members, like the one between local politicians and constituents, invoked paternalistic overtones in which John L. Lewis was cast as the benevolent protector of miners and their families (see also Portelli 1990; Yarrow 1982, 265).

Daniel Norton thought that the entire community should be grateful to the UMW for the services and wealth it brought to the county. His narrative reveals the salience of community identity and interests, among Harlan's miners. The UMW did not promote the miners' interests alone, but the entire community's well-being. He noted:

> Right now, the only reason you got a Harlan County is because of the United Mine Workers of America. The UMW got your black lung [benefits] and that has brought fortunes into Harlan County. United Mine Workers of America pensions, UMW health care cards, United Mine Workers of America built your hospital. And, if you hadn't had no pensions, no black lung, and no health cards coming into this county for thirty years, you wouldn't have had a Harlan County. . . . I don't know what the figures would be, but it would have to be up in the millions, that have come through here because of the United Mine Workers of America.
>
> Now, the hospital has felt the pinch in the last few years, especially since Brookside has closed down. That took away a lot of their business, because people simply do not go to the doctor if they don't have the money. Of course, all the service jobs that have come in here since: if this [United Mine Workers of America] money hadn't have been available, they wouldn't have come in here.

This being the case, it was difficult for them to understand why other local business owners opposed the union. As one miner said, "That's why I can't see why that the merchants and the business people down in Harlan do not go all out to support United Mine Workers of America. It seems like their pride holds them back from that. . . . [They think] you've got to be a Republican and hate the United Mine Workers of America. . . . [But] you should be supporting something that is making your dollar." Three factors are worth noting here. First, miners identified their interests with that of the whole community; theirs was not a selfish interest or primarily a class-based one. Second, they did not seem to recognize the class-based interests that united other business owners with the coal operators or, at least, they chose to ignore or downplay them. Finally, they cited individual characteristics, in this case "pride," as the primary motivation for class behavior (see also Yarrow 1982, 279–80). As we shall see, "greed" emerges as a central social problem for which there is no apparent solution.

Miners recognized that, as individuals, they wielded less influence than the coal operators did. Although they resented this inequity, they did not elaborate it into a critique of American individualism per se (Yarrow 1982, 330). They simply took the pragmatic step of pursuing their individual interests through collective activity. Daniel explained:

> Any coal miner that's got common sense would want to be represented by the United Mine Workers of America, because you're going to have somebody to bargain for you. You're part of a group. An individual can't go complain and get any results. But, as a body, as a whole group of people, you can do that.
>
> To be in a coal mine and to be on your own is one thing but to be in a coal mine and to be represented by a union that can *dictate* [my emphasis] to a company what they're going to do and what they're not going to do is a world of difference.
>
> If you're just an individual and you tell a boss that you don't want to go in that water hole, if you're afraid, he says, "Hit the road! Either get in it or get out." But if you belong to the union, you can tell him to pump that water hole or you're not working in it. He has to pump that water hole. That's the difference. A poor person don't have anything if he can't have organized labor. I mean, if you can't belong to an organization and have somebody to bargain with you and for you, how are you going to bargain for yourself? There's no way. It just can't be done.

The use of the word *dictate* here, I think, overstates the UMW's power in the coal industry as well as the workers' power over management. Nevertheless, it does capture the extent to which contractual agreements, such as the protection of the jobs of miners who refuse overly dangerous work or report safety violations, have empowered Daniel and other union miners. They have experienced this as an almost revolutionary change in their working conditions in which they can sometimes veto management decisions and orders. Under certain circumstances and in a limited way, then, unionized miners could "dictate."

A central theme in my conversations with local miners and businessmen as well involved the global restructuration of capitalism, particularly global corporate dominance, capital flight, and the loss of American jobs. The nation-state increasingly danced to the tune called by multinational corporations, they observed. In the United States, everyone, even the politicians, feared for their jobs. So, they "towed the line" for energy corporations, thereby subverting the democratic process. Daniel complained, "The government don't run this country and the people don't run it. The corporations run it. . . . If there's 100 million people said, "Don't sign this bill" and an oil company come up and says, "I want it signed," it'll be signed. I'll guarantee it. . . . That oil company can make or break [a politician]. . . . It takes money [to be heard]. . . . but that's all cut and dried. That'll never be no different. There's no way you can change it. It'll never be changed. That's a fact of life. Your big corporations runs the country, runs the world. No doubt about it." His insistence that the current situation of global corporate domination is a "fact of life" that will "never be changed" clearly sounds fatalistic. Interestingly, however, his fatalism has not decreased Daniel's love for his country (Anglin 1992) nor diminished his political activism. It did, however, reveal his pessimistic and limited vision of the future (see also Yarrow 1982, 265).

Joe Phipps's vision was not quite as pessimistic or limited as Daniel's. He conceded that corporations had emerged victorious in the struggle against labor, thus far; but Phipps had not given up the fight for control of the discursive terrain. That was one reason why he had agreed to be interviewed: this project offered a mechanism by which his pro-union voice could be heard. During our conversations, he repeatedly emphasized the important role that education and the media played in maintaining capitalist hegemony (see also Maggard 1983–4). Elementary and secondary school history textbooks did not include much labor history, he told me. Also, corporations donated collections, materials, and moneys to schools and libraries, thus, preserving and promoting their point of view. Finally, the media channeled information and manipulated public opinion, thereby crushing dissent. As he put it:

> You see, you never got the negative press that the police and John Rockefeller, in 1914, hired people to massacre people. It's always been the American coal operator [that] has his voice heard. And we've [United Mine Workers of America] been the voice crying in the wilderness. . . .
>
> [Yet the United Mine Workers has always gotten bad press, sometimes deservedly.] There have been some bad situations, some very terrible situations in our union and [the Yablonski murders] was one of them; and we'll never live that down. . . . That [murder] should have never happened. Nobody benefited from it; it don't make sense. You can't figure a legitimate reason for that thing [the murder]. It was stupid and we're paying the price for it. . . .
>
> Always, always, the corrupt, management-controlled press . . . will blow [the union's corruption] out of proportion. . . . That is selling the public a negative image about unions.

Phipps shared notions of community reciprocity, fairness, and egalitarianism with his fellow Harlan County miners. He thought corporations should follow these standards as well. Their complaints of economic recession and global competitions were exaggerated, according to Phipps, who said:

> [The coal operators] always give a hardship story. Now, if anybody has to take a cut, it's always the laboring people. Always, always, always! That's union, nonunion, whatever. Management never, never, never even considers cutting their margin of profit or cutting management's wages. Who do they always hone in on? The bottom of the pile. Go after labor! Cut their wages. Let *them* work for nothing; but it's unheard of for them to say, "Let's cut some corporate profits to compete, let's cut some corporate head's salaries to compete." And this is something that's always mystified me. You're a professor, or something, so tell me why that it takes so darn much money for a corporate head to live, in the millions per year, and so little for me? . . . Why do they

justify $11 million for Lee Iaccoca last year, for Chrysler, and they gave to corporate heads bonuses for production and good work and all that bit. Yet they turned around and forced the auto workers to make wage concessions so they could give these bonuses to these people? Their profits raised each year, yet my folks [workers] have got to take cuts.

Daniel made a similar point, when he criticized the "self-made men" narratives that coal operators used to justify their wealth and power. "These people that claim that they worked hard for their millions. I don't care if they worked twenty-four hours a day, they didn't work no harder than a coal miner works, if he works eight hours. So, that's an old story: 'So-and-so's got it but he worked for it.' But there's millions that don't have it that *worked* for it. So, I don't buy them kind of stories," he said.

Phipps did not "buy" those stories either. His accounting of the economic balance sheet resembled Daniel's. In lean times, he complained, "It's always the miner that suffers. The miner has to go without food for his family, he has to starve his children, keep his pregnant wife barefoot [during a strike]. . . . and he has to suffer to get a contract he can live with. . . . and the only thing we want is to be able to earn a living, working in the coal industry, with dignity" (see also Michrina 1993). He continued by noting that progress had come only through class struggle: "Everything we have ever asked for, in any contract at any time, was brought on by somebody dying. Somebody bled for it."

Phipps saw federal elections, particularly presidential ones, as an important arena for class-based political action. Most of the Harlan miners with whom I spoke agreed that electoral politics was the most direct mechanism for economic and political reform. Most of them, like Harlan Countians generally, identified themselves as Democrats. Daniel cited key philosophical differences that prevented him from voting Republican, even when he knew and respected the candidate. "The Republicans' philosophy, for a fact, is to get rich, for the rich to get richer and the poor to get poorer," he noted. "I never voted for a Republican, because, even if he was a good man, he'd probably be a friend to a bad one." Most miners agreed that the Republican presidential victory in 1980 had hurt the cause of labor, locally and nationally. As one put it, "Reagan has hurt unions more than any recent president has. He started off with these air traffic controllers and, of course, that was their goal: to do all they could in four years. Then, they had four extra years to do just a little bit more and they've bit a hunk into organized labor. They've done a pretty good number on it. It'll take years to get back what's been lost in these six years."

While Harlan's miners generally acknowledged the reality of social stratification and political domination and often depicted the world as a struggle between the "haves" and the "have-nots," they did not conceive of themselves primarily in class terms. They neither regularly used the terms *class, proletariat,* or *working class,* nor did they primarily identify with other workers beyond fellow coal miners and union members (see also Yarrow 1982, 231–47). (Joe Phipps and other UMW officials and activists are an exception to this rule, however.) To most folks, the primary units of analysis were the individual, the family, and the local community, which, as noted before, was defined by egalitarian, kinlike relations, and paternalistic overtones. They recognized common material interests with other manual workers, whom they referred to as "common people" (Yarrow 1982,330–50) and "regular folks" (see also Michrina 1993, 143, on the "little man"), but most of my interviewees did not seek to form a larger union or broader political coalition with people from outside the community, as UMW President Richard Trumka had suggested.[1]

In my conversations with miners on this issue, it seemed that a general suspicion about the corrupting influence of power and the difficulty in sustaining democracy in large-scale organizations lurked behind this hesitation. In a discussion about the possibility of the UMW joining with other unions in the oil industry to strengthen their bargaining position with energy conglomerates, I asked what Ernie thought of all labor unions merging or coordinating their efforts. He did not like the idea:

> Unions cannot merge together and just become one big union. I'm not for that because they can get too demanding. I'd rather be in a position to negotiate; and you can negotiate much better than you think you can when you're dealing with responsible people in the companies.
>
> It seems like if they made just one big union—let's just think if half of this nation was one big union—what that union said [would go]. That wouldn't be right. Besides, you don't never know what you got running that union. You don't never know. It's awful.

A cursory glance at this answer might lead one to conclude that Ernie's experience with the corrupt Boyle regime had eroded his confidence in unions and democracy to the point that he could only place his faith in face-to-face relations with his employer (see also Yarrow 1982, 265–73). This is not necessarily an incorrect reading of Ernie's response; but I would like to offer a second interpretation. Ernie's answer, it seems to me, combined several elements that were common to the political ideology of Harlan miners. First, he both began and concluded his statement with a comment on the impersonal and corrupting nature of power in large organizations. A national labor union, he argued, would not only destroy the family-like relationship within the local community, it would unbalance pluralistic democracy at the national level. He was especially concerned about corruption, since it had been endemic both in his labor union and in his community. Finally, he said that a single labor union would *demand* too much, it would upset the balance of pluralistic democracy (Gerstle 1989, 310–18) and simply reverse the patterns of inequality and injustice that already existed. Ernie's utopian vision did not include a "big bully" who could call the shots, whether in the form of a union or a multinational corporation. Rather, he envisioned a multiclass, locally based community in which bosses, workers, politicians, and citizens interacted as equals. Everyone would cooperate in a mutual (kinlike) reciprocity; everyone would be sensitive to the needs of the community.

Generally, miners agreed that human greed posed a significant obstacle to this communitarian vision. They were most critical of, and hostile to, coal operators when they talked about profit rates and safety programs, often accusing bosses of caring more about mules and money than people. Yet apparently many had not apparently achieved an understanding of the social processes by which such greed is constructed, as the following excerpt illustrates:

> I'd say to anybody that's going to work, a company is definitely *not* looking out for you. They may say, well, Yarborough would tell you they would; but they ain't going to do it. They're looking for their profit and, if they don't have profits, they ain't going to be there long. Of course, the bigger the profits, the better. They're not going to kick these profits back to the employees. . . . As a rule, a company doesn't consider employees. They don't [even] consider *management* employees. They consider the stockholders and the owners and that's it! If you're poor and unorganized, you're just

up the creek without a paddle. It's just their philosophy is that way. A company, for some reason or another, just don't recognize the employee!

Attributing the capitalism's profit motive to personal philosophy and individual greed obviously does not get miners very far along the road toward imagining an alternative society.

Nevertheless, it is a journey that many of them have begun. For one thing, the miners I interviewed clearly recognized their labor as the source of coal operators' profit. This recognition lay behind many of the demands they made upon their employers, not only tangible material benefits like adequate wages, benefits, and a safe working conditions, but also more intangible items like respect, dignity, and recognition (see also Michrina 1993). When Harlan Collieries put senior workers on nonunion wages, they were not only cheating these workers out of pay, they were insulting their dignity. When Ernie recounted that incident, he complained more about the inhumanity and lack of gratitude than money. "They didn't respect that man," he explained. "He worked his life for them but they were taking advantage of him." Similarly, Joe Phipps pointed out that operators owe miners a debt for making them into wealthy men and that that debt should be repaid in job security and wages for a "decent living." As he explained, "We're up there [at Lynch] because of these coal companies. We mine their coal for them. Certainly they ought to give us the security of knowing we have a job. That's all we're asking for. . . . There's nothing wrong with that. We've been there, in Lynch, working for those people as coal miners since 1915. . . . [and] it's not wrong for us to ask for job security." Instead, he noted, operators treated miners "like animals" and these workers routinely wound up at "the bottom of the pile."

Daniel Norton wished that he could trade places with the operators, he claimed, so that miners would finally receive wages, working conditions, respect, and gratitude that they deserved. His idealized version of labor-management relations also included reciprocity and paternalism:

If I was going to run a mines, I'd call 'em [UMW] and tell them to come and sign me [my employees] up, because I'd want my men to be happy and I'd want to provide for them. And another thing, if I was an employer, no matter how rich or how much money I made, my employees would know it. I'd *give* it back, in some form or another. If a group of people makes your rich, you're *indebted* to those people, *even* if you paid them wages to make you rich. Share it. Give 'em some of it. Give 'em a bonus, come out of a blue sky and give 'em a bonus. Don't just wait 'til Christmas. Give 'em one in September. Give 'em a good one. If you made plenty, *give* plenty. I never could understand why employers didn't want to share some of their wealth with the employees. . . . It's just beyond me. . . . You know, anybody who's poor could say that and you'd say, "You'd have a different thought if you was rich." But not me.

In other words, the basic dynamics of capitalism—the profit motive and exploitation (i.e., the extraction of surplus value from workers)—can be transformed by a simple change of the personnel (personalities) involved. Once again, this proposition rests upon the underlying assumption that individual characteristics and personalities structured social problems, but not the reverse.

Perhaps it comes as no surprise, then, that none of these miners challenged the central assumptions of capitalist political economy: free enterprise and market competition, private ownership of property, the capitalists' right to hire, fire, and manage, or the inevitability of profit motive and greed. Even the union miners argued in favor of labor unions on the grounds that they were actually *good* for a capitalist economy. Unions, they said, stabilized industries and labor forces by regulating and codifying their relations (see also Yarrow 1982, 350–97). As Daniel explained:

> Even the president [Reagan], your coal operators even, speak of how important it is to have organized labor, because it stabilizes the workforce. For example, in coal mining in this area, especially up until the 1950s when everything was union, it's different; if owners had been allowed to pay different wages, some of your bigger mines could have hand-picked all their men. And the way it turned out, there were enough men to do all the jobs at all the mines; and one man wasn't going to leave one mine to go to another because his wages and everything (benefits) are the same. . . . That was good for the companies. . . . Once the unions got organized, they [the companies] saw it was really a better way. Of course, any costs that a union cost, was always passed along [to the consumer]. So, they never lost nothing. They [the companies] made money from it.

According to Daniel and Ernie, union workers were more productive than nonunion employees. In fact, they were much better workers than the younger generation of nonunion miners, who were the slipshod, lazy men who did "not understand unionism." They furthermore regretted that, in the process of representing good workers, the union was forced to represent the interests of poor ones as well. Daniel reflected, "A union has to protect people that don't really deserve to be protected. I always said that a good union man would be a good worker. If he understands his union and understands [that] his company has to make a profit. . . . but it's just like church, I guess, you see a lot of people in church that's not good Christians. You see a lot of people in the union that aren't good union men. They're lazy. And they're sorry. And they take advantage. And that makes you look bad."

Ernie similarly condemned workers who did not work hard on the job, stating that they "don't know what union is about." To his thinking, lazy workers hurt *all* workers because they decreased production and reduced profit. After the Brookside strike, he said:

> [Duke Power] has been the greatest asset to the county and state that I know of. . . . It put a lot of men to work. It made miners out of a lot of people but it hurt some. What I mean [by] "hurt" is that [at Brookside] it . . . put young people in there where they don't have to work; they got the union protection. They're going to be good union men, see, until the time comes and they don't even know what union is all about. This kind of men don't produce too well. See them young men that's never known what union is, they don't think about it in terms that I would. Like I would always think to myself, "Let's try to beat that other shift. If they loaded 400 tons, let's get 450." Now, if you're doing that, you want to see high production. Anything you see in the mines that will help production, do it, because you're going to get paid for it. That's where your pay day comes from: their profits. So, if the production ain't there, he [the boss] ain't going to have your wages. So, the young men don't see that any more; they just go in there and get by with what they can.

To Ernie, then, workers and their bosses functioned like an athletic team, in competition with other teams on the playing field of the market. Everyone had to do his part if the team was to succeed.[2]

Put simply, Ernie and Daniel could not yet imagine a noncapitalist economy, because, to them, the human "nature" constructed in capitalism seemed to be the only human nature possible. Like most other Harlan miners, Ernie and Daniel believed that the capitalist free-enterprise economy, competition, profit motive, greed, and exploitation were the inevitable results of the individual's need to compete, to achieve, and to pursue one's interests. Still, both Ernie and Daniel agreed, that individualism, profit, greed, and exploitation could get "out of hand" and ultimately harm the community. In the 1980s, Ernie saw signs that this was indeed occurring. "Used to be," he remembered, "people seemed content with making a fair return on their money. Now, if they can't make it all this year, they want to sell it and let someone else try it. I mean, people are just greedy and you can't satisfy them."

The most common example of greed run amok, cited by Harlan's miners and businessmen alike, was the behavior of multinational corporations during the 1980s. Their vast reserves of capital, diversified holdings, influence over government policy and public opinion, and ability to transfer holdings and shift operations across national boundaries made them both free agents and superstars in the global playing field, to elaborate on the sport analogy. Their ability and willingness to abandon local and national communities in pursuit of profit posed a serious threat to democracy and community as most Harlan Countians imagined it. Multinational corporations had no home-team spirit and no community conscience; they cared about nothing but profit and were accountable to no one (see also Bluestone and Harrison 1982; Couto 1993 Gaventa 1990). Joe Phipps complained most bitterly about the situation:

> They talk about going to the nonunion South, the right-to-work states. Indeed, that's what has occurred. And every year, there's been more jobs in those states; and every year more folks have got to work ten and twelve and fourteen hours at below-poverty-level wages. . . . If you're working for nothing, it's just like it was back in slave days. . . .
>
> Is it fair for me to compete with a Chinese coal miner at $30 a month? Is it fair to me to try to compete with somebody in Colombia that's mining strip coal for $45 a month? Do I bring myself to that level or do I try to bring them up to my level? We've got a choice. If the choice was mine, then I'm going to bring them up to my level.
>
> I believe that every man, woman, or child in this country, in this *world*, is entitled to a fair wage pay for a fair day's work. I believe that with all my being. And it's *wrong* for me to have to

give up my fair day's work for a fair day's pay to compete with somebody in China or South Africa, where there's slave labor conditions. Those people don't make $20 a month, on the average. They [South African blacks] live in compounds and they're driven to work and drive back from work and don't even get to see their families. . . . That's what apartheid's all about. . . .

The concept in this country is, "Hey, we're going to compete. Let's get down to their level." And this is the greatest country in the world [he says, with shock in his voice]. No! No! Let's help them come up to our level. That makes so much more sense to me.

[The prevalent attitude is] Let's take wage cuts and let's go back to groveling in the dirt again. And, if we take 'em like we're doing and making concessions like we're *doing*, we're going to be right back to child labor and everybody's going to be starving. And only the rich is going to get richer.

There's never been a time in corporate history that they really and truly lost money because of the workers. Never! They're not losing money right now. Today, in this state, they're going to break [coal] production records and we've got over half our workforce in the coal mines in the street [unemployed]. We got folks that are working in Harlan County right now for $4 an hour. . . .

But it does not help us at all to bring ourselves down to somebody else's level. We strived all our life to get where we are. It's certainly *wrong* and it's economically infeasible for us to go back to $30 a day or $30 a month. We can't do that. . . . When a man can't feed his family and doesn't know where his next bite is coming from, that's wrong.

Yet this is what American industry is trying to tell us. "Let's get down to their level and compete." . . . There's people starving to death in minimum wage and they're working every day. Now, what does it get us to work every day, seven days a week for $3.35 an hour? And we're living below the poverty level [on that wage] in this country. . . . Nobody in this country should live [at poverty level]. We are *all* supposed to be dedicated to that [eliminating poverty]. . . .

But our industry leaders say, "No!" . . . The corporate leaders justify it and it's perfectly all right; President Reagan said it was. "I'm a millionaire and I think anybody should be." But everybody can't be an actor! Lee Iacocca says, "I'm worth every penny of it!" Well, I feel like my coal miners are worth $500 a day but I can't convince nobody to pay them that. But they're worth it. They're worth just as much as Lee Iacocca is to his company or the president of the United States. . . . I can't justify that and I resent it.

Phipps's discussion of capital flight, while empassioned and critical, also included paternalistic references, such as "my coal miners." In addition it rested upon patriarchal assumptions, casting men in the role of "breadwinner" and then using this role to lodge moral claims upon the bosses. "When a man can't feed his family . . . that's wrong," Phipps tells us (see also chapter 3; Anglin 1992; Maggard 1988, 1990; Pudup 1990b; Yarrow 1985). The complex and sometimes contradictory relationship between patriarchal constructions of masculinity and class identity among Harlan County miners will be discussed further in Chapter 6 (see also Chapter 3).

The issues of capital flight and community responsibility unite Harlan's miners with local coal operators, including the president of the HCCOA. In a discussion with my Appalachian Studies class, HCCOA president Jay Barlow railed against capital flight but not necessarily against corporate wealth:

The thing that bothers me about it, Shaunna, is that they take American money and American ingenuity and take it to Central America to develop it. Why don't they do it here? There's things that could be done here. They could take coal and make oil out of it. This is what irritates me. They could take that same money and utilize coal in the U.S. and get the same benefits. But it's too tough; it's harder. It's much easier to go down there and get cheap labor and all that coal. That's my reasoning behind it.

Now, they go to Iraq and all those places to develop oil and, then, what do they do? They turn around and belt us in the mouth when they want to. The point I'm trying to make is: it'll come back to haunt you. The oil people in the Middle East can control this world. And who developed them? The United States, 99 times out of 100. We just don't learn our lessons right. And I think those big corporations, which are fine, get up into the billions, they forget about where they got it. . . .

[Using cheap Third World labor] is a case of, in my opinion, taking advantage of misery. And what irritates me is that they could care less about how many people die. . . . When it comes to the dollar, they don't give a damn.

Of course, miners make similar complaints about small, locally owned companies: that the operators are greedy and that they forget that laborers produce company profits. Still, multinational energy corporations provided the favorite targets for scapegoating.

It was no coincidence that, when Daniel complained about the inordinate power of corporations in this country, he specifically mentioned oil companies. Daniel and Ernie agreed that American oil companies caused the so-called energy crisis of the early 1970s. Daniel's conspiracy theory included the xenophobia and anti-Semitism that have been generally and sometimes unfairly associated with rural southern parochialism and white working class identity: "If they want coal to go, coal will go. If they say, we're going to use oil, we'll use oil. Just like, them Arabs didn't raise oil from $2 a barrel to $4; they ain't got that much sense. The Rockefellers, Armand Hammer, and some of them Jews up in New York City, Kissinger, Nixon, they're the ones that raised the price of oil. . . . and it all went out of sight."

Phipps concurred, claiming that oil corporations had destroyed government programs that would benefit the coal industry. "Big oil has controlled every president since 1923. . . . Obviously, they do right now because they stopped. . . . the coal [liquification and gasification] programs. . . . They've slowly but surely bought up all the coal reserves . . . and producing coal mines, one way or another. In this area [southeast Kentucky] alone, the only two [independent operators] I can think of, off the top of my head, are the Harrisons . . . and the Abbotts [both of Harlan County]."

This pervasive local distrust of oil companies has been nurtured throughout a seventy-five-year battle of market competition between coal and oil, a competition that coal and, by extension, Harlan County has generally lost. Most local residents, regardless of their class position, agreed that the fight had not been a fair one. It was not competition they opposed, for that is a natural human drive and a dynamic force that makes society and, especially, politics and the economy operate. As youngsters, Harlan Countians competed mostly in athletics. But, as adults, they competed for jobs, for markets, for profits, and for political office; they competed to produce, to impress the boss, and to get ahead. Operators competed for market shares, flooded the coal market, and drove prices down. Higher and higher numbers of unemployed miners competed for fewer and fewer jobs. Competition was the "name of the game" in Harlan County. But in an ideal world the playing field would be level. With multinational energy companies in the mix, however, not even the most naive person could be fooled into thinking that the playing field was level. And, in fact, one could scarcely say they were competing at all—not with each other, not with other coal companies, and certainly not with the union that they were increasingly driving into the ground. "Oil companies, if they control the oil, the coal and the gas, what else is there?" asked Ernie. If Harlan Countians could agree on one villain upon which to pin the blame for local travails, it was the multinational oil companies, who had abandoned their communities, subverted free enterprise, eroded democracy, busted the union, and betrayed the nation.

ఇ⋅

In summary, Harlan's vulnerability to cyclical industrial fluctuations allied miners with small operators in a competition with oil corporations and a quest for individual and regional economic stability. Local miners and operators publicly advocated a policy of personal and community loyalty, based on paternalistic, patriarchal family values as well as broad-based reciprocity. While miners generally supported the free-enterprise economy, based on private property and animated by market competition in pursuit of profit, they also criticized operators who prioritized profit and individual greed over reciprocity, teamwork, and loyalty to the workers. And, finally, they recognized their labor as the source of capitalist profit.

In their ideal vision of society, management and workers would cooperate to produce efficiently and safely; and workers would labor in dignity by participating in decision making. Corporations would distribute profits and hardships evenly among shareholders, managers, and employees, and they would not forsake their home communities in a global quest for cheap labor and high profits. Miners lacked a systemic explanation for individual and social problems: they blamed social problems on "greed," "pride," or "philosophical differences" and, for this reason, did not conform to the definition of class consciousness that I carried with me to Harlan County. On the other hand, they clearly had an alternative vision against which they judged the present political economy. And some were willing to act collectively to achieve these goals, through either labor unions or the growing number of grassroots organizations emerging throughout the 1960s, 1970s, and 1980s, to address community and regional problems.

The dialectic relationship between kinship, community, and class has historically been a key element in forging and informing class consciousness in Harlan County. To the extent that kinship networks and class communal bonds overlapped, they reinforced class solidarity. To the extent that the entire community was defined and idealized as an egalitarian kinship network, family and community identity undermined class solidarity. Nonetheless, the ideologies of community egalitarianism and kinship reciprocity informed an alternative model for organizing the local political economy. This model engendered political corruption, nepotism, and administrative inefficiency at the same time as it personalized and humanized potentially rigid, alienating bureaucratic organizations. This rather mixed bag of structural and ideological tricks is reflected by this book's ambivalent title, *Two Sides to Everything*.

ॐ

In his own examination of class relations in Harlan County, Alessandro Portelli (1991, 234) argues that class struggle there has historically been waged upon the terrain of culture. Harlan miners and their employers, unlike capitalists and workers in his native Italy, have contested the meanings of shared texts and symbols instead of employing alternative symbolic systems to legitimate their actions. In his analysis of the "cultural class struggle of 1931–32," Portelli identifies the key symbols that animated and, in the end, short-circuited the transformative potential of this conflict. These include patriotism, patriarchy/paternalism, religion, and racial/ethnic identity. While I did not deal adequately with the issue of race/ethnicity (as will be discussed in the Afterword), I recognized that all of these factors were still at play in the political ideology and struggles of the Harlan miners of the 1980s. Nothing I observed contradicts Portelli's basic argument.

As Portelli notes, Harlan County coal miners and coal operators have historically identified themselves as patriotic Americans and have advanced their causes through appeals to the ideals of democracy and free enterprise and the symbol of the American flag (Portelli 1991, 216–26; see also Corbin 1981) while they variously debated their rights according to the U.S. Constitution. In the 1930s, for example, miners viewed the company town-guard system as an infringement upon their constitutional rights (see also Corbin 1981, 176–94; Gerstle 1989), whereas operators, simultaneously, interpreted the miners' unionization efforts, particularly through the NMU, as seditious acts. The elite justified jailing and prosecuting union organizers because, in their view, such men were committing treason. Fifty years later, Harlan coal operators and miners labeled multinational energy corporations "un-American," because they valued profits over national energy independence and the provision of jobs and economic security for American citizens. In the long run, the HCCOA president predicted, investment in foreign operations did not serve American interests.

Second, miners and their employers shared a commitment to the system and symbols of patriarchy and paternalism. In a 1990 article, Portelli links the (authoritarian) paternalism of coal-camp managers and UMW president John L. Lewis to the passivity and dependence of Harlan miners. As a group, he says, Harlan miners continue to view the world in personalistic terms, failing to see themselves as socially structured members of an exploited class. This theme was echoed in my own interviews with Harlan miners: they did not know why coal operators were greedy but assumed that this characteristic could be traced to a personality flaw. In addition, coal operators have successfully appealed to notions of patriarchal responsibility (breadwinning) and cultural constructions of masculinity (competition) in order to discipline their employees and encourage higher rates of production (Yarrow 1985). I previously noted that this ideology appeared to have been counterproductive duriing the 1970s, when women entered the mining workforce. Nevertheless, coal operators seemed unwilling or unable to see through this patriarchal line of reasoning.

To a significant extent, Harlan's miners "bought into" into this logic as well. They viewed mining as "men's work" and expresssed the belief that "real (union) men" should work hard to maximize coal production and, thereby, support their families and the companies run by their father-managers. Yet, it is not clear whether this patriarchal paternal ideology has benefited coal operators miners, or visa versa. While operators may mobilize patriarchy over paternalism to keep miners hard at work or "in line," miners have used the same ideology to point out that their employers have been very poor fathers indeed—willing to sacrifice the health and well-being of their miner-sons in order to make a profit. And when these miner-sons are themselves fathers with families to support, this same patriarchal logic provides them with an incentive to demand safety programs, health benefits, and higher wages from their employers. Finally, the cultural construction of masculinity as competitive, physically strong, and aggressive can manifest itself in competition against the coal operators as easily as it can encourage miners to compete with one another for jobs and production (Yarrow 1985, 1990).

In sum, Harlan County coal operators and miners share a similar set of cultural beliefs through which they view the world around them and justify their actions within it. One of the most important set of beliefs and discourses animating political ideology's power struggles in Harlan County centers upon religion. Consequently, it should come as no surprise that the relationship between religion and resistance and protest, on the one hand, and passivity and fatalism, on the other hand, provided the initial impetus for the next chapter. However, it was through my attendance at Harlan's churches and my analysis of religious discourse there that I came to realize more fully the relationship between patriachy and working-class identity among Harlan miners and, finally, to see how gender was emerging as an important terrain of local political struggle. Appropriately enough, church provided the setting for an intellectual conversion experience of my own.

CHAPTER 6

They Don't Have to Live by the Old Traditions

This chapter, which focuses on religious discourse at two working-class churches in Harlan County, continues the same themes of contradictory tension introduced in the previous chapter. Included among them are themes of community and conflict, reciprocity and greed, corporatism and individualism, democracy and authority, egalitarianism and stratification, and femininity and masculinity. These oppositions arise from the structural contradictions within the current patriarchal capitalist political economy, from internal ideological tensions, and from the oppositions between ideology, social structure, and material reality. They, in turn, both underlie and resonate from the religious discourse that takes place in Harlan County's churches. After all, the contradictions enumerated above cannot simply be relegated to the political arena: they pose religious, spiritual, ethical, and moral questions as well as political ones. Church, then, as an arena through which people act and interact, seek and offer support, and make meaning, is a central place to observe and investigate political ideology and symbology.

While it is important to remember that religious institutions and discourses can not be *reduced* to their political or economic "functions," I maintain that it is equally important to explore how churches and religious discourses are dialectically and dialogically linked with other social institutions and discourses. The desire to explicate such connections and patterns is a defining feature of the discipline of anthropology, and a characteristic that attracted me to the discipline in the first place. One does not have to view religious ideology as a pale reflection of economic or political forces to be interested in examining its economic and political assumptions

Portions of this chapter appeared previously in *American Ethnologist*, May 1994.

and ramifications. Religious ideology and discourse, like all ideologies and discourses, seek to explain a multifaceted social reality. Therefore, they cannot escape being profoundly social, economic, and political (Genovese 1974, 162).

Nowhere is this truer than in Harlan County, where local churches have historically reinforced class solidarity and imbued class struggle with religious legitimacy (Billings 1990; Garland 1983; Hevener 1978; Portelli 1993; see also Corbin 1981). Dwight Billings (1990), for instance, specifically cited Harlan as one of the coalfield counties in which local churches provided strikers with organizational resources and the "free space" to develop pastoral leadership from their own ranks (20–22). Miner-preachers, in turn, provided leadership in unionization struggles during the 1920s and 1930s and continued to play key roles in Harlan County's Brookside strike over forty years later. However, as labor historian David Corbin (1981, 146–75) has pointed out, the miners' struggle for organizational and ideological independence, even at church, was a hard-fought one. Coal companies hired men to take the pulpits of company churches, where they launched sermons against unionism, condemned protest and violence, and emphasized salvation and the hereafter over social justice issues (see, for example, Pope 1942).

Despite the opposition from "company preachers," union activists, in the 1920s and 1930s, generally succeeded in rhetorically aligning themselves with the Christian values of brotherly love, generosity, justice, and righteousness. Miners composed union anthems and work songs based on traditional religious hymns and referred to Biblical passages in their speeches and letters (Corbin 1981, 154; Portelli 1991, 228; see also Gutman 1976, 93–94). This discursive strategy could offer an effective mobilizing tool, as evidenced by the enthusiastic response received by this conclusion to a sermon: "Now I lay down my Bible and take up my rifle in the service of the Lord," the preacher closed; to which, a miner replied, "By God! That's what I call preaching" (Corbin 1981, 159). A similar sentiment was expressed by Harlan miners in 1973, when they resurrected Mother Jones's old slogan, "Pray for the dead and fight like Hell for the living!" and held religious tent meetings on the Brookside picket line (Ewen 1979; Wooley and Reid 1974). Many of the miners I interviewed in the 1980s attributed religious and moral significance to their union participation, framing past strikes as fights, for justice, goodness, and righteousness. Finally, Daniel Norton likened the union to a church, which also had trouble with hypocrites and "backsliders." "[The union's] just like church, I guess. You see a lot of people in church that's not good Christians. You see a lot of people in the union that aren't good union men," he analogized.

Although religion provided a basis for social critique and class solidarity in Harlan County, its translation into pro-union political activism was sometimes problematic. Jim Garland, a local miner, Missionary Baptist deacon, and NMU organizer during the 1930s, found it difficult to reconcile the Christian edict to "turn the other cheek" with his anger and desire to fight back against injustice. "You must remember that I was a religious man at this time, a deacon of the church, and that most of my family was quite religious. But when a person gets involved, truly involved, in a labor struggle, it's hard to keep his religious beliefs primary, mainly because he gets so damn mad," he explained. "And I was mad. I was burned up and hitting out in every direction even though I didn't know actually where to hit. . . . It wasn't that I was fighting for higher wages; I was just trying to fight against further cuts in a starving situation" (Garland 1983, 152–53). Daniel Norton's wife, found it too difficult to combine the two sets of beliefs and, so, refused to join the other Brookside women on the picket line. She was not alone in her belief that the troubles of this world could be addressed only through spiritual means (see also Greenhouse 1992; Maggard 1988).

A miner-preacher, active in the Brookside strike fifty years later, found a way to resolve the contradictions, by prioritizing his commitments. He explained:

> I've always been active in the union, and I will be right on. I'll always be a hundred-percent union man. The operators made a union man out of me, the way they treated me. They made me what I am, and I'm glad of it. . . .
>
> I was saved in '41. The eleventh day of September, nineteen hundred and forty-one, I was saved. The church where me and my wife got saved is tore down and moved now. On June eleventh of '44, I was ordained as a minister of the Gospel and on the fifteenth of August I took a church. And I'd go to the head of these hollers and have prayer meetings with the people night after night. . . . That was after we organized the union. We had

time then to come out and go to church and do things. We was getting along awful successful in our church. . . .

But in all my work and all my ministry, I never did get away from how I was treated [as a miner]. . . . I helped pave the way to get the coal mine where it is now, and I'm proud of that. The hard times just made a good union man out of me, and I'll always be one. It's just in me. I'm proud of being a United Mine Worker.

You know, the Lord is first. His saving grace is first. I don't let nothing get between me and my church and my Lord's work. Nothing. And then my Mine Workers is next. It's second. That's the way I feel. That's my conscience. And, you know, I feel like I've got a clear conscience. I feel like I've been fighting for something great. (Wooley and Reid 1974, 84–86)

Alessandro Portelli (1991) recognizes this contradiction in the religious ideology of Harlan's miners, as well. As he put it, "The miners religion, in fact, seemed to oscillate in perpetual tension between otherworldly resignation and radical criticism of the world, and between subordination to the status quo and egalitarian solidarity" (228). To further complicate matters, the coal operators themselves shared many of the same religious traditions and beliefs of their employees. And, of course, operators could cite the Bible in support of their own political aims as easily as the pro-union miners could. For instance, Portelli argues that, in 1931–32, religious discourse played an important part in derailing the (atheistic) NMU organizing effort (226–32). My observations indicate that religion continues to be a hotly contested political terrain in Harlan County, as it does elsewhere (Billings and Scott 1994).

ᶎ

If Christian religious ideology can alternately strengthen or undermine social protest among miners, a similar argument can be made about the ideological connections between Christianity and patriarchy. When one compares Christianity with pre-Christian and non-Western religions—ones that have female deities and allow women expanded spiritual and leadership roles, for example—Christianity appears to buttress patriarchal social forms (Lerner 1986, 9). Christianity's deity (or dieties) is (or are) male, and its creation myth could be described as misogynist. And although some denominations have begun to ordain women as pastors, most continue to relegate women to nonleadership organizational roles and to secondary spiritual ones. Nevertheless, scholars have noted that the Christ figure includes many characteristics that have been culturally defined as feminine, including love, mercy, sacrifice, and forgiveness (Cucchiari 1990). Church membership, in most Western countries, including the United States, has been predominantly comprised of women, who consistently score higher in sociological measures of religiosity than men (cf. Argyle and Beit-Hallahmi 1975, 71–79). Indeed, it seems that spirituality is a component of American (and Appalachian) constructions of femininity.

In summary, religious belief, political ideology, class, and gender interact in a complex dialectic, each informing the other. Christian beliefs do not *automatically* translate into a radical political ideology, but neither is it fated to be a conservative ideology that legitimizes patriarchal or capitalist ruling-class dominance, focuses attention on the next life, and nurtures fatalistic passivity amongst the masses (Durkheim 1965; Gerrard 1970; Marx 1975; Weller 1965). Religious ideology articulates with political ideology and, like it, represents an ongoing collective attempt to make meaning out of life. To continue a metaphor from the previous chapter, religious ideology informs our "provisional map" of social reality. Before examining the religious discursive construction of class, community, and gender in two case studies, let me provide a brief and general historical overview of religion in Harlan County.

≈

In the nineteenth century, Harlan had few permanent church buildings or regular, formal religious services. Traveling preachers and missionaries, called "circuit riders," visited periodically to preach sermons, hold revivals, and win converts. It took some time for Harlan's communities to construct their own churches and develop a community-based clergy. When local men did become preachers, they were responding to a "calling" from God. They received neither formal training nor a salary for their religious work. They earned their living, like everyone else, by farming. The concept of a "calling" continues to be important among Harlan's Christians (cf. Weber 1976, 79–92). Several local preachers, including the one at Small Branch Pentecostal, carried out their pastoral duties free of charge.

During the early nineteenth century, Harlan Countians and other marginal, poor southerners flocked to Baptist and Methodist denominations, which arose out of the Great Awakening revivals in the postcolonial era. After a few decades, Baptists and Methodists had displaced some of the well established denominations, like Episcopal and Presbyterian, in the South. By 1820, for example, 21,000 Kentuckians had affiliated with the Baptists and 21,000 with the Methodists, while only 2,700 still belonged to the Presbyterian denomination. In the South generally, Baptists rose from being a minor sect in 1800 to being a major denomination ministering to between one-fourth and one-third of all southern church members by 1860 (Bruce 1974, 37).

In the process of gaining converts and establishing themselves as organized, permanent organizations, both the Baptists and the Methodists broadened their base of appeal. They adapted their message and mission to appeal to *all* southerners, not just to marginal mountaineers, tenant farmers, and African Americans. As their membership base broadened, Methodists and Baptists eventually replaced emotional camp meetings with well-reasoned sermons delivered by seminary-trained clergy. As Dicksen Bruce (1974, 59) explained, "The same impulse which led to camp-meetings led to their demise. The practice was begun to increase the outreach of the sects, and it succeeded admirably; but the same evangelistic outreach could not be promoted by a practice which belonged only to the marginal folk of the frontier. Evangelism dictated that the church broaden its social base if it were to continue to grow, and the camp-meeting was too much a part of the frontier church-folk to satisfy such a dictate. The denominations, unlike the sects, did not belong to the plain-folk, but to Southern society in general."

Around the turn of the twentieth century, Holiness and Pentecostal splinters broke away from mainline denominations such as these (Anderson 1979). Several Harlan County believers joined this revolt against ritual routinization in the Southern Baptist and Methodist faiths by converting to Pentecostal and Churches of God, which were more emotional and charismatic in their worship practices. Baptist and Methodist churches remained popular in Harlan County, however.

The influx of nonlocal capital, capitalists, and laborers changed the religious landscape of Harlan County during the 1910s and 1920s. Several large churches were constructed in downtown Harlan and Cumberland, with the influx of coal capital. These new churches served coal operators, managers, and business owners who sought an escape from the "emotionalism" and "informalism" that characterized many of Harlan's existing churches (HDE, 15 September 1922, 2). In addition, two Catholic churches—one near Harlan and the other in Cumberland—were established for immigrant employees. Coal companies also sponsored and sometimes funded the construction of churches in smaller coal camps throughout the county. In many cases, the preacher was also hired by the company, with salaries provided by deductions from the miners' pay packets.

In 1980, the National Council of Churches of Christ in the U.S.A. reported that 47.1 percent of Harlan's population were church members. That was slightly lower than the Kentucky state average of 54.2 percent. Unfortunately, the directory omitted several churches in its survey, including all the Pentecostal churches and the small Episcopal church downtown. My own survey of local telephone directories indicated that there were 42 churches, or about 1 per 1,000 population. However, the local newspaper advertised 60 churches, or about 1 per 800 residents. In order of popularity, local denominations included 23 Baptist (mostly Southern Baptist), 13 Churches of God, 6 Churches of Christ, and 6 independent churches. There were two each of Presbyterian, Pentecostal, and Catholic, and one each of Christian (Disciples of Christ), Episcopal, Mennonite, Mormon, and Nazarene churches. Several churches, one of which I describe below, did not appear in any published sources.

I attended services at fourteen Harlan churches before I selected a "home church" near my own community of Ages, a Southern Baptist church that I will refer to as "Old Home Baptist Church." I observed Old Home services for approximately 11 months. This chapter has also been informed by three weeks of participant-observation at a revival at the Small Branch Pentecostal Church, some forty miles from my home, in the Martin's Fork Community of "Small Branch." In addition to my tape recordings of twenty-nine church services and field notes from an additional sixty-three services, I interviewed five local ministers about their ministries and other religious topics. Formal interviews with clergy and visits to various churches provided me with an overview of the local religious scene, but most of my analysis is based upon observations of the public discourse at Old Home and Small Branch. By "public discourse," I mean sermons, testimonies, prayers, Sunday School class discussions, and conversations at church gatherings.

I chose to worship and study at the Old Home Baptist Church because it was located near the community in which I was based and did most of my research, and also because its size and typicality made it attractive to me. As a Southern Baptist church, it represented the most popular denomination in Harlan County and in Kentucky generally. The congregation was small enough for me to become well acquainted with the members. Since it was located near Ages-Brookside and drew much of its congregation from the mining families there, it provided a suitable setting for me to investigate the relationship between the local church and the formation of class consciousness. In contrast, I did not select the Small Branch Pentecostal Church as much as it selected me, a point that will be discussed later. For now, let us start at Old Home Baptist Church, where I spent most of my time.

≥

The Old Home Baptist church building was a modest brown brick building, surrounded on three sides by a blacktop parking lot. The church's small lot was located by a creek bank, leaving little room to park. The parking situation was further complicated by the presence of a large covered picnic table area for dinners-on-the-ground. The picnic shed eliminated almost one-third of the parking spaces, so that, on Sundays, parked cars lined the highway for almost a mile in front of the church. Nevertheless, almost every member of the congregation drove to meeting on Sunday, no matter how close to the church they lived.

Old Home Baptist Church was established in 1928. Its current building had been constructed in 1952. Members remodeled, expanded, and bricked the structure following the 1977 flood. Since then, it has boasted a fully carpeted auditorium with modern, cushioned pews and a seating capacity of about two hundred souls. It also had central heat and air conditioning, a study for the pastor, two bathrooms, a dining room, a fully equipped kitchen, and four Sunday school classrooms. The pale brown paneled walls and pastel, swirl-patterned stained glass windows gave the auditorium an airy, expansive feel in spite of the relatively low eight-foot ceilings. The pulpit stood front and center on the stage behind a small oak table that held the communion and offering plates. Communion was served three times a year: at Christmas, at Easter, and when out-migrants return for Evarts's homecoming in late August. To the left of the stage was a piano and behind it, was the baptistery. In short, the building was typical of many local working-class and middle-class churches. Although in architecture and size it was not as grand as the downtown church buildings, the congregation was proud of its church.

The Old Home congregation included eleven retired miners (including Ernie Norton), four active coal miners (including Bobby Carson), four educators (three teachers and a principal), three health-care professionals, three retail clerks, two store managers, two school cafeteria cooks, one insurance salesman, one carpenter, one financial advisor, and their families. Among these, only the financial advisor, Richard Milton, was "well-to-do." The son of a Bailey's Creek coal miner, he lived with his wife and two children in a middle-class subdivision on the outskirts of Harlan. Like Cindy Carson, he returned to Old Home every Sunday to worship in the church in which he was raised.

In 1986, social relations within the church were relatively smooth and conflict-free. In the past, the church had more than its share of infighting and interpersonal conflict. Six ministers had served there since 1970, the most recent one having just departed in 1985, four months before I arrived. The church's attendance had declined from 110 to 62 during his short tenure at Old Home. The congregation laid the blame for the church's decline on the previous minister, whose sermons lacked "fire." A non-native, highly educated, aloof man, the previous pastor just did not "fit in" at Old Home. After some difficulty in locating a suitable replacement, the congregation finally recruited a seminary student willing to make the hourlong commute from the seminary in Bell County to the church in Harlan County. A "Hoosier" (from Indiana), Bill Mason had recently married a women from neighboring Bell County and intended to settle in eastern Kentucky.

People were skeptical about Mason at first. He was not from Harlan County, and he was born in "the city": those were two strikes against him. Much to everyone's surprise, however, the new pastor boosted the church attendance by 38 percent within a year. The congregation could see that he was a sincere, determined young man who would have no trouble "fitting in." They particularly enjoyed his passion and his "fire-and-brimstone" preaching style, although they frequently complained when he preached past noon. Usually their complaints were in jest, they told me; they did not mind getting out of church late when the preacher delivered a "strong" sermon. A "strong" sermon was marked by the pastor's enthusiasm, confidence, and passion, as well as his ability to inspire similar emotions in his congregation. A noncontroversial, nonthreatening theme served to strengthen sermons as well. A sermon about salvation or grace, for example, would usually considered "stronger" than a lecture on the importance of tithing.

Every Sunday just before 10 A.M., the congregation convened in the auditorium for opening announcements. The pastor would recognize those who had birthdays or anniversaries that week. Those so honored stood at the front of the church while the congregation sang a song wishing them well, whereupon they were expected to make a special offering to the church. After this, members adjourned to age-segregated Sunday school classes where volunteer teachers led discussions based upon readings from the Southern Baptist lesson book. Each class also took up an offering. At 11 A.M., everyone returned to the auditorium for worship services, which included an opening greeting and hymn, announcements, a prayer, an offertory hymn, and the collection of another offering. Then the preacher read from the Bible and delivered a thirty-minute sermon, based on his selections. A clock hanging over the door in the back of the auditorium assisted the pastor in the timing of his remarks. The service closed with an invitational hymn inviting "sinners" to step forward and dedicate themselves to Christ.

Services at Old Home were generally quiet, reserved, and meditative—very similar to services in the middle-class Christian church in which I was raised. Very few people spoke out in church, and then they only murmured a soft "amen" to underscore the pastor's point. For the most part it was men who said "amen," although the pastor's wife and the (female) pianist sometimes joined in the chorus as well. When the individuals prayed individually, they did so silently. But most of the time the minister, elder, or deacon (all men) led the congregation in prayer. Although sermons and services were described as emotionally moving, I rarely saw overt displays of emotion (in particular tears), during services at Old Home. Sunday worship service had a predictable pace: the congregation convened at 11:00 A.M. and adjourned an hour later. The sermon started at about 11:20 and ended by 11:50.

There was also a regular pattern to seating at the church. Most people, including me, sat in the same pew every Sunday. Some of the devout preferred the front pews but most gravitated toward the center rows. Nuclear families sat together on a pew with extended kin seated nearby. As a non-native with no local family, I provided one of two exceptions to this kin-based seating pattern. There was also one group of teenagers who had taken over the third pew for socializing and flirting.

⁊◖

Upon arriving at Old Home in April 1985, Bill Mason faced a formidable task: to reunite and inspire a congregation that had been characterized by spiritual apathy and interpersonal bickering. Furthermore, he had to convince them that he was a legitimate spiritual leader, in spite of his youth, lack of formal training, and "outsider" origins. He won the congregation over through a combination of actions that endeared him to the community. First, he did not impose heavy financial demands upon the congregation: he accepted a modest salary and remodeled the pastoral study himself. Second, he spent every weekend in the community visiting both congregation members and the unsaved. And, finally, he regularly ministered to hospital and nursing-home patients as well as those "shut in" at home. To be bluntly materialistic on the topic, Bill Mason was a real bargain to Old Home: he offered a large spiritual and social return on the congregation's material investment.

Like most local preachers, Mason explained his extreme devotion and willingness to sacrifice material gain for spiritual well-being as a "calling" from God. "God has never been wrong. It's we that are wrong," he preached. "It's me that's wrong. I thought in my life that God made a few wrong decisions. I said, 'Lord, you don't want me to preach.' . . . He said, 'Yes, I do.' And I'm glad he did because I'm having me a time; and I like it. I like preaching. I told the church Wednesday night I could do other things as far as occupations; but preacher's what God called me to do. And I'd rather preach than eat." The reference to God's calling explained and, more importantly, legitimated his leadership position. It lent credence to the moral claims and material demands that he was to make on the congregation in the days to come.

It took Bill Mason almost a week to prepare each sermon, but by Sunday morning he had typed index cards and a sermon outline on

TABLE 6.1
Old Home Baptist Church
Sermon Themes,
Ranked by Frequency

	Rank	Frequency	Proportion
Submission to God's will	1	30	13.4
Sin and the necessity of repentence	2	24	10.6
Evangelical mission and witnessing	3	22	9.8
Salvation brings personal happiness/ Christians are happy people	3	22	9.8
Congregational conflict	4	20	8.8
Inherent human weakness and vanity	4	20	8.8
Anti-materialism and -worldliness	5	18	6.2
Tithing	6	14	6.2
Gender	6	14	6.2
Anti-rationality/pro-faith, and emotion	7	6	2.6
Social Problems	8	5	2.2
Backsliding	9	4	1.8
Troubles of this world	9	4	1.8
God as source of wealth/God rewards Christians with good fortune	10	3	1.3
Parable of the rich man	10	3	1.3
Pastoral legitimation	10	3	1.3
God's omnipotence and perfection	10	3	1.3
Salvation through grace, not good works	10	3	1.3
Limitations of formal education	11	2	0.8
Benefits of formal education	12	1	0.4
Prayer for instumental purposes	12	1	0.4
Fundamentalism	12	1	0.4
Criticizing the separation of church and state	12	1	0.4
Using the Lord's name in vain	12	1	0.4
Satanism	12	1	0.4

the pulpit. He had also marked all of the relevant scriptural references in his Bible. Although he relied on his outline as a guide, Mason nevertheless frequently "ad libbed" and joked during his sermons. As a fisherman, he loved to tell fishing stories to spice things up. He also examined the assembled congregation for something upon which to jokingly remark. He especially liked to tease men about their beards, their haircuts, or their fashion choices. He hoped that his sermons were as natural, unpretentious, and accessible as he was. Nevertheless, he tried to avoid grammatical errors and nonstandard English, as he wanted to serve as a good role model for the young people. He expressed regret at having dropped out of high school at seventeen. His seminary teachers, he revealed, were quite adamant in their quest to improve his grammar. The Old Home congregation, on the other hand, did not seem to mind poor grammar in the least. He was grateful that they were more concerned about substance than "flash."

Mason's sermons generally reflected his desire to legitimize his spiritual leadership and to avoid conflict within the church. In fact, all but one of eighteen recorded sermons were aimed at one of these two goals (see table 6.1; see also Greenhouse 1986, 1992 for an analysis of conflict resolution at another Southern Baptist church). In one sermon, for instance, he informed his congregation that God wanted them to support their pastor. After all, he pointed out, God had sent him to the community so he would stay as long as God willed him to be there. "It always tickles me when I take a new church and all the members, when they voted me in, they'll come by and shake your hand and hug your neck and say, 'Brother, you're just what we need. We're going to pray for you. We're going to support you. We're going to help you.' . . . And, then, two weeks after you're there, they're not anywhere around. What happened to all the promises they made?" he asked, before concluding, "God expects you to keep your word."

ॐ

After legitimating his pastoral authority and maintaining harmony within the church, Bill Mason seemed most concerned about rampant materialism amongst his followers. The Old Home congregation, it seemed, was more interested in financial security and worldly pleasure than in Christian charity and spiritual commitment. It was not that he was opposed to people's enjoying themselves. Indeed, he had repeatedly remarked that Christians should to be the happiest and most cheerful people of all, since they looked forward to the promise of everlasting life. And church should definitely be a fun place—a place for enthusiasm, joy, and love. To that end, Old Home hosted pizza parties, picnics, and dinners-on-the-ground. They sponsored a softball team and staged a Christian play. During the summer, the church took the youth group to amusement parks and ball games. The pastor also encouraged members to take part in family recreation activities, such as athletics, vacations, picnicking, hiking, hunting, and fishing.

Nevertheless, the pastor reminded, people were not put on Earth just to have a good time. Mason's sermons repeatedly emphasized that "man" should tend to his spiritual side as well as his physical side and that Christians, in particular, should prioritize God's will over their own satisfaction. God's Scriptures clearly instructed Christians to be generous to those less fortunate than they. More specifically, Christians were commanded to donate 10 percent of their income as a tithe to the church. Mason seemed convinced that the Old Home congregation was cheating God by giving low offerings each Sunday.

He warned them, however, that God would not allow himself to be cheated. In the long run, he would collect his 10 percent. Mason was sympathetic to his congregation's struggles and temptations, he said. In the past, he sometimes failed in this struggle to put God first. One week, he said, he decided to use his tithe money to buy a fishing rod that was on sale. He really wanted that fishing rod and it would not be on sale for long. He figured he could make it up to God, in the long run, with the savings he realized from buying on sale. That very same week he got so sick that he had to go to the emergency room. He wound up spending his fishing rod money on the doctor bill, thus, leading him to the conclusion that "God got the money anyway."

Most of the time, Mason did not emphasize the spiteful, vengeful God who took his due from his weak followers. Rather, he highlighted the caring, paternal God who would provided for his people's needs. "Consider the lilies of the field," he told them; they neither worked nor worried but were clothed in the finest garments (Luke 12:15–34). Mason offered his own life as a testimony to God's benevolence toward those who would put God first. Mason had given up both his job and his house in order to study at the seminary. And, so, God had taken care of him by providing him with his pastoral post at Old Home church. I might add that God also found employment for the preacher's wife. Mason failed to mention this fact, just as he also neglected to report that she earned more money than he did.

Usually when Mason preached about tithing, he was met by an

awkward silence. The only congregation member who typically offered an approving "amen" to these sermons was the upper-middle-class financial advisor. The remainder of the congregation did not regard sermons on tithing as particularly "strong" ones. However, Mason was a determined, young, maverick preacher who did not back down from controversial topics. A full one-third of his sermons warned against materialism and worldliness, and included some reference to the importance of tithing.

Initially, Mason tried to shock and embarrass the congregation into donating more money. For instance, one Sunday he snatched the collection plate from a deacon's hand and began to count the money in it. All of the bills were singles, except for one ten-dollar bill. When he discovered the ten, he held it up to the congregation and remarked loudly, "Oops! Somebody made a mistake. They thought this was a one." He frequently joked to the congregation during the offertory hymn. "Get out your billfold," he urged. "Every Baptist knows where it is. I know you get it out every now and then—to count your money!" This brand of humor seemed to catch the congregation off-guard. Few members laughed aloud at these jokes.

Through time, Mason found a different rhetorical strategy. This one shifted the focus from ridicule and shame to reassurance that God would take care of them in *this* life, as well as the next. The following sermon excerpt demonstrates the combination of strategies that Mason used in preaching on tithing as he struggled to find the correct note to strike with his congregation:

> If you ever needed a job, the Lord will give you a job. A lot of people say, "I can't tithe. I just can't get a job. I can't afford to tithe." Honey, you can't afford *not* to tithe if you're a child of God. [The financial advisor said, "Amen."] That's [tithing] not God's plan for building the church; that's God's plan for raising children, really. People say, "Preacher, I can't afford to tithe. I only make $100 a week! You expect me to give $10 of that to *God?*" God *expects* you to. Personally, I don't care what you do. God's going to get it one way or another. I mean you can put it in the plate or he'll get it down in the emergency room or somewhere else. He always does. You can say, "Oh, that preacher! Start preaching about money!" I don't care *what* you think. That's what the Bible says.

His closing remark indicates that he was sensitive to the reaction of his congregation and that he realized that his remarks were unpopular. After about nine months at Old Home, Mason evolved a position on materialism and wealth that his congregation could tolerate. Although he continued to threaten the congregation, he stopped ridiculing their frugality. At the same time, he increased the stakes in his threats against nontithers. Punishment might not be restricted to a temporary expense or inconvenience, like a trip to the emergency room. It could also involve a personal tragedy: the death of one's family or eternal damnation. The following excerpt represents a transitional phase in Mason's preaching against materialism and worldliness:

> John 2:15 [incorrect cite] said, "Love not the world, nor the things that are in the world. You may love the world and love not the Father. Any man who loves the world, the love of the Father is not in him." You see, I'm not saying it's not right to have a nice home and have possessions and have money. Some people I've heard preach that money can send you to Hell. Money can't send you to Hell. I believe God blesses us with money.
>
> We all know we have to live. You see, the problem is when you get to loving money more than you do God; and that money becomes your God and that money controls you.
>
> I've known people that got a new car and they were afraid to go to church because somebody might open a car door against it. I know people that went out and bought them a new home and they're afraid to come to church because somebody might break in their home and steal something. People go out and buy a new boat and they'll take off one Sunday and go to the lake, you know, just to try it out. Then, before long, they're there every Sunday. They forget God. They world takes the place of God. It always amazes me. It's never the people that are having a hard time making a living. It's always the people that God really blesses *and* God's the one that blesses that walk off and leave God.
>
> If you've got possessions, praise the Lord for them and realize that's where it comes from. Don't put it before God. Worship God first. Because, if you're not careful, one day you might lose everything. . . . God says He'll chastise people and He will. Maybe you'll lose everything that you got. I know people who have lost their homes, their jobs, their family—not through divorce, through death. And, then, they sit down and they bawl out God. They say, "God, why did you do this to me?" God's Word says He'll do that to you.

Serve the Lord. Don't worry about the world. If you serve God and put God first, everything is going to be in place. . . . God supplies your needs. . . . You see, money can't buy happiness. Money can't get you to Heaven. I don't care what they say. You ain't going to take it with you.

Through time, as he developed a line of argument that reassured his congregation, Mason began to win his congregation's approval. He received "amens" and nods of agreement from a broad range of the congregation, instead of stone-faced silence and nervous chuckles. Gradually decreasing his reliance on ridicule and threats of divine retribution, Mason began to concentrate almost exclusively on how God took care of his flock and especially rewarded those who tithed regularly. A favorite example of this was the founder of the J. C. Penney department store. As a good Christian man, Penney devoted 10 percent of his store profits to the church. Clearly, God had rewarded Mr. Penney with success and wealth. He would do the same for the people of Old Home.

This was a message that the people of Old Home desperately wanted to believe, during the mine layoffs of the 1980s. The congregation at Old Home was mostly managing to survive without government aid but were becoming increasingly concerned about their financial stability. Although some had worked their way out of the coal mines into white-collar jobs like insurance agent, principal, financial advisor, and teacher, most still remained in either insecure mining jobs or low-paying service/retail positions. Increasingly, families required two incomes to survive. And a large component of the retirees were devoting their stable but limited, fixed incomes to the support of their adult children as they coped with forced vacations, work schedule reductions, layoffs, and disabilities. Although the congregation cared about those who were less fortunate, they could not afford much charity. If they gave away too much, then they ran the risk of becoming furture "charity cases." Needless to say, offerings were down throughout the 1980s. And, not surprisingly, the most common topic of conversation around the church involved the state of the local economy: the latest layoffs, the newest plan to revitalize local industry, or the smartest way to save and invest limited funds.

My "young" adult Sunday School class, for instance, seemed particularly preoccupied with financial issues. Perhaps it was because our teacher was Richard Milton, the financial advisor. More likely, it was because all of us felt vulnerable as we planned our careers and retirements, and prepared to raise children and provide for their educations. The class included a broad age spectrum— just about any adult who was not a senior citizen or retiree. At twenty-five, I was the youngest member (and the only unmarried person) in the class. There was also the church pianist and her husband, a couple in their forties, with three kids, one of whom had just started college. He worked for the railroad, and she was a housewife. There was a couple who were about my age, hoping to start a family soon; he was sporadically employed as a miner and she was a salesclerk. In addition, there was an unemployed miner and his wife, who worked as data processor to support their three children.

Regardless of our official lesson plans each Sunday class's conversations generally drifted toward economic and financial matters. Sometimes members debated the meaning of a scriptural reference to wealth, poverty, or charity. More often, they simply complained and sought sympathy, shared information, discussed public policy, or speculated about how their lives might be transformed by a change in financial status. One Sunday, the railroad employee remarked he was glad not to be rich because he doubted that he could be a good Christian as a wealthy man. He would be tempted by the things of this world, he explained. The young miner did not share this man's point of view. On the contrary, he thought that wealth would be a blessing. He would use his money for God's work, he predicted. His first priority would be to construct a community center in Ages to keep the young folks engaged in wholesome activities.

A New Testament parable (Matthew 19:21–24) posed a special dilemma for this class. The debate over this passage lasted three weeks and eventually became a general topic of church conversation that was ultimately addressed in a sermon. In this parable, a young rich man, who refused to sell all of his worldly possessions, was not allowed to become a disciple of Christ. Jesus, noting that it is more difficult for a rich man to get into Heaven than for a camel to pass through the eye of a needle, regretted the young man's decision. One Sunday, our "young adult" lesson book featured this passage. The class discussed it during three consecutive class meetings before, finally, reaching the conclusion that Jesus was simply testing the wealthy man's dedication. The teacher speculated that, if the rich man *had* agreed to sell his possessions, Jesus *would* have accepted him as a disciple. He did not even have to go through with it, then. This conclusion soon came to express the congregation's consensus on this passage. And the preacher subsequently offered that interpretation of the parable in three different sermons over the next year (see table 6.1). This innovation, combined with the evolution of his sermons on tithing and the group's interpretation of the parable of the rich man, illustrate the congregation's collective discursive effort to reconcile economic interests, financial conservatism, and quest for upward mobility with the antiworldly, antimaterialistic teachings of Christ.

ðŸ¦

In addition to financial security and materialism, Mason's sermons also reflected his congregation's growing concern over the breakdown of the nuclear family, which they saw as the cornerstone of Christian society. Many of them linked the women's movement with abortion rights, sexual promiscuity, and rising divorce rates. All of these were viewed as facilitators and indicators of the decline of the American family. Locally, the strains of economic hardship and urban migrations had also taken their toll on family life. Sometimes fathers left families in search of work in other areas. Economic uncertainty and money problems caused marital problems. Most people perceived a rise in domestic violence and drug and alcohol abuse. Mine layoffs put men out of work and forced women into the workforce, thus challenging traditional gendered division of labor and threatening patriarchal authority, both at home and in the community. This was most clearly indicated by the unprecedented increase in female-headed households in Harlan County from 1980 to 1990 (Louisville *Courier-Journal*, 4 August 1991, A1, A19).

In addition to the sermons that explicitly addressed gender issues, many of Mason's sermons on materialism included a gender component as well. When I first started going to Old Home, for example, Mason preached against working on Sunday, explaining it by reference to people's growing materialism. To him, the issue was clear-cut: Sunday was God's day and people should not let a lust for money prevent them from observing it. He expected his congregation to follow God's straightforward command against working on Sunday. For those congregation members who were asked to work on Sunday—mostly women in retail/service sector jobs—this posed a difficult dilemma, however. Their wages were low; they had no benefits; and many of them worked only part-time schedules, as it was. Since their husbands' jobs were at risk and some were already underemployed or unemployed, these women could not afford to either lose a shift or alienate their bosses.

Mason, recognizing that his appeal was falling on deaf ears, evolved a more elaborate argument against working on Sunday. First, he developed a rationalistic and utilitarian logic for his appeal, and then he "upped the ante" by impugning the parental dedication of Sunday workers. Here is what he said:

> People say, "I got to work every day of the week." How come? Anybody with any sense knows if you work seven days a week, that seventh day is going to be overtime or doubletime. And 90 percent of that is going to Uncle Sam. What have you gained? Time you count your gas and pay a baby-sitter and buy your food to go to work and all. What do you really gain?
>
> I went to work for a radio station about two and a half years ago and he said I might have to have you work on Sundays. And I said, "I ain't going to work on Sunday." He said, "Well, it would be between church [services]." I said, "I don't work on Sunday. That's the Lord's Day." I ain't going to. . . .
>
> Some people would rather work on Sunday than go to God's house because they want that extra three or four dollars. It's going to look bad when you bury your children; and they go to Hell because you've not been to church and taught the things of God because you worked on Sundays.

Within this sermon excerpt, I see an implicit critique of dual-earner households and women's labor-force participation, even though it does not explicitly criticize women workers and does, of course, touch upon several issues. First, it is important to note that Mason's utilitarian logic rests upon erroneous assumptions about local employment opportunities—both for women *and* for men. Most working-class laborers, in Harlan County, were happy to get to work full-time, five days a week in 1985; not many were called upon to work six- or seven-day weeks. Although working men had in the past gotten overtime work opportunities, women rarely had such opportunities. The majority of these women worked part-time in the service/retail sector, where there was no possibility of earning "double" pay. In fact, their employers made it a point to keep them working part-time in order to avoid paying for vacation leave and health and pension benefits. By working on Sunday, Old Home women were merely supplementing a minimum wage income and protecting their jobs in an economically deteriorating situation, not placing themselves in a higher tax bracket.

Mason's sermon against working on Sunday, while ostensibly aimed at everyone, it was most readily applicable to women workers and dual-earner households. The most likely Sunday workers at Old Home were women. In fact, the only man in the congregation who could elect to work on Sundays, in 1985, was the railroad worker. The rest of the men were on reduced work schedules, worked a five-day week at white-collar jobs, had retired, or were unemployed. Furthermore, the high cost of baby-sitting was most relevant to families in which the mother was no longer available 24 hours a day to take care of the children. And even the remark about the high cost of lunch out related more to working-class women than to their coal miner husbands, who ate their home-packed lunches underground. Finally, Mason's threat of eternal damnation for the children of parents who worked on Sunday was particularly stinging to local mothers, who have traditionally been the primary physical and spiritual caretakers of children. The local construction of motherhood included self-sacrifice for the children and, in fact, most women explained their entry into the labor force as necessary for the welfare of their children. Yet the possibility that these jobs could threaten the souls of their children placed the working mothers at Old Home in a difficult double-bind.

Mother's Day provided Mason with another opportunity to preach on women as mothers. The deterioration of the nuclear family, breakdown of patriarchal authority, changing gender roles, and regional differences in homemaking were among the topics he addressed in this Mother's Day sermon. Unlike his sermons on Sunday work, this one focused more explicitly upon patriarchy and gender, still it echoed similar themes:

> If it wasn't for women, a lot of our homes—and a lot of our homes are being destroyed in the United States today. The divorce rate is just about 50 percent nationwide; and that's because homes aren't working. . . . It's extremely hard for a home to be held together in today's society. And it's hard for a person to live

a good Godly life, to be a Christian. It's hard for them to live like a Christian.

I know it's hard for my wife, sometimes, to keep her mouth shut and quit talking back to me. She doesn't always have to keep her mouth shut. Don't think I'm an Adolf Hitler or something. The Bible says to keep your wife under subjection. The Bible also says, "Husbands, love your wives as Christ loves the Church." [Amen.] And I believe, if your husband's a Christian and you're a Christian, you should be under subjection to your husband.

But, at the same time, you know these ladies who are in the Equal Rights movement, ERA, whatever you want to call it. All these ladies want to be equal. If you're a Christian and in a Christian home, you've got better rights than anyone even dreamed of. [Amen.] You do because that home is built on Christ. [Amen.] We don't have to worry about Equal Rights. We don't have to worry about subjection. We don't have to worry about all these different things that we like to fuss and fight and argue about some times. . . .

I like to kid, especially, Mike about being under subjection, you know. He didn't wear his pink shirt today, I believe. I like to kid him and he knows I'm kidding. I hope Darlene [his wife] knows I'm kidding, too. [Mike was an unemployed miner who took care of the family's three children while his wife supported the family financially.]

But, uh, a good Godly lady is a real blessing from God. And they can't be the mother they should be without the Lord. . . . If we stop to think about it, mothers and wives, they do more work than we ever dreamed of. You men, I know we all like to think we've been out and making a living and we come home at the end of the day. And we want to sit down in front of the TV and read the paper and want them to wait on us and them to cook supper and all this. But have you ever stuck around home one day and seen exactly what your wife does? You children, have you ever stuck around and seen exactly what your mother does? . . . I got news for you. The lady that runs the home has a full-time job. . . . Women really work hard.

I realize *some* women *don't* do anything all day. I've been in some homes where you can tell they don't take care of the homes. You can tell. I hate to go up North. I don't know whether it's all the Yankee places, or the ones I visited but I hate to go up North because they just won't feed you! Them women up there don't know how to cook. [Laughter.] Brother Willie, you been up there. Are they all like that? ["Just about," Willie replied.] . . . Most of the homes I've been in around here, you ladies, I can tell you care about your home. You care about your family. . . .

I know a lot more women that go to church and serve the Lord than men. Have you ever thought about that? Every church I've ever pastored, we had more women in church than we did men. We did. Now, some of these guys have said, "That's why women are allowed to preach, you know, because you can't get the men to do any of it." I don't go along with that. [Amen.] If God calls them [men] to preach and they ain't going to preach, you ought to take fellows like that out and hang them somewhere. They should. [Laughter.] I ain't kidding you. I'm serious. I'd pull the lever and let them drop. If God tells you to do something and you don't do it, then you ought to be strung up! . . .

It seems like God works through ladies. You go out and knock on doors. Most times, it's easier to win the woman over to the Lord. [Amen.] It is. They have a softer heart. They do. That's why the man is supposed to be leader of the house. You see, women need a spiritual leader of the house. [Amen.] That's you men. If you're not man enough to get up and say, "We're going to church and we're going to serve the Lord." And you're not man enough to get saved yourself, then you're not much of a man. I don't care how big you are. . . . If you're the spiritual leader God wants you to be, then you won't have to worry about your wife rebelling against you or doing something different. She'll go right on along with you. [Amen.]

Here, Mason attempted to shore up deteriorating local patriarchal authority by grounding it in Biblical references and in women's inherently emotional nature. The type of patriarchy that Mason advocated, however, did not involve a cruel or arbitrary exercise of power but, rather, the patriarch's assumption of a loving, spiritual leadership role in his family. Mason's sermon defined the woman's place in the home, cooking, cleaning, and caring for her family. Yet he nevertheless recognized traditional woman's work as interminable. He realized that it had been culturally devalued. And he urged his congregation to demonstrate their appreciation for all that women do, as housewives and mothers. But, significantly, his sermon did not include a single word of praise for working mothers. Nor did it recognize the fact that, for increasing numbers of local families, the demands of motherhood pushed women into the work-force. Afterward, most shouldered the double burden of public employment and the "full-time job" of housework and family care (Hochschild 1989). His so-called jokes about Mike's pink shirts and his own wife's propensity to "talk back" reveal a crisis in patriarchal authority and local constructions of masculinity. Mason attributed this crisis, *not* to economic sectoral shifts, changing gender roles or women's demands for equality, but to men's failure to assume the spiritual leadership demanded of them as heads of patriarchal, Christian families.

ਣ

In 1986, then, Old Home Baptist religious discourse centered upon four topical main areas: (1) the elimination of internal bicker-ing and construction of a harmonious church community; (2) the legitimation of pastoral authority; (3) the debate over materialism and tithing; and (4) changing gender roles and the subsequent erosion of patriarchal authority. Notably missing from the discourse were constructions of a class-based collective identity (class con-sciousness), a pro-union political agenda, or a critique of capitalism. Neither did materialism, individualism, and the increasing econom-ic disparity between rich and poor, emerge as significant topics of religious discourse at Old Home.

Initially, I was surprised by the lack of overtly political discourse at Old Home. I knew several congregation members to be avid pro-unionists and local Democratic Party activists. Furthermore, the church's working-class membership base and its location near Ages-Brookside, the site of the 1973 Brookside strike, made this church a rather likely candidate as source for religiously based working-class resistance. However, if the church had ever served as a font for class consciousness, the congregation and its pastor gave no indication of that in 1986.

How might we understand this apparent lack of class-based, transformative religious discourse at Old Home Baptist Church? One contextual factor to consider was the Eastover Mining Com-pany's demolition of the Brookside camp houses after the success-ful 1973 strike. This move splintered and scattered a relatively active and unified core of pro-union miners. Many of the workers who remained in the area had, since that time, retired from mining. Second, the lack of overtly working-class religious discourse may, in part, be due to families' success in achieving upward mobility for their children. Most have at least moved them out of the physically dangerous coal industry. This, in combination with a growing local pessimism about the future prospects of the local mining industry, seemed to have precipitated a decline in interest in both mining careers and miners' unions. In the context of coal industry decline and increasing class and occupational differentiation within the congregation, the old fights between miners and coal operators may no longer be salient.

At Old Home, the desire to put aside personal and political differences in the reestablishment of a faltering church no doubt influenced the political tone of religious discourse as well. Bringing up past conflicts would not heal old community wounds. And at any rate the new preacher, who was neither a local man nor a coal miner, might have been largely unaware of the community's history of class struggle and solidarity. Such conflicts were not a part of the experiental base upon which Bill Mason's sermons drew. In fact, Mason brought with him a rather apolitical version of the Christian ministry: he opposed Pat Robertson's and Jesse Jackson's presidential bids, arguing that preachers should remain aloof from worldly matters. And he personally restricted his political activism to issues with an obvious moral dimension, such as the debate over reproductive freedom, women's rights, legalization of alcohol sales, gambling, and the proposed state lottery (which was later established by the state legislature).

Finally, economic sectoral shifts threatened the financial wellbeing of local families, forced women into the labor force, transformed gender roles, and threw local patriarchal authority into crisis. Thus, much of the limelight had shifted from class to gender conflict, by the mid-1980s. At Old Home, gender had clearly eclipsed class, both as the basis for political and personal conflict and as a subject for sustained religious discourse. Old Home was not unique in this regard, as the following discussion of the Small Branch revival indicates.

❧

I was introduced to the community of Small Branch by my friend Kathy Black, whom I met through various civic activities and in my position as an instructor for Southeast Community College. Kathy had grown up in Small Branch, although she no longer lived there in

1986. She often invited me to accompany her on the hour-and-a-quarter drive to the community, mostly to see her teenage daughter Dawn, and to visit her mother, sister, and nieces. Kathy's mother was looking after Dawn while Kathy recovered from an abusive marriage and a difficult divorce. Since Kathy had periodically sought refuge at her parents' home during the breakup of her previous two marriages, Dawn felt quite at home in her grandmother's house. It was larger, more comfortable, and safer than Kathy's cramped Cumberland apartment, where she periodically received visits from her bat-wielding ex-husband. Kathy was always prepared to defend herself with a handgun.

Still relatively isolated, Small Branch was a working-class community on the southeastern edge of the Harlan County. It had originally been an agricultural settlement, similar to Holmes' Mill, where the Brown family settled in the early 1800s. Many of the 180 Small Branch residents were related to Kathy, and over half were descended from four original settling families. During most of the twentieth century, Small Branch men had earned their families' living by mining coal. The church was established by local, pro-union miners, in 1938, as the Harlan "mine wars" were concluding. The first three pastors were all UMW miners and the pastor in 1986, Robby Gardner, was also an unemployed UMW miner.

The 1980s coal slump was taking an even worse toll on this community than it had on Ages. The population, for instance, had declined from 203 since the beginning of the decade, as men and sometimes entire families left the community in search of work. A majority of the residents received some sort of financial support from the government: unemployment benefits, food stamps, Social Security benefits, Aid to Families with Dependent Children, or workers' compensation and disability payments. Over half the children qualified for free meals at the school. About one-third of the men in the community were out of work, one-fourth were retired or disabled, and the rest worked as coal miners, construction workers, truck drivers, and mechanics. In addition, there was one merchant and one bootlegger. Approximately 50 percent of Small Branch households were headed by women: half of these by elderly widows, and half by single mothers, mostly divorcees. Of the women under forty, around three-quarters had full-time or part-time jobs, mostly as data processors, waitresses, and sales-clerks; there were two nurses and a teacher's aide as well. Four of the women attended Southeast Community College while they worked part-time. Small Branch's working-class population had suffered more from the decline in the local coal industry than had the Old Home Baptist congregation. Their community had more poverty, higher unemployment, more out-migration, and a greater proportion of female-headed households than the Ages area had.

Until the winter of 1986, my trips to Small Branch consisted primarily of informal family visits, Sunday dinners, and other family events, such as birthday parties, funerals, and holidays. On these visits, Kathy introduced me to the residents and showed me around the community. In January, she telephoned me about a revival that was about to start in her home church, the Small Branch Pentecostal Church. I recall being surprised to learn that, not only had she been raised in the Pentecostal church, but her late father had been the pastor there. Neither she nor her family conformed to my stereotypical image of Pentecostals. Even more surprising, none of them were currently attending worship services there. I thought it was noteworthy that the widow of a former pastor had stopped going to the church. Kathy did not attend church at all and, as near as I could tell, was quite skeptical about organized religion. Her daughter, mother, sister, and nieces periodically attended a Southern Baptist church located about two miles from the Small Branch community.

Kathy's cousin Robby Gardner pastored the church in 1986. Many of her relatives and former neighbors continued to attend services there. The issue to her, however, was not her family's history in or connection to the church, but the bid to introduce snake-handling to the local church. It was Kathy's curiosity about the "exotic" ritual of snake-handling that introduced me to the Small Branch Pentecostal Church—although, as I now see it, snakes were not the central factor in the local revival or the events leading up to it. Before we delve into the revival and one interpretation of its discourse, a brief overview of Pentecostalism might be helpful.

❧

Historians trace the origins of Pentecostalism to a 1906 Los Angeles revival during which the practice of speaking in tongues emerged as a central spiritual experience. To Pentecostals, speaking in tongues signaled the Baptism in the Spirit, a second Pentecost for the Church, and the Second Coming of Christ (Anderson 1979, 4). This denomination is historically and doctrinally related to Holiness groups that split from the Methodist church after the Civil War (Dieter 1980). Like others labeled "Holiness," Pentecostals are considered to be fundamentalists who believe in the literal interpretation of the Bible. They generally observe behavioral and dress codes that set them apart from "worldly" people. For instance, most Pentecostal groups prohibit the use of alcohol and tobacco and allow neither dancing nor gambling. At Small Branch, members were expected to wear modest, conservative clothing— the women in dresses, the men in sports or work pants and an open-collared shirt (no tie, no T-shirts). The women were not allowed to cut their hair or wear makeup or jewelry and the men were expected to keep their hair trimmed short and their faces clean-shaven.

Much of the academic literature associates Pentecostals with poverty, social marginality, and rapid social change. It explores political implications of Pentecostalism and for the most part concludes that the religion is either apolitical (Anderson 1979; Holt 1940), conservative (Annis 1987; Pope 1942), or reactionary (Stekert 1963). Some argue that its primary function is to offer an emotional catharsis and personal escape for its practioners (Anderson 1979; LaBarre 1962). The Small Branch case, as we shall see, contradicts these general conclusions, thus adding to a growing literature documenting this religion's potential to reinforce cultures of resistance (Billings 1990; Gerlach 1974; Gill 1990; Lancaster 1988) and its contradictory ideological connection to patriarchy (Cucchiari 1990; Scott 1994).

ॐ

The Small Branch church met every Saturday and Sunday evening in a small white frame building that had been erected in 1947. The building was heated by a coal stove and had no indoor plumbing. There was an outhouse located beside the church. Small Branch Pentecostal services varied considerably from the structured, quiet, meditative services at Old Home Baptist. At Small Branch, congregants sought to recreate the events documented in Acts 2:1–21, during which Peter and other early followers of Christ were said to have achieved spiritual unity with the Holy Spirit, who allowed them to perform several superhuman feats, including prophesying, speaking in tongues, and healing the sick. To Small Branch Pentecostals, gifts like these both signified and reinforced the saintly "sanctification" of believers. To achieve such gifts, one had to surrender oneself to the Holy Ghost through prayer (usually aloud), fasting, and worship.

Even though worship services appeared to be noisy and chaotic, there was an underlying order to them. Each service began with a short period of informal conversation before the pastor called the congregation to order with an opening prayer and announcements. Then the pastor or, in this case, the evangelist would take the pulpit to preach a sermon. Following the sermon was a period of singing and dancing that culminated in speaking in tongues and testimony. The service was adjourned with a prayer, some two to three hours later. Occasionally the congregation had a healing ceremony before the final prayer, and sometimes the pastor called for an offering before the sermon. Neither were regular features of Small Branch services, but they were done when there was some specific need expressed: a congregation member was ill or money was required to buy new guitar strings for the instrumentalists, for example. Small Branch Pentecostals did not traditionally endorse snake-handling and, until the revival of 1986, snakes had never been handled in this church.

The origins of snake-handling can be traced to eastern Tennessee, where, in 1909, George Went Hensley handled a rattlesnake as a sign of grace and sanctification, much the same as healing or speaking in tongues. Hensley cited Mark 16:17–18 as the spiritual basis for this practice. It reads: "And these signs shall follow them that believe: in my name shall they cast out devils; they shall speak with new tongues. They shall take up serpents; and if they drink any deadly thing, it shall not hurt them; they shall lay hands on the sick, and they shall recover" (Mark 16:17–18). Snake-handling is not a common ritual practice, even in Harlan County or other areas surrounding its eastern Tennessee birthplace (Kimbrough 1992; see also Kane 1974; Stekert 1963). Officially, Kentucky state law prohibits this religious ritual, but local law enforcement officials do not strictly enforce this law. Just before the Small Branch revival began, for example, a woman was killed while handling a snake at her uncle's funeral in the Harlan County community of Baxter. No charges were filed in the incident. Nevertheless, her death reminded local residents of the physical and legal risks of snake-handling. All of this was fresh on people's minds when Gardner invited snake-handlers into the Small Branch church, their first appearance there in the church's forty-seven-year history.

❧

Many people, including my friend Kathy and her family, explained Gardner's controversial decision to allow snake-handling in the Small Branch church as the result of stress brought on by a combination of personal, community, and church problems that had erupted during the previous decade. According to her, the community, its church, and the pastor had been plagued by a remarkable run of "bad luck," including (1) the departure of the previous popular pastor, John Gardner (Robby's father and Kathy's uncle), who had left his wife to marry a younger woman from outside the community; (2) the decline of membership in the local church; (3) Robby's layoff from his mining job; and (4) community-wide economic decline and population loss. As Kathy saw it, the divorce of his parents and moral downfall of his father had hit Robby particularly hard, because he had so idolized his father. Then losing his job, on top of all that, had also upset Robby.

While Gardner agreed with much of what his cousin said, he did not share her view that he had suffered a run of "bad luck" that threatened his mental stability and intellectual faculties. Rather, Gardner explained his father's downfall, the church's decline, and other problems in the Small Branch community by reference to a supernatural struggle between God and Satan, a struggle that the Small Branch community and church had been losing on account of their moral weakness, lack of faith, and increased materialism and attachment to the "things of this world." The opposition between the psychological and spiritual explanations of community dynamics animated the discourse that was constructed throughout the three weeks of the revival. Before one can make sense of the revival discourse, however, some local historical context is necessary. The next section includes a narrative reconstruction of incidents that Kathy Black and her cousin Robby Gardner have identified as central to understanding the broader conflicts that crystallized into a theological debate over snake-handling.

❧

This entire affair started, Robby Gardner explained, when he received a phone call from a Pentecostal miner-preacher, Samuel

Chandler. Chandler had no church of his own but instead served God as a traveling evangelist. He informed Gardner that God had called him to preach a revival at the Small Branch church. This, in itself, did not surprise Gardner, for he knew that his church and community were in trouble. Not long ago, the church's pastor (his father) had left in disgrace, and since then church attendance had dropped dramatically, from around 80 to 33 per service. Most of them were retired and unemployed miners and their families. Conspicuously absent from active membership were young and middle-aged adult women, whom one would expect to comprise the core of the church's congregation (Cucchiari 1990, 689; Gill 1990, 708; Lancaster 1988, 103; Lawless 1988a, 6–7; Roberts 1968).

In addition to this decrease in church membership, Gardner also noticed a departure from traditional "Holiness" ways among his remaining congregation. They were becoming more materialistic, worldly, selfish, and vain. His sister, for example, trimmed her long hair so that it would not get in her way when she sat down. Even worse, she belonged to a bowling league and participated in tournaments with cash prizes, a practice that came dangerously close to gambling. Her husband, a man from outside the community, was not a Pentecostal "saint" and did not attend church with his family. Gardner attributed some of his sister's moral backsliding to her husband's "sinner" ways. Likewise, Gardner's mother had also become more vain and worldly recently, particularly in the months since her husband left her for a younger woman. By 1986, she was no longer winding her long hair into a tight bun at the nape of her neck. Instead, she had it styled at a Harlan beauty salon. Moreover, she seemed to be investing more time and money in her appearance than she had in the past; she bought new dresses and shoes and a stylish winter coat. And they were not the only ones, Gardner admitted. Many of the women in the community cut their hair short, got permanents, pierced their ears, and wore makeup, blue jeans, shorts, and over-the-knee skirts during the 1980s.

Most local young people had stopped going to church altogether and were allowed to attend sporting events, dances, and movies in town. Many men and women in the community publicly drank alcohol and smoked cigarettes; and young folks were increasingly experimenting with drugs and premarital sex. Marriages were growing increasingly fragile as well, it seemed. Not only had his father divorced his mother, but most of Gardner's cousins and neighbors had also been divorced. For that matter, Gardner himself was in his second marriage. The proportion of female-headed households was rising. Gardner found it regrettable that so many women had to work outside the home to support their children. He thought children needed a stay-at-home mother. His own wife, for instance, stayed home to take care of their two school-aged children even after Gardner lost his job in the mines. He supported his family with food stamps and his income from odd jobs, preaching funerals, presiding over weddings, church offerings on his behalf, and the sale of washing machines that he had retrieved from the county dump and repaired. Gardner knew that he was not alone in his economic struggles. The entire community had been affected.

In spite of this fact, the community had not responded to the economic challenges as they had in the past: with increased Christian charity and community reciprocity. A couple of generations earlier, it seemed that families were more willing to cooperate in their work and share goods, particularly meals and garden produce. During the Depression, according to Gardner, nearly everyone lost his job, and still each family suffered together and shared equally. The families who still owned land shared food from the gardens that the women tended. Local men joined the UMW to protest wage cuts and poor working conditions, eventually fighting for their rights in pitched battles against "company thugs." Back then, it seemed to Gardner, local folks responded to problems by "pulling together." But by 1986 only the old people gardened and "put up" food. Women with jobs, especially those heading households, did not have time to keep gardens. Housework, child care, jobs, and, in some cases, schoolwork kept this new generation of Small Branch women busy enough.

Included among these shirkers of Christian charity and abdicators of community reciprocity was Robby's sister, whose employed husband did not approve of her giving his "hard-earned money" away when they had four children of their own to raise. Kathy's sister, who remained in the community, had no surplus to share; she could barely "make ends meet" for her two children. And in her rush to work in Harlan, attend community college in Cumberland, and get back home to Small Branch, she had no time to chat or deliver food to sick neighbors. She barely had time to cook for her daughters. She relied on her mother's garden to stock her pantry, but did not grow her own. Then, of course, there was Robby's other cousin, Kathy, who had moved away from the community altogether and only visited about once per week. She contributed to her daughter's upkeep, of course, but felt little responsibility toward others in the community.

The economic hardships facing his community and church were many, but Gardner was primarily concerned about moral and spiritual issues. In fact, he thought that the economic troubles might have been caused by the community's increasing moral laxity and decay. And even if they were not so directly related, he proposed, the best way to handle economic adversity was through cooperation and seeking God's guidance. Facing unemployment and poverty would not be so difficult if the community had its priorities straight, emphasizing spiritualism over materialism, heaven over earth, God over Satan, and others over self (see table 6.2). That is, after all, what he had done. Gardner discovered that the loss of his

TABLE 6.2
Small Branch Pentecostal
Revival Themes,
Ranked by Frequency

	Rank	Frequency	Proportion
God as source of comfort in a troubled world	1	69	22.0
Anti-materialism and -worldliness	2	51	16.2
Pastoral legitimation	3	44	14.1
Congregational conflict	4	40	12.8
Egalitarianism and reciprocity	5	32	10.2
Anti-modernity, nostalgia for past	6	18	5.8
Threats against backsliders	7	14	4.5
Fundamentalism	8	12	3.8
Anti-rationality/pro-faith, and emotion	8	12	3.8
Snake-handling	9	8	2.6
Limitations of formal education	10	6	2.0
Ethics	11	5	1.6
Faith healing	12	2	0.6

job, although difficult for his family, made it possible for him to devote more of his life to his spiritual calling to do God's work at home, in church, and throughout the community. Maintaining a positive outlook, though, was a strong point of Gardner's. As he put it, "If you fall down and break your arm, jump up and praise the Lord! You could've broken *both* your arms." Gardner thought that, perhaps, this revival could set both the local church and the community back on track.

Unfortunately, the evangelist's open practice and proponence of snake-handling put Gardner in a difficult position. After all, the Small Branch Pentecostal church had never condoned snake-handling. After a three-week period of prayer and consultation with the dwindling Small Branch congregation, the pastor allowed Chandler to schedule a revival in their church. Neither Gardner or the remaining Small Branch "saints" intended this invitation to be an endorsement of snake-handling. None of them planned on participating in the ritual themselves. Nevertheless, Gardner thought it was advisable to "keep an open mind" on the topic and to seek God's will in the matter. In the wake of the former pastor's disgrace, the decline in the congregation, and widespread community problems, this revival offered Small Branch a chance for reassessment and revitalization.

Those who no longer attended the local Pentecostal church, whom Gardner referred to as "sinners," did not share Gardner's open-mindedness on the snake-handling issue. Snake-handling was against the law. And furthermore it was physically risky, as evidenced by the recent demise of a snake-handler in the Harlan community of Baxter. While they thought adults should be free to take the legal and physical risks of snake-handling, many "sinners" opposed exposing the children to these dangers.[1] Last but not least, "sinners" cited local tradition in their arguments against snake-handling. The church's founders were against snake handling, and even though "sinners" no longer regularly attended the local Pentecostal church, they felt bound to defend the religious traditions of their mothers and fathers. In some sense, they continued to regard Small Branch Pentecostal as "their church," perhaps because they had been raised there and their parents had founded it.

When the revival started, "sinners" like Kathy Black attended, not only to witness the snake-handling, but also to register their protests against this departure from local tradition. One evening, even the former pastor, John Gardner, appeared at services amid rumors that he had notified the authorities about the snake-handling. The entire congregation waited in fear, anger, or eager anticipation of a police raid that never materialized. Still, the brief return of the "prodigal" father, along with the other prodigal sons and (mostly) daughters, added to the drama of the revival, an event whose discourse centered as much upon constructing a spiritual and moral basis for the community and its church, as it did upon winning souls to God.

Immediately preceding this revival, a regular worship service would have attracted about thirty worshipers. They would seat themselves in a sex-segregated pattern, with women on the right and men on the left. In addition to gender differentiation, seating patterns reflected variations in spiritual status as well. "Saints," for instance, sat near the front of the church while "sinners" sat in the back. The pastor and musicians, all men, located themselves on the elevated platform, behind the pulpit. Children sat with their mothers but were generally free to wander about during services, which lasted from two to three hours.

Once the revival started, however, attendance rose to over a hundred worshipers per night. The "saints" maintained the traditional seating arrangement, but "sinners" did not—often electing to sit together as nuclear family units instead of following the sex-segregated seating pattern. One divorced mother even took the daring step of sitting on the men's side of the aisle in the back row. And when former pastor John Gardner appeared, he took a seat in the middle row of the men's side of the church, where he was joined by several "sinner" women and men. This was the only occasion on which women broke the same-sex seating barrier *en masse*. Finally, Kathy and (sometimes) her sister elected to sit with me at the revival, instead of with their relatives and former neighbors, signifying their growing distance from the local community and its traditions. Such spatial arrangements and disruptions were neither coincidental nor trivial; they constituted but one strategy in the symbolic battle between Small Branch "saints" and "sinners."

In fact, such spatial disruptions were a central means by which "sinners" registered their disapproval during services, since they could not or would not speak out in church. Of course, their spiritual status precluded them from testifying, preaching, or speaking in tongues. Yet much of the time they refused to pray and sing as well, apparently as a silent protest. The silence of the "sinners" during services, however, was matched by their verbal expressiveness outside of the services. They spoke frequently to one another and to "saints" during the three-week revival period: reminding everyone of their anti-snake-handling heritage, recalling their youth in the church, expressing concern over the danger of snake-handling, and requesting information about the financial and emotional well-being of pastor Robby Gardner. In conversations with me, they questioned the intentions of the visiting evangelist: what was his interest in Small Branch, and why did he fail to "look them in the eye" when he preached? They ridiculed his poor grammar and joked about how ill at ease he seemed to be with women. Kathy, in particular, noted the phallic symbolism of the snakes and remarked upon the sensuality of Pentecostal worship services: the gyrating dancing to rock gospel music (played by electric guitars, a piano, a drum trap set, and tambourines), writhing on the floor, touching, and the "laying on of hands" to heal. She said that it reminded her of Saturday night at The Club, a Cumberland dance spot that she frequented after her divorce.

In contrast to the "sinners," who did most of their talking outside of church, "saints" restricted their remarks to the spiritual arena, where they prayed, testified, and, in Gardner's case, preached to the unbelievers. Testimonies usually ranged from two to three minutes in length, although the pastor frequently dominated testimonial services with fifteen-minute minisermons. On the night his father attended church, for example, the pastor testified at length. He began with the accurate observation that "sinners" had gossiped more than they worshiped during the revival. "There's a revival going on and a lot of talk going on, going around," he observed. Then he shifted to his primary target: his father. "A man, claiming to be a preacher, said he was going to call the law on me because I let them bring the box [containing snakes] in. You know what? He don't believe the Word of God, like he said." By questioning the legitimacy of his father's "calling" to preach, he challenged his father's authority as a man of God and church founder. And, regardless of its accuracy, the charge that John Gardner had "called the law" cast him in the role of "Judas," highlighting his previous betrayal of the community and, if possible, alienating him even further from his family, former neighbors, and congregants.

The most striking aspect of the Small Branch revival discourse, however, was the extent to which it was dominated by men (see table 6.3). Men occupied the central positions of authority in the church as pastors, evangelists, and musicians. Consequently, they had more opportunities to speak, direct action, exercise authority, and command attention than women did. Men occupied the front, center stage area from which they preached the sermons, called the congregation to order, dismissed services, took prayer requests, and invited the congregation to pray. Only men handled snakes, as well, although there were women snake-handlers elsewhere in the county. Men also selected and initiated 69 percent of the hymns. Anyone in attendance could initiate a song of worship, but the chances of having one's song heard and completed by the group were increased if the singer also played a musical instrument. Except for the piano, only men played the musical instruments in the front of church. Women primarily played tambourines from their seats in the pews. The single woman guitarist was a visitor who sat in the pews with other women, not on the stage with the men. Hers was the only guitar that was not electrified. Most remarkably, men also dominated the testimonial segment of the service, a portion of Pentecostal worship services that others have described as typ-

TABLE 6.3
Small Branch Revival
Worship Activities, Ranked by Frequency
And Compared by Gender of Initiator

	Man Initiated		Woman Initiated	
	Frequency	Proportion	Frequency	Proportion
Song	69	69.7	30	30.3
Testimony	51	85.0	9	15.0
Prayer	67	100.0	0	0.0
Prayer Requests (outside of testimonies)	29	45.0	36	55.0
Sermon	21	100.0	0	0.0
Snake-handling	18	100.0	0	0.0

ically female-dominated (Cucchiari 1990, 693–4; Lawless 1988b, 85; see also Gill 1990, 713). Here Small Branch men broke the general, documented Pentecostal patterns (Cucchiari 1990; Lawless 1988b), delivering 85 percent of the testimonies. Men's revival testimonies outnumbered women's, fifty-one to nine. Only one local woman, the pastor's mother, testified during this three-week period.

Since Gardner saw the world as a battlefield for a polarized struggle between God and Satan, most of his testimonies revolved around identifying signs of the supernatural struggle and aligning himself with God's side. He warned his congregation, "The Devil is getting people's spirit today. I feel like Satan is here. There's a lot of things that's not of God that the Devil put off on people." He continued, adding that Satan won only when people succumbed to their weaknesses. "Do you know why [Satan is winning]? Because [people here] are wanting it. They're wanting it. They're wanting an easier way," he observed. As for Gardner, he still wanted "the old path." "What was right, then, is still right tonight," he concluded. This equation of Pentecostalism with the community's past traditions continued throughout the revival; it was a discursive linkage that may have been the revival's "undoing," as will be discussed later.

As with most revivals, the one at Small Branch sought to convert "sinners" to God's side of the struggle. Yet this one seemed to be remarkably successful at attracting a large turnout of "sinners." Even the evangelist, a man who regularly preached revivals throughout southeast Kentucky, expressed surprise at the event's success. He remarked on the first night of the revival, "I thought, tonight, about the 'sinner' people who are standing up and wondering what's a going on. Brother, there ain't nothing going on. There ain't nothing going on in the House of God that is much interest to them. But, brother, we need the power of God to move on their souls. You know what this is all about? Saving people. You know, tonight we got 'sinner' people that are shut out from the power of God."

The evangelist drew a distinct boundary between "saints" and "sinners," contrasting their positions ("shut out from the power of God") to his own ("vessel of God"). Most of his sermons began with an assertion of legitimacy, in which he claimed that God had "called" him to preach. Repeated refrains were: "That's the only thing there is: to preach the Word of God tonight"; "When I leave here, I'll say, 'God, I done what you sent me to do'"; and "When I'm here, I do what God wants me to do." Like many Pentecostal preachers, neither the evangelist nor the local pastor received any formal education to preach. Neither did they receive a salary for their work. The "calling," then, served as both a motive and a legitimation of their spiritual leadership.

Because his church was in decline, Gardner seemed even more anxious to legitimate his pastoral authority than Chandler was. He referred to his "calling" repeatedly, in statements such as this: "I didn't choose to preach the Word of God. God chose me." It was his unfailing submission to God, he thought, that had alienated him from neighbors who no longer wanted to hear the word of God. "A lot of times, I preach pretty hard. Preach what the Lord told me. And a lot of people takes offense at me. 'It's not right for Robby [Gardner] to preach that way!'" he complained, observing that local "sinners" were increasingly hostile toward him. "Ah, but somebody else could come along and they'd say, 'They're preaching good!' I'm just giving you an example. It's easy for somebody else to stand up and they [sinners] don't get so hurt. I wonder what's wrong. I ain't doing nothing except preaching the Word. Just preaching the Word."

Alas, Small Branch "sinners" had "gone to the things of the world. They've gone away from God. . . . They don't believe no more. They don't have to live by the old traditions." And, as they continued on this journey, Gardner feared that his former congregation members had become confused. They had erroneously interpreted Gardner's sermons as personal assaults. Their feelings had been hurt, and therefore they wanted to hurt their pastor in return. But Gardner had no personal grudges against them; he was just relaying a message from God. "I don't want people to take my word for nothing, do you? Let God tell you. This is the good way," he urged. As a servant of God, he had suffered more than "sinners." "A lot of people torment you because they left what they knew was right. . . . People get something in their heart and can't worship." So great was this pain that he prayed to God, "I said [to God], 'The people they've stood against me.' And he said, 'They've not stood against *you;* they've stood against *me.*'" Throughout the revival, Gardner portrayed himself as a Jesus-like martyr. Like Jesus, he was child of God. He was chosen by God to preach and, in doing so, bore the sins of an increasingly worldly congregation that ultimately betrayed him.

The evangelist and pastor utilized two basic strategies to convert lost "sinners." First, they threatened "sinners" with eternal damnation. Second, they promised "sinners" love, fellowship, and eternal salvation if they "returned to God's fold." The initial strategy predominated during the first half of the revival. On the opening night, for instance, the evangelist preached harshly to the crowd of "sinners," capitalizing upon his status as an outsider with no history of interpersonal conflicts or unresolved grudges with them. "I don't know anybody. I don't know a lot of people. I never seen them before," he remarked. Nevertheless, he recognized "sinners" when he saw them. He noted, "I'd rather have two or three good ones than a house full of bad ones. You can do more with a few believers in the Word of God than a house full that won't believe the Word of God. Anybody that don't believe the Word of God the way it is, there ain't much use for them!"

His dismissal of "sinners" as "useless" laid the groundwork for the pastor, who already had a history of personal conflict with local "sinners," to threaten them again with eternal damnation. Gardner once again portrayed himself as a Jesus-like martyr, whom the community rejected and tormented. "Oh, there are a lot of people kindly hurt at me," he explained. "And it's because I believe the Word of God. That don't matter." Then, crying, he recalled the sting of gossip. "I've heard a lot of people say a lot of things. Only that weren't right, brother. And I'll tell you something, God is going to judge folks, like it was said before, and you'll get what's coming to you. You'll get exactly what's coming to you," he warned. "Hell's going to be awful. I wouldn't wish that on nobody, would you?" He hoped to save the "sinners" from such a fate, but it was not ultimately in his hands. "God will be your judge. Anybody that comes against the spirit of God, anybody that blasphemes the Holy Ghost, you're in trouble," he told them. "Bad trouble."

As the revival continued, Gardner's testimonial pleas to "lost sinners" became increasingly emotional and tearful. Gradually, he stopped threatening his congregation with damnation and began to emphasize the positive aspects of salvation and church fellowship, painting a picture of a merciful, loving, and comforting Pentecostal God. One night, toward the end of the revival, Gardner singled out each "sinner" by name, saying that he loved her and wished she would return to church. He spoke of the reciprocity and goodness of love. "I try to live close enough to the Lord so I know who loves me and who really don't. Love is something that'll reach back. Amen. It'll reach back. It'll reach back. Love is not a one-way thing. It'll reach back. It'll reach back." He reassured them that they could live a "Holiness life" on the "straight and narrow," noting that "God never asks nothing beyond reason. Everything he tells us to do, we can do." Ultimately, the image of a nurturant, loving, and forgiving God dominated revival discourse. Sermons and testimonies elaborating God's traditionally feminine characteristics, such as mercy and love, outnumbered mentions of God's masculine, vengeful side (Cucchiari 1990, 689–91) by more than five to one. The tension between these two sides of God was evident throughout the revival, however, and was never fully eliminated.

Although many local "sinners" returned to church to witness and protest the experimentation with snake-handling, local "saints" provided little fodder for their moral outrage. They did not handle snakes or defend the practice in testimonies, prayers, or personal conversations. The pastor referred to the snakes only one time, and even then he did not say the word *snake*. His single reference to the practice occurred in a testimony against his father in which he claimed to have been threatened with arrest for allowing "the boxes" (which held the snakes) into the church. Only the evangelist and a few male guests handled the snakes, which were taken out during six of the twenty-one worship services.

In short, the issue of snake-handling seemed more salient to local "sinners" than to the "saints." The "saints" focused upon other issues, predominantly the decline in community neighborliness, harmony, reciprocity, and solidarity in Small Branch. During testimonies, they complained that people no longer socialized *within* the community. They could not "count on" neighbors, as they had in "the old days." They accused "sinners" of ignoring them when they ran into one another "in town" (Harlan). According to Small Branch "saints," the "sinners crossed the street" in order to avoid "saying hello." Obviously, they were "ashamed" of their poor saintly neighbors. "Snobby" behavior like this indicated an elitism that violated egalitarian ideologies that have been associated with Pentecostalism and with Appalachian community generally (Beaver 1986; Feine 1990; Schwarzweller, Brown, and Mangalam 1971), as well as Harlan County specifically (see chapter 2).

Contemporary Small Branch, marred by community cleavages and conflict, stood in contrast to "saints'" memories of past egalitarian social relations and neighborly reciprocity. In the eyes of Small Branch "saints," Pentecostalism provided the primary basis upon which such a community was built. "God's people are a peculiar people," they said, not only because of their spiritual gifts and physical appearance, but because of the way they behaved toward others. God's people were generous and kind. They followed God's Golden Rule, doing unto others as they would have others do unto them. The pastor articulated the linkage between Pentecostalism and communal reciprocity, in the following: "You know, the Bible says, 'Love thy neighbor as thyself.' You know what that means? That means, if I got a meal on my table and I know Brother Larry [like Gardner, an unemployed miner], he ain't got a meal on his table. He ain't eating so good. That means I take the meal off my table and put it on his," he reminded his congregation. But such communal solidarity extended beyond acts of Christian generosity; it manifested itself in community involvement and concern, in putting others' needs ahead of one's own. Gardner acknowledged the difficulty of the task, as he testified. "There's a lot of things that's not of God that the Devil put off on people. . . . Do you know why? Because they're wanting it. They're wanting it. They're wanting an *easier* way. They *keep to themselves* [my emphasis]," he complained. Nevertheless, he declared, "I still want the old path, don't you?" In other words, the "easy" path of individualism ("keeping to oneself") was not the route to Heaven.

Although Small Branch "saints" rejected the modern world in which "sinners" had immersed themselves, they often alluded to it in testimonies. It yielded innumerable examples of sin and corruption and provided a rich source for testimonial metaphors. Salvation is the best "insurance policy," "saints" said, reminding "sinners" that, when they faced God at Judgment, they could not hire a lawyer to "plead their cases." From the world of work came the following observation: Heaven is the best "promotion"—a promotion from worldly pain and trials. Although "sinners" emphasized the importance of education, "saints" knew that it provided no substitute for salvation. They reiterated the superiority of faith over intellect by the remark: "I received my education at the brush arbor!" ("Brush arbor" refers to a grove of trees or bushes where one seeks privacy to pray.) Anecdotes about the uselessness of "book smarts," the inadequacy of reason, and human impotence dominated sermons and testimonies. These themes prevailed in narratives about illness and healing, which extolled the virtues of faith and Pentecostal healing rituals. Doctors could not heal people, "saints" proclaimed, only an omnipotent God could. Unfortunately, "sinners" had placed their faith in medical science, insurance, legal statutes, careers, and educations. Having allied themselves with "worldliness" and against God, they were condemned to an eternity in Hell.

Of all the worldly concerns, however, wealth received the "saints'" most consistent and hostile condemnation. Eighty-five percent of the sermons included a personal anecdote or Biblical allegory about the eternal damnation of a rich person that was later elaborated in saintly testimonies. Although no one specifically testified or preached that wealth brought damnation, sermons and testimonies portrayed an inverse relationship between one's material well-being and one's spiritual well-being. Personal anecdotes about the wealthy inevitably ended in the wealthy person's suffering a painful death, usually caused by cancer (see Sontag 1978 for a discussion of cancer as a metaphor for evil). Sometimes the rich realized the error of their ways on their deathbeds; but it was too late to be "saved." In other cases, they remained misled, asking to be buried in their Cadillacs or trying to "take their money with them." Either way, they spent an eternity in Hell. From the Bible, local "saints" retold the story of Jesus ordering a wealthy potential follower to sell all his worldly goods. Unable to do so, the wealthy man was turned away. "It is more difficult for a rich man to enter the Kingdom of Heaven than for a camel to pass through the eye of a needle," Small Branch "saints" warned. Also popular was a parable of the wealthy man who, after being condemned to Hell for refusing to give scraps to beggars, pleaded to return home so that he could warn his brothers of their fate; he was refused. In testimonies about "witnessing" to non-Pentecostals, Small Branch "saints" reported their ability to recognize "lost souls" by reference to their characteristic stylish clothing, expensive jewelry, and late-model cars.

ౚ

The symbolic identification of wealth and wickedness facilitated working-class solidarity in Small Branch by differentiating miners from owners and informing a critique of capitalist hegemony, as others have noted (Billings 1990; Corbin 1981). But while local Pentecostal discourse was critical and potentially radical in its class politics, its gender ideology was far from progressive (see also Cucchiari 1990, 687–88). This is true, in spite of the fact that Pentecostalism has been regarded as a "woman's religion" because of a high proportion of female believers and the expanded leadership opportunities for women offered by some Pentecostal churches. To understand this apparent paradox, we must know something about the local socioeconomic context in which this unaffiliated Pentecostal church operated and to which its discourse referred.

The Small Branch Pentecostal Church was born into a political economy dominated by coal and men. This economy was run primarily by and for men (Pudup 1990b). Working-class solidarity had been built upon and reinforced patriarchal gender relations (Yarrow 1985). The emergence of new class- and status-based cleavages in the 1980s coincided with transformations of traditional sex roles and gender ideology, apparently at the expense of Small Branch working-class men. The relationship between class and gender in this community—where men worked in (or were laid off from) blue-collar jobs and women worked in white- and pink-collar jobs—was complex but important.

During testimonies, class-based themes often slid imperceptibly into gender-based themes. "I thought about people . . . a-wearing their suits and their ties. You can read in the Book of God about the love of the flesh," Gardner began, implicitly linking professional dress with personal vanity and worldliness. He continued, "But, brother, I tell you what. I'd be happy up here it I didn't have nothing but a pair of over-hauls [overalls]. I'd sing 'Glory to God,'" thus, elevating the work clothes of farmers and miners to a symbol of Godliness. "People want to be looked upon now. 'Look at me! Look at me!' That's what gets a lot of people: pride. Glory to God!" he further complained, before turning his attention to the most vain creatures of all: women. "Nowadays, people has to go to the beauty shop. Everybody got to get their hair fixed right good. Thank God! I don't want a look that'll please the world." Thus, the interpenetration of Pentecostalism, working-class identity, and patriarchy emerges. In the end, physical appearance provided a terrain on which the battle between "saintly" men and "sinner" women became intense and hostile.

A brief review of Pentecostal beliefs illuminates the dynamic that propelled Small Branch men and women into debates over seemingly trivial matters, such as beauty shops and fashion aesthetics. Recall that, in addition to moral and behavioral proscriptions banning smoking, drinking, dancing, and gambling, Small Branch Pentecostals required men and women to present a modest, unworldly appearance. For men, this meant keeping their faces clean-shaven and their hair trimmed shortly. Pentecostal men, as Gardner noted, were expected to wear simple, unpretentious clothes, such as work clothes, dungarees, blue jeans, and open-collared shirts. None of this set Pentecostal men apart from their non-Pentecostal neighbors and co-workers. Nor did it substantially diminish their chances on the marriage market, a market that had traditionally included an oversupply of Pentecostal women in search of sanctified mates.[2]

Pentecostal women, however, were not allowed to wear pants, blue jeans, shorts, short skirts, makeup, pierced ears, or short hair; and they could not curl or perm their hair. Their dress code was purposely old-fashioned and "out of style," erecting many barriers between them and their non-Pentecostal friends. This was not a burden to previous generations of Small Branch women, whose lives centered on the community, where they attended school, went to church, married, and set up housekeeping. In 1986, though, women worked and attended college and consolidated schools outside the community. Young women had been raised on U.S. advertising and mass media definitions of feminine beauty. Like other American teenagers, they used modern fashions (especially jeans), short haircuts, and triple-pierced ears as ways to differentiate themselves from their parents and to express their "individuality" amd youthful rebellion. Older women "updated their looks" when they went to college and started careers in town. Some did it "for themselves," saying they enjoyed "looking their best." Others had to "look professional" for their careers. Finally, many thought that attracting a mate (or keeping one) hinged upon their physical beauty. This was true of both non-Pentecostal men, who dominated the county dating scene, and of Pentecostal men as well. After all, the former Pentecostal minister had left his wife for a younger, more attractive woman. Subsequently and in spite of her son's protests, Mrs. Gardner had her hair styled at the beauty shop. For better or worse, Small Branch women were adopting more modern fashions.[3]

This change in physical appearance accompanied and symbolized a broader range of behavioral changes among local women, as well. Just as women took their fashion cues from TV and from town, they also sought friends, jobs, and entertainment in town. Single women hoped to marry town men with steady, clean, and safe jobs—not coal miners, like their fathers or ex-husbands. After high school graduation, young women often moved to apartments in town where they could escape the watchful eyes of the community to befriend and date whom they pleased. They also went to movies, dances, bars, ball games, and bowling alleys for entertainment, scoffing at the idea of a God who forbade happiness and beauty. In short, many Small Branch women were no longer "under subjection" to the patriarchal authority of the family, church, and community.

In addition to challenging local patriarchal authority, these women's behavior upset the traditional gender ideology, which associated masculinity with independence, strength, assertiveness, and rationality while it linked femininity with dependence, weakness, passivity, and emotionalism. By 1986, things seemed topsy-turvy in Small Branch. Women were active, strong, independent, and rational. They functioned as "breadwinners" and also as "household heads" after divorce. They took the initiative in attracting mates, by investing more in their appearance and socializing more actively. They insisted upon choosing their own companions. They sought education and fulfillment away from the community and their families. They even quit going to church. Put simply, women had traveled a long way toward the masculine pole of the traditional gender spectrum; and their haircuts and fashions embodied their journey.

Ironically, the revival, which was aimed at establishing the status quo ante, further intensified the process of gender inversion. The (male) pastor wept openly and begged "sinner women" to return to church in testimonies that highlighted God's feminine traits of love, mercy, and forgiveness. The female "sinners" met his tears with a stone-faced silence: they did not cry, sing, pray, "speak in tongues," or seek the Holy Spirit, thus, distancing themselves from the emotional "feminine" characteristics of Pentecostal worship (Cucchiari 1990, 691–92). "Sinner women" responded with alarm to the pastor's decision to allow snake-handlers in the church, but they analyzed it in a dispassionate manner. Adopting a stance typical of male medical experts discussing an "hysterical" female patient, "sinner" women complained that the local pastor was "overly emotional" and apparently incapable of coping with the stress of unemployment and his parents' divorce. Another applied her expertise as a college psychology student, observing that the phallic symbolism of snakes and the sensuality of Pentecostal worship services probably accounted for its appeal to local congregants, who otherwise lived impoverished, sexually repressed lives. Clearly, she, and others like her, no longer inhabited the pastor's patriarchal, bipolar Pentecostal world of God versus Satan.

The revival at Small Branch Pentecostal Church ended rather anticlimactically after three weeks, resulting neither in revitalization nor in the adoption of snake-handling. On my return visits to Small Branch in 1989, 1991, and 1993 I found little changed in the community: the church struggled on with a small, aging congregation, while some "sinner" women had joined mainstream denominations but most had remained apostates. Other outcomes were and still are possible, as evidenced by Pentecostalism's contemporary appeal to a variety of populations and continued popularity among women. In an attempt to understand the failure of the 1986 Small Branch revival, however, several points can be made.

First, Small Branch "saints" and "sinners" did not share the common language or paradigm necessary to construct a dialogue about their mutual personal and community problems in 1986. The "saints'" polarized version of the world left little room for discussion and debate with "sinners." Their worldview included only God and Satan, right and wrong, good and evil. Since the "saints" were on the right side, they could not and would not compromise with evil "sinners." They lectured, testified, and preached to "sinners" but rarely listened to them. Theirs was a discourse centering, not upon snake-handling, but upon saving "sinners" from Hell and, in doing so, revitalizing the church and community.

Working from a non-Pentecostal paradigm, "sinners" concentrated upon the snake-handling issue as an indication of the instability of the local Pentecostal pastor and as a rejection of their shared theological roots. Church fathers and mothers had opposed snake-handling. By inviting snake-handlers into the church, the current pastor had forsaken their common traditional past and thereby lost his claim upon both their present and their future. Somehow, the pastor had become "unhinged." Allowing snake-handlers in the local church was not only "irrational and hereti-cal," but also against the law. Having captured what they saw as a clear moral and legal high ground, "sinner women" remained aloof from a revival discourse that condemned their modern vanity, worldliness, and individualism while lodging traditional moral claims upon them. They did not listen to the "saints" so much as analyze them. The "saints" could not sway them from their current course partly because the "sinners" thought the "saints" were "nuts" anyway.

The Small Branch revival's failure also resulted from contradic-tions between the "saints'" idealized vision of a patriarchal past and the contemporary situation. "Saints" hoped to revitalize their church, reconvert their lost neighbors, and reconstruct a commu-nity based upon Pentecostal egalitarianism and reciprocity. How-ever, with an exclusive focus on the spiritual basis of communal solidarity, "saints" ignored its requisite material and social foun-dations. Their romanticized images of the local community harked back to the nineteenth and early twentieth century, when Small Branch remained a relatively undifferentiated patriarchal commu-nity whose families engaged in reciprocal exchange of goods and services that had been provided primarily by the unpaid work of women. But by 1986 women had jobs in town. They were not available to grow the gardens, preserve the produce, cook the meals, and make the quilts that had been shared and jointly pro-duced by the community. After coal mines layoffs, local men could no longer support stay-at-home wives to do this type of "commu-nity work." In addition, the loss of men's jobs also robbed them of important opportunities to socialize and form a gender- and class-based community solidarity at work. And, finally, these economic transformations introduced new social cleavages into the commu-nity: between employed and unemployed, among blue-, pink-, and white-collar workers, and between men and women. The tearful testimonies of the "saints" did not address these structural ob-stacles and by themselves could not overcome them.

As "saintly" discourse criticized individualism, materialism, and commodification, it was potentially radical in its class politics. Yet it was both conservative and traditional on the topic of gender. The community that Small Branch "saints" idealized was based upon not only agrarian and working-class solidarity, but also patriarchal domination. It was a community in which men owned the land, earned the wages, headed the households, and led the church; and women stayed at home, raised the children, brought in crops, cooked the meals, cleaned the houses, depended on men's wages, and remained "under submission" to men, both at home and in church. These may have been the "good old days" for Pentecostal men, but "sinner" women did not wax nostalgic about this past. They had bid farewell to the Pentecostal church on their way to a future that this religion, in its present form at least, failed to address.

❧

In summary, sectoral economic shifts transformed the material bases for community and class solidarity and patriarchal authority in working-class communities like Small Branch and Ages. Subsequent stresses and conflicts, in turn, animated the religious discourses at two working-class churches, Small Branch Pentecostal Church and Old Home Baptist Church. Sermons, prayers, lessons, testimonies, and conversations that unfolded at these churches during 1986 primarily concentrated upon the issues of materialism, financial insecurity, charity and reciprocity, and gender roles. Small Branch, the historically more isolated and more impoverished of these two congregations, took a hard line against materialism, worldliness (hedonism and consumerism), and commodification. Particularly critical of the wealthy, whose riches appeared to pose an obstacle to salvation, Small Branch sermons articulated a logic of hope for the "saints" and formed an important part of this working-class community's culture of resistance. Yet, as Gardner preached it, the Small Branch Pentecostal vision revolved around a romanticized version of the community's patriarchal past that was impossible to achieve in the mid-1980s. This, I argue, was an important factor in the decline of the Small Branch church, and helps account for the ultimate failure of the 1986 revival.

The discourses at Old Home Baptist and Small Branch Pentecostal had both similarities and differences. Like Small Branch pastor Robby Gardner, the Old Home minister Bill Mason warned against the dangers of increasing materialism, worldliness, and individualism in his congregation. Yet he and his congregation discursively negotiated an interpretation of the Christian critique of wealth, materialism, and worldliness that resonated with the needs and experiences of this working- and middle-class population. Also like Gardner, Mason sought to reestablish patriarchal gender relations by countering challenges to his patriarchal authority over the congregation with reference to his "calling" by (a male) God. Mason's sermons, even more explicitly than the ones preached at Small Branch, extolled the virtues of traditional gender roles and the patriarchal nuclear family. Yet, unlike Gardner, whose testimonials evolved into tearful, emotional appeals based upon Christ's "feminine" traits of love and mercy, Mason's sermons had an assertive, vengeful, masculine tone that reinforced his patriarchal leadership. Mason even went so far as to ridicule male congregation members who allowed their patriarchal authority and, by extension, their masculinity to slip from their fingers. The most striking example of this was Mason's regular teasing of Mike, an unemployed man whose wife supported the family and who sometimes wore a pink shirt to church. Nevertheless, he had not alienated his women members who, by and large, have kept both their marriages and faiths intact.

In the areas of patriarchy and pro-union class solidarity, at least, the people at Old Home and Small Branch have made it abundantly clear that "they do not have to live by the old traditions." As they continue to chart and rechart their provisional maps during their the struggle over the language, symbolism, and meaning of their religions, their collective and individual courses may ultimately change. And it is difficult to predict what new experiences and demands their volatile political economy might introduce along the way. In 1986, the Old Home church had negotiated a tenuous balance between materialism and otherworldly concerns as well as patriarchal traditions and authority in the face of gender transformation; Small Branch had not. Their futures, as constrained as they may be, are ultimately undetermined.

CHAPTER 7

Dead Work

Thus far, this ethnography has focused on two major areas: first, the elucidation of the material, structural, and ideological forces in the dialectical construction of class consciousness among Harlan's miners during the mid-1980s; and, second, the analysis of public discourses as collective negotiated interpretations of the present and past that inform plans for the future. Although gossip was discussed, both as a social control mechanism and a means by which miners made claims upon local coal operators and government leaders, the important distinction between "frontstage" and "backstage" (Goffman 1959) discourses has not been emphasized. This is mainly because I did not, in my primary role as researcher, have access to much "backstage" discourse. People recognized, particularly when tape-recording and note-taking were involved, that their words were "public record." As a result, they might censor themselves and qualify their remarks. On the rare occasions that they "slipped up," they could ask me to keep their remarks "off the record." And I, of course, complied.

Still, eighteen months is a long time to keep one's guard up. And in settings where I functioned largely as a participant, my access to backstage discourse increased. At church, for example, I witnessed the construction of the adult Sunday school class's backstage discourse on the parable of the rich man, which in turn influenced frontstage sermons delivered by the Old Home pastor. Regarding the Small Branch church, I argued that the public discourses of the "saints" failed to engage the private discourse of the "sinners" in a meaningful dialogue or debate. In addition to church, I participated even more actively in other institutions in the community (Adler and Adler 1987), most notably as a teacher in community college courses and as a Jaycees club member involved in the construction of the Harlan Miners Memorial. This chapter discusses data gathered in the latter setting.

My active participation in and intense commitment to this project might concern readers who would prefer a more distanced, disinterested ethnographic account, one that could adequately attend to "both sides" of this story. While I do my best to summarize and explain the position of those who opposed the construction of a memorial, I do not pretend to do justice to "their side" of this story. I was positioned, both socially and ideologically, on the other side of the conflict. In spite of my sincere concerns about the effects of such bias, I remain convinced that my participatory role offered more of an advantage than a disadvantage. My immersion in backstage discourse illuminated "the tendency of public discourse to make some forms of experience readily available while ignoring or suppressing others" (Lears 1985, 577). To me, it seemed well worth the trade-off in illusory "objectivity."

ે

The Harlan Miners Memorial Project was only one of several projects undertaken by the local Jaycees chapter in 1985–86. This project, however, differed from the noncontroversial activities typically performed by such civic organizations—fund-raising for cancer research and prevention or the promotion of bicycle safety, for example. The memorial project involved constructing a monument dedicated to workers who were killed while mining coal in Harlan County. The title of this chapter, "Dead Work," thus, alludes both to commemoration of the dead and to the labor that is required to construct a safe workplace for underground miners (see chapter 1).

With the exception of a few monuments dedicated to victims of large mining disasters, I know of no other memorial of this kind in the United States. Certainly, Harlan County had no other memorials commemorating common workers—except, of course, those who had been killed in war. In addition to the column of coal honoring the coal industry erected on a small roundabout in the old highway into town, Harlan County's monumental statuary included the following items, all located on the court house lawn in the center of town: (1) a wall of coal commemorating the first carload of coal shipped out of Harlan County; (2) a prominently located, tall, realistic statue of a charging infantryman in honor of local World War I casualties; (3) a series of plaques commemorating the local casualties in World War II and the Korean Vietnam Wars; (4) a historical marker noting that the local court house had been burned down during the Civil War; and (5) privately donated benches in memory of local notables. The Harlan Miners Memorial Project, thus, elaborated upon an established local tradition of commemoration, but with a new twist in its potential political implications.

To understand this unprecedented project, some background discussion is necessary—first on the topic of its sponsoring group, the Harlan County Jaycees. It seems somewhat counterintuitive that a civic organization, such as the Jaycees, would even propose such a project. The key to unlocking this mystery, however, lies in the relatively (though not racially) diverse composition of the Harlan Jaycees. Formerly a club for men only, the Jaycees had opened its membership to women in the 1980s. By 1985, women had become among the most active members of the club. More directly relevant, however, the club's membership boasted a rather large proportion of coal miners, including that year's president, Randy Head. The rest of the club consisted of mining and construction engineers, civil servants, retail and restaurant workers, data clerks, educators, an extension agent, one small businessman, and one anthropologist—not the mix of small business owners and political leaders that one might expect. When miners Jerry Laws and Rick Boggs, both Jaycees members, were killed in a coal mine accident, the chapter voted to build the miners memorial.

Second, it is important to recognize the extent to which coal mine safety is a collective concern in Harlan County. Although safety is of primary interest to miners and their families, almost everyone in the community has been touched by coal mine deaths. They worry about the problem and genuinely hope that coal mine safety will improve. Generally speaking, underground coal mining has consistently been one of the most dangerous industries in the United States (Braithwaite 1985; Caudill 1977), often ranking first in fatality and accident rates.[1] Since 1900, over 103,000 American miners have been killed at work (Wallace 1987, 338). An additional 1.75 million have been afflicted with disabling injuries, at least since 1930 when collection of nonfatal injury statistics began (338). To add insult to these injuries, the health and safety of American miners compares quite unfavorably to miners working in similar industrialized countries. For instance, the U.S. coal fatality rate was four times that of Holland in 1986, when the Harlan County Miners Memorial was built (360). Health and safety issues

usually rank high among union miners' concerns and strike demands, and have been cited as a primary source of pro-union
attitudes and class solidarity (see also Braithwaite 1985).

Harlan County is no exception to these generalizations. When
Jaycees examined death certificates at the county health department to identify the names of miners killed in Harlan's mines, they
found that over 1,300 miners had died in the industry's seventy-
five-year history. That is, on the average, 17 each year. In the years
before mines were federally regulated and inspected, a miner died
each week in Harlan County. Starting in the late 1930s, however,
mine fatalities slowly decreased, so that, by 1985, only 8 Kentucky
miners died at work, less than 1 per month (Kentucky Department
of Mines and Minerals [KDMM] 1985, 1986); two to three of
these are usually from Harlan. In spite of this progress, safety
remained a prime concern to the miners interviewed for this project. Even Bobby Carson, who enjoyed his work and had congenial
relations with his boss, characterized mining as "the worst job in
the world" because it was the "dirtiest and most dangerous." In
hundreds of oral history interviews, miners discussed how they
overcame their fear at work (see also Fitzpatrick 1980; Yarrow
1985, 1990). Others fretted that women would be unable to cope
with the danger and risk inherent in mining. In response, women
like Linda Taylor and Beth Walker argued that their presence
would enhance workplace safety because women did not feel compelled to take unnecessary risks to prove themselves.

Many miners and their families credited the United Mine Workers with improving mine safety. In the estimation of Harlan County
miners, the union's lobbying efforts for mine safety legislation, its
role in implementing and regulating federal safety standards, and
its protection of miners who report safety infractions or refuse
dangerous work were among the primary benefits of union representation. As Daniel put it, "If you're just an individual and you
tell a boss that you don't want to go in that water hole, if you're
afraid, he says, 'Hit the road! Either get in it or get out.' But, if you
belong to the union, you can tell him to pump that water hole or
you're not working in it."

To miners, the relatively high national mine accident rates demonstrated that coal operators cared more about profits than about
people. This is regularly reiterated in the much-repeated anecdote
in which a coal operator expresses more concern for the mule he

bought than for the worker he hired. Shared danger at work was a primary factor uniting Harlan's miners against coal operators. Coal operators, on the other hand, protested their depiction as coldhearted profiteers. On the contrary, they argued, they did their best to insure their workers' safety. The primary problem, in the their eyes, was not operator greed but employee error. The workers caused their own accidents, operators claimed, and then tried to blame the management. The president of the Harlan County Coal Operators' Association, Jay Barlow, put it this way:

> It [coal mining] is dangerous work but, as you know, there are some people who wouldn't do anything but that. I think in most cases, in most medium-sized to large mines, I think the real thought in their minds, not only the people who work in the mines, but the management, is safety.
>
> And I think, if you'll go back and check the accidents in recent years, that 99 percent of them are [the result of] some human error, like a guy picking up a cable and cutting it with a knife and he hasn't turned the power off. These things happen. . . . It happened up at Eddie Karst's mines maybe a month and a half ago. . . . With all they can do, it's still impossible to keep people from being hurt.
>
> They interviewed me after the tragic accident up at Bailey's Creek where about five men got killed in a rock fall. ABC [American Broadcasting Corporation] . . . called me from New York and I . . . said, "Do you have any idea how many people have been killed on a farm tractor here in Kentucky?" She said, "What are you talking about?" I said, "They're just as dead as those people [the miners] are. There have been forty-two killed [on tractors]. You don't see that anywhere in the newspaper."[2] I know that [for] the majority of [coal operators], it's just devastating to them when somebody gets killed in the mines.

Clearly, the Harlan community was divided in its explanation of mine deaths even as it was united in its desire to reduce them.

Constructing a monument to Harlan's fallen miners meant, among other things, opening up old wounds from previous class conflicts, conflicts that the public discourses of community harmony had systematically skirted during the recession-plagued 1980s. It required a revisitation of painful memories. It meant erecting a permanent, concrete reminder of industrial death, violent struggle, exploitation, and injustice in the court house square, the town's most public legitimating space.[3] The problem of meaning, then, animated the conflictual discourse surrounding the project from its inception. What did the Jaycees mean by proposing such a monument? What did the community mean by building it? Why did its opponents oppose it? What would the monument symbolize for us, for others in the community, and for future generations? Everything about this monument—its design, whose names could be placed on it, who could be invited to the dedication ceremony, and what could be said about it—was open for debate and negotiation.

&

By the time I had joined the club in October 1985, the memorial project had already begun. The chapter had proposed construction of a miners memorial to the community, through the local newspaper. After receiving expressions of support, it secured the county fiscal court's permission to build the monument on the court house square where other county monuments had been erected. Then club members selected a design from a pool of local submissions to a contest, which had been sponsored and organized by the local newspaper, the *Harlan Daily Enterprise*. The contest offered a $100 prize. The winning design received almost unanimous approval from the membership (see figure 7.1). It called for a six-foot-tall cross, with a diagonal break across its middle (see figure 7.1), to be laid on the south lawn of the court house. The names of mine casualties were to be engraved on black granite plaques that would be installed on the cross's sides. When viewed from ground level, the memorial appeared to be an abstract, disjointed wall of names. The cross shape would be visible only when viewed from above—from the top floors of the court house and surrounding businesses, for example. Club members approvingly noted the design's resemblance to the Vietnam Veterans Memorial, which had been constructed in Washington, D.C., three years previously.

Having selected the design, the club then set about identifying mine casualties. As a researcher who was already conducting oral history interviews with local miners, I provided a natural conduit for information about mine accidents and fatalities. The people whom I interviewed expressed strong support of the project and were happy to cooperate in the club's efforts to identify miners to be honored on the memorial. No single institution had consistently documented mine casualties over the seventy-five-year period of the industry's local history, so the club had to tap several sources

FIGURE 7.1
The original design of the Harlan Miners Memorial, by David Harp.

for information, including company records, newspaper archives, and governmental sources at all levels. The following groups assisted the club in this task: the county health department, which allowed club members to research their death certificates; the local newspaper, which published mail-in forms for their readers to submit information to the club; and Arch Minerals and Bow Valley Coal Company, two coal corporations that offered the club not only their records but use of their copiers and computers as well.

Even with considerable community and corporate cooperation, the compilation of an accurate casualty list posed a challenge. But it was a challenge that could be met only after the club agreed upon a set of inclusion criteria for potential honorees. Although the group had no authority or tradition to cite in developing a set of selection criteria, Jaycee members nevertheless achieved a remarkable degree of consensus during the process. First, they decided to restrict their attention only to coal-mining deaths that had occurred *within* the boundaries of Harlan County. This decision excluded victims of the locally significant 1976 Scotia disaster, which had occurred in nearby Letcher County. Also omitted were miners who died while en route to or from work, as were those who had died from work-related diseases such as black lung. Finally and most significantly, miners who had been killed during the unionization drives of the 1930s and 1970s were excluded from consideration as well.

The first two exclusions reflected practical limitations. The club could not afford to launch an areawide search for all of Harlan's commuting miners. Nor could it afford to purchase plaques on which to engrave the thousands of local black-lung victims, even if it had been feasible to identify black-lung victims, whose deaths may have been officially attributed to a number of respiratory diseases. To include those who died in the "mine wars" and Brookside strike, however, introduced a different set of practical and political concerns. Including these men would not have added significantly to the time or money spent on the memorial, but the political expense of honoring unionization fatalities was potentially astronomical. First, of course, there were the politically tricky definitional questions. If the group included pro-union activists on the memorial, should it also include the anti-union company casualties? After all, these men were company employees. But could they really be considered miners? Then, the ultimate question remained: What sort of backlash could the club expect from anti-union community members? Unable to resolve such questions and unwilling to confront deep anti-union sentiments in the county, the club elected to ignore unionization casualties.

This was just one strategy by which the chapter attempted to minimize the controversy and conflict engendered by the Miners Memorial. The club's refusal to discuss the issue of mine safety, to attribute blame for mine accidents, to offer credit for recent safety improvements, to explain the causes of workplace accidents, or to recommend steps to improve mine safety also represented an attempt to minimize the conflict caused by the memorial. Club president Randy Head, who did most of the public speaking on the memorial, consistently emphasized the project's simple, apolitical goal of paying tribute to the *individuals* who had died in the mines.

೩

The construction of such a monument required money, a commodity that was in rather short supply in Harlan County during this period. The county fiscal court donated $500 to the memorial, about 5 percent of its projected cost. The rest had to be raised by the Jaycees themselves. The most enthusiastic support for the project came from the community members who could least afford to donate to it, so the Jaycess were forced to solicit funds from the lukewarm to hostile sectors of society: business owners, coal operators, and middle-class professionals. Successful fund-raising depended upon the club's success in assuring potential donors that the memorial would meet their political and aesthetic criteria—not an easy task. It called for nonthreatening, socially adept fund-raisers. Only women were assigned to this task. I was one of them.

In some cases, the club's pledge that the Miners Memorial design, its execution, and its dedication would withstand the community's apolitical litmus test met with skepticism. One local bank president, for example, said that he would consider donating money only *after* he inspected the final product. The skepticism and hesitation, encountered by the fund-raising committee, stood in stark contrast to the enthusiastic expressions of support that I had received during my interviews with miners. Fortunately, my participation in the fund-raising efforts enabled me to correct my initial, erroneous conclusion that the memorial enjoyed wide community support.

After the first day of fund-raising, club members detected a pattern to their rejections, which they quickly shared with one another. Businesses that were owned by one prominent coal operator, his family, and his political allies unilaterally refused to donate to the project, while others lent at least minimal support. Having tentatively identified the primary source of opposition, teams began to concentrate their funding requests upon the political and economic rivals of the memorial's opponent. These included businesses that competed directly with this operator's holdings, as well as political patrons who sponsored candidates running against his in races for locally important offices, such as magistrate, school board member, sheriff, and county judge executive. While visiting these businesses, Jaycee fund-raisers discreetly informed these owners of their rival's lack of support. They circulated this information via the route of "small talk," often among themselves, on the difficulties of fund-raising during a recession. Times were so hard, they would complain to one another, that Bank A or Store B could not spare a single cent for the memorial. They assumed that no one who overheard them would actually take their remarks literally. That is, not many local business owners would believe that a prosperous bank's refusal to offer token support to the memorial was motivated entirely by economic considerations.

Upon completion of the first day of "targeted" fund-raising, I asked the local fund-raisers to explain this coal operator's opposition to the memorial. Had he not been convinced of the memorial's apolitical purpose? Did he oppose it because, regardless of its intent, the memorial would inevitably call attention to the industry's poor safety record? These explanations, they agreed, were plausible. But they saw the dispute primarily as a reflection of local political dynamics and individual personality flaws. The whole conflict demonstrated, to them, that the members of the local elite were petty and egocentric tyrants who suffered from status anxiety and could not bear to have "common folks," like coal miners, usurping their control over their court house "turf."

In the eyes of local memorial fund-raisers, the Harlan Miners Memorial Project presented a grassroots challenge to the elitist political status quo. In that sense, the project constituted a counterhegemonic discourse and practice, though not a strictly class-based one. In almost every facet, the memorial project ran counter to the nepotistic, smoke-filled room, deal-making "politics as usual" that has characterized Harlan County at least since 1920 (see, for instance, Hevener 1978; Titler n.d.; Scott 1988). The Jaycees had, at least temporarily, opened up a democratic "free space" (Evans and Boyte 1986) in Harlan County. They sought approval for the memorial concept from the public, not from the court house "gang" or coal operators. The design was chosen from within the community and without the approval of business leaders or elected officials. The memorial plaques not only incorporated input from miners' families, but success in creating the memorial required miners' active participation. Even more importantly, as local analysts astutely pointed out, this memorial staked a claim to a space in the symbolic and political center of town for the purpose of paying homage to common, working people. Its ritual and symbolic elevation of workers to the same level as war heroes and political leaders further added to its counterhegemonic impetus (see also Wagner-Pacifici and Schwartz 1991, 408).

In addition, the Harlan Miners Memorial threatened to perpetuate this politically counterhegemonic discourse indefinitely, or at least until the coal industry either shut down or dramatically improved workplace safety. Barring these two eventualities, memorializers would periodically add to the fatality list. What would be the cumulative political impact of such a ritual exercise? How would people react when there was no more space left for the ever-expanding list of names—would townspeople build a new monument? These questions remain unanswered today, as they were in 1986. Yet it seems obvious that this monument's representation of *ongoing events* has enhanced its symbolic and interpretive plasticity and, possibly, added to its counterhegemonic potential. So, while this would not be the first memorial to provide an arena for future symbolic reinterpretation and political protest (see, for example, Inglis 1987; Sandage 1993; Schwartz 1982), the design's demand for revisitation enhanced its counterhegemonic possibilities inasmuch as it offered memorializers additional discursive opportunities in a central, symbolically important public space.

❧

When the Jaycees club voted to construct the Harlan memorial in September 1985, members selected Memorial Day weekend of the following year as the target for completion of the monument. Inasmuch as Memorial Day is a national holiday set aside for remembering the dead, it clearly offered the club a symbolically appropriate choice. But pragmatic considerations were at work here as well, for the Memorial Day holiday weekend has traditionally provided an opportunity for Appalachian out-migrants to return home to visit, decorate family graves, and contribute to the maintenance of family-owned cemeteries. Although the dedication date best served both the symbolic and the pragmatic demands of the occasion, the club eventually came to regret its ambitious deadline.

Unable to raise sufficient funds, the project participants consistently searched for ways to "cut corners" on the design construction. Instead of requesting money, fund-raising teams accepted donations of construction materials, tools, labor, and landscaping supplies—some of which may have been of questionable quality. The club's fund-raising effort fell short by almost half the required amount, forcing the chapter to secure a loan from a local bank— one that was not associated with the coal operator who opposed the monument, of course. Unfortunately, by then the group's relationship with the plaque company had deteriorated due to disputes over payments, delivery schedules, spelling errors, and the quality of the engravers' work.

As the Memorial Day deadline approached, the Jaycees began to devote every evening and weekend to the project. The club had publicized the memorial dedication date and contacted media months in advance, so the ceremony date could not be easily changed. Local and regional reporters had already committed to covering the dedication; TV news teams, from as far away as Knoxville, Tennessee, were scheduled to arrive. And, more importantly, high-ranking government officials had already accepted the group's invitation to speak at the ceremony. As club members worked diligently to make this deadline, unexpected spring showers delayed the construction process for several days. Finally, a local funeral home lent the group a tent. The construction team could then pour the concrete foundation so that work could proceed.

During the week of the dedication ceremony, some of the men took "sick days" from their jobs in order to complete the monument's construction. Three of them, including Randy Head, were employed by the coal operator who opposed the project. Each had managed the conflict with their employer by never discussing the memorial during work or in the boss's company. Hitherto, they had kept their "work lives" and "civic lives" neatly separated. But when they "skipped" work for the monument, they produced a potentially volatile mixture of work and civic lives—one that provided the topic of much speculation. What would happen if they got caught? Was it ethical to lie to one's boss, even in pursuit of such a noble cause? Was it wise to risk being fired in such an uncertain economic climate? These questions animated community gossip on Monday and Tuesday. By Wednesday, the group's worst fears had been realized. While driving through town, the coal operator had spotted his employees at work on the memorial and radioed an inquiry to his office staff. Upon learning that they had "called in sick," he was said to have replied, "I thought so! Those sons of bitches are in town working on that damned memorial." For two days, the men's fate provided the topic of community speculation until, finally, as a relief to everyone involved, the men accepted a dock in pay.

Offsetting this good news, however, was the bad news that the plaques would not arrive in time for the ceremony. As disappointing as this was, the club could not afford to indulge in self-pity just two days before the ceremony. While the men continued construction, a few of the women turned their energies to the production of a program for the ceremony that would include, in addition to the ceremonial agenda and acknowledgments, a description of the monument, an explanation for the missing plaques, and a complete list of the thirteen hundred miners whose names would eventually appear on the monument.

Having primarily occupied myself with research and fundraising efforts, I had not taken part in the planning of the Dedication Day activities. I had remained ignorant of the details until the night before the ceremony, when I helped to type and copy the programs. Upon learning that no United Mine Workers representatives had been invited to the ceremony, I asked for an explanation. Club members furtively whispered that it would "too risky" to include union officials in the ceremony because the "word around town" had been that certain Jaycees members would find themselves unemployed if even *one* United Mine Workers' official "set foot on the speakers' platform." Most people believed this unverified rumor, which sufficed to keep the planning committee "in line." The bad economic climate had heightened the atmosphere of fear surrounding the monument enough so that certain boundaries to the commemoration process—particularly the taboo against publicly discussing the miners' union—were not open for challenge. The freedom of the memorial "free space" terrain was limited and constrained, as the Dedication Day discourse reveals.

&

On Saturday, 31 May 1986, the Jaycees arrived early to the court house square to prepare the site for the arrival of onlookers and dignitaries. Much to everyone's surprise, "bums" were discovered sleeping on the benches by the memorial. The men escorted them away, just before the most important visiting dignitary, U.S. Senator Wendell Ford, arrived to the speakers' platform. As the crowd gathered, a woman began to distribute handwritten, mimeographed flyers that cited coal operator greed as the cause of dangerous working conditions. A local business man and Jaycees member snatched the flyers from the woman's hand, depositing them in a secure trash bin. I never actually saw the flyers, but I could see the tension and anxiety in club members' faces as they attempted to control the discursive direction of the day. There could be no uninvited speakers, no unplanned commentary, no unseemly guests, and, most importantly, no reference to the conflict that permeated this monument or the events it embodied.

The Harlan community band provided the musical program for the day, a mixture of patriotic anthems and popular tunes. Assembled on the speakers' platform were Jaycees President Randy Head, Jaycees Vice President Karen Ayres (Phillips), Kentucky State Senator Charles Berger, U.S. Senator Wendell Ford (KY), Kentucky Department of Mines and Minerals representative Willard Stanley, Assistant Secretary of Labor for Mine Health and Safety David Zegeer, and State Representative Roger Noe. Their speeches and remarks were conciliatory and noncontroversial. The most potentially disruptive maneuver came from State Senator Charles Berger, who read a poem, which had been composed for the occasion, by well-known local union activist John Deaton. It read:

> Of the many projects in Harlan County,
> This one exceeds all others.
> What an honorable way to show respect
> For the coal miner and his brothers.
> We're proud to give thanks to those involved.

Your thoughtfulness is sure to please.
Not enough can be said toward appreciation
For the Harlan County Jaycees.

As an apolitical expression of gratitude, it confirmed, rather than challenged, the community consensus evoked by the carefully crafted dedication ceremony.

After the poetry reading, Willard Stanley from the Kentucky State Department of Mines and Minerals stepped to the podium to discuss advances in local mine safety programs. He spoke of the importance of "teamwork" in creating a safe workplace, noting, "It's a *team* effort that makes the industry work safely. It's that team effort between operators, miners, and the state that has led to improvement in the mines. It's that spirit of cooperation that has helped the number of injuries and death to drop." Strikingly absent from this "team" was the miners' union, the United Mine Workers, which many workers and industry analysts credit for improving the mine safety in the U.S. (Wallace 1987).

David Zegeer, from the Federal Mine Safety and Health Agency, continued in this vein. Pointing to a recent downward trend in mine fatalities, he credited the many parties who were instrumental in securing safer working conditions for miners. It seemed that everyone *but* the United Mine Workers had stormed the barricades to demand protection of the miners' health and safety. "Through the years around the early part of this century, 2,500 to 3,200 people a year were killed in coal mining alone. That was uncalled for; and society demanded, the people demanded something to be done. The industry demanded something to be done. And it has been done. . . . The number of mining deaths in the United States, and in Kentucky, and in Harlan County has reduced to the point where we are reaching zero." According to reports by his own agency, Zegeer's claim is, at best, optimistic. In the two years preceding his remarks, 191 men had died in coal mine accidents—102 in 1984, and 89 in 1985 (U.S. Department of Labor 1988).

Finally, U.S. Senator Wendell Ford inadvertently captured the underlying conflictual dynamic behind the monument project when he said, "Our miners go to work each day knowing the dangers they face; but they *choose* [his emphasis] to take the risk so they can care for their families, so they can work in the community they love, so they can improve the quality of life in Harlan County, and, yes, in the Commonwealth of Kentucky. This monument project *touched a nerve* [my emphasis], I believe, in this community. It set off an outpouring of their heartfelt loss into a magnificent tribute that will stand for generations to come. God, in making the mountains of eastern Kentucky, provided a very special people to preside over it." Senator Ford seems to have misspoken. He probably intended to state that the memorial had "touched the hearts" of the community, although his actual words certainly described the project just as accurately.

After the ceremony ended, miners and their relatives went back to their family holiday festivities. Visiting dignitaries were escorted to the local country club, where the Harlan County Coal Operators' Association provided them with refreshments. Everything returned to normal for the town and for weary project sponsors, who were pleased that the dedication ceremony had gone so well. They had successfully handled the "bums," the lone protester, and the missing plaques, so that, by the time the actual dedication ceremony started, few signs of conflict or disorder remained. And none were articulated. Eighteen months passed by before anyone publicly mentioned the conflict surrounding the Miners Memorial. The new Jaycees president Karen Ayres (Phillips), a woman from outside the community who had no ties to the coal industry, acknowledged that the memorial "project was one where there was no middle ground. People were either all for it or totally against the idea." She added, "I personally am proud to have been a part of the club that accomplished that" (HDE, 25 January 1988, 1).

è▲

I left Harlan in December 1986 and the name plaques still had not been installed upon the memorial. But when I visited Harlan during the summer of 1988, I found the memorial almost complete (see figure 7.2). The plaques had been inserted, and only the installation of the top finishing piece remained. But by then hardly anyone was willing to work on the monument. The Harlan chapter of the Jaycees had dissolved, ostensibly in response to a national dues rate hike that had placed the cost of participation out of the financial reach of most Harlan members. Rumor had it that the local representative of the monument company had absconded with the down payment on the memorial, that the club had defaulted on a loan from a local bank, and that threats from local coal operators prevented their employees from reinitiating the project. Many former club members continued to socialize together

FIGURE 7.2
The original Harlan Miners Memorial, as it appeared in June 1988, after the name plaques were installed but before the concrete cap and stucco finish were added by memorial designer David Harp and two Harlan County jail inmates in November 1988.

and express pride in the memorial, in spite of the difficulties. The club's last president, Karen Ayres (Phillips), witnessed the monument's popularity each time she arrived at or departed from her court house county extension office. There was always someone paying a visit to the monument, she reported.

❧

In 1991, I escorted a group of university students on a field trip to eastern Kentucky, which included a brief stop at the Harlan Miners Memorial. Steering the university van into town, I became momentarily disoriented. The monument was not there. In its place stood a large light-gray granite wall, which bore a striking resemblance to a tombstone. My initial reaction of confusion soon gave way to anger, as I hastened to the conclusion that the new monument had neither the symbolic power nor the aesthetic appeal of the original broken-cross monument.

Upon a closer and more sober inspection, I found that the new monument represented a rather interesting combination of elements from the original design and those associated with a more traditional memorial genre, as outlined by Wagner-Pacifici and

Schwartz (1991) in their analysis of the Vietnam Veterans Memorial. Although not much taller than the original, the new monument was significantly thinner and more linear in its dimensions. Its vertical alignment, along with its lighter color, clearly moved it closer to the traditional memorial genre. Equally important, the new memorial included a realistic engraving of a coal miner's face as he gazed upon the mountains of his homeland. Beneath him an inscription read, "IN HONOR OF THE HARLAN COUNTY COAL MINERS WHO SACRIFICED THEIR LIVES WHILE SUPPORTING A FAMILY AND A NATION" (see figure 7.3). A cor-

FIGURE 7.3
The new Harlan Miners Memorial, as it appeared in July 1993.

FIGURE 7.4
The new Harlan Miners' Memorial cornerstone in July 1993.

nerstone, placed in a prominent front-and-center position at the new monument, gave credit to the elite sponsors of the new memorial but included no mention of the original Jaycees effort (see figure 7.4). Finally, the new memorial's abandonment of the broken-cross shape removed the questioning reference to Christianity, thus robbing the memorial of much of its ground-breaking ambivalence. In spite of these changes, the replacement memorial retained many of the original's qualities. Most significantly, its "wall of names" remains, preserving much of the first monument's individualistic emphasis. The new monument, in addition, utilizes the original foundation, benches, and landscape design, perpetuating the welcoming, comforting, sanctuary-like ambiance of the Jaycees' memorial.

But, in the end, the monument leaves little upon which to reflect. Why did these men die? The monument answers this question in its proclamation that these coal miners sacrificed their lives in *support* of their families and country. Both are worthy causes, of course. But could we not also consider whom else their labor may have supported? Coal operators or the stockholders of absentee-owned, multinational energy corporations, perhaps? Or should we not ask what caused their deaths? Is anyone to blame? Did anyone help these men or their survivors? Can anything be done to assure that future generations will not meet a similar fate in Harlan's mines? These alternative questions lead more directly to counterhegemonic discourses, such as those articulated in earlier eras when local union activists wrote songs declaring their hatred for the capitalist system and demanding that local residents choose sides in an apparently inevitable class battle.

After the field trip, I phoned Harlan to find out what had happened to the original monument. Randy Head, Karen Ayres (Phillips), and others who had been active in the project had received no advance notice or explanation for the monument's replacement. The monument switch had occurred just weeks before my field trip, and there had been no opportunity to notify me in advance. At the time, Head and Ayres were concentrating their efforts upon locating and repossessing the remains of the original monument. They worried that the name plaques may have been destroyed or lost.[4] Their second priority was to obtain an adequate explanation for the monument's replacement. They found the Harlan County Fiscal Court's reversal on the memorial issue to be particularly curious. Five years previously, the court could afford only a symbolic show of financial support. Yet in 1991, the magistrates committed $20,000 of the taxpayers' money to erect a new memorial—twice the cost of the original and forty times the amount that they devoted to the initial effort. Why? What had changed since then? It certainly was not the economy, which, if anything, had declined further.

Three explanations for this remarkable turn of events emerged from the interviews following the monument's replacement. First, the fiscal court maintains that the original memorial, although built with the best of intentions, was flawed in its execution. Always aesthetically unappealing, its poor construction and inferior materials had caused the monument to age poorly. It had become more of an eyesore than an inspiration. What is worse, the plaque's spelling errors disturbed monument visitors. In their opinion, the miners and their community deserved a more professional monument. A second explanation poses the following scenario: The county judge executive and magistrates hoped to "cash in" on the widely appreciated monument now that the risk of alienating its powerful opponents had passed. In coming years, the original sponsors of the monument would be forgotten, while the cornerstone giving credit to the 1991 fiscal court would remain prominently displayed in front of the memorial. Finally, others proposed a more conspiratorial theory. They claimed that at least one local politician had privately pledged to replace the original monument in order to secure the financial backing of its original opponent. For the time being, at least, this latest move by the local political elite to reclaim their court house "turf" from the usurpers has been successful.

৯

Anything as complex and multivalent as the Harlan Miners Memorial can be interpreted in many ways. For example, the monument project as well as its design had important gender implications in addition to its class-based one. For one thing, the project had been almost completely male-dominated. The Jaycees president and primary symbol and sponsor of the project was a man, as was the memorial's primary opponent and its designer. And because the coal industry had been historically male-dominated, no women had been killed in underground mining accidents. By necessity, then, the monument honored men only.

Not surprisingly, the memorial project also had patriarchal overtones. The previously all-male Jaycees Club, for example, relied primarily upon a gendered division of labor to carry out its work. Women, for the most part, participated in fund-raising, landscaping, food preparation, typing, writing, and other support activities. Men, on the other hand, engaged in high-profile activities—providing interviews and posing for pictures for the media, constructing the monument, and holding all but one of the formal leadership positions.

Nevertheless, the masculine nature of the Harlan memorial project was countered by the monument's feminine sensibility, a feature it shared with the Vietnam Veterans Memorial, which it clearly resembled (Wagner-Pacifici and Schwartz 1991, 397). While the Harlan memorial's topographical situation did not permit it to be embedded into the ground as the veterans monument had been, the Harlan version nevertheless retained its horizontal lines. At six feet in height, its inverted enclaves and a passageway further intensified the embracing, womblike mien that the Vietnam monument had introduced. A visitor could, in fact, enter the passage and find him- or herself virtually enveloped within the monument. The Harlan memorial's incorporation of plants and benches into the memorial layout further amplified its open, welcoming, comforting ambience, thus transforming it from a potentially awe-inspiring spectacle into a sanctuary, or free space, for reflection and solace.

There are two points to be made here, as in the previous chapter on religion: First, by concentrating upon the class-based political implications of the memorial, I do not mean to restrict or reduce the memorial to its class-based political elements. And, second, the construction, reconstruction, and discourse surrounding the memorial—once again, like religious discourse in Harlan County —suggests a complex interchange between community- and class-based ideology in the ebb and flow of working-class resistance and acquiesence.

Finally, the memorial case surely demonstrates, as William Murphy (1990, 25–26) has pointed out, that there are many social contexts that require only the *appearance* of consensus, not its actual achievement. In looking beyond these appearances, we might locate a "complex lamination to reality in which divergent, un-sanctified ideas and practices become relegated to the 'backstage' domains of social life" (Murphy 1990, 25), where they may be rehearsed and adapted for possible frontstage delivery (see also Billings 1990, 21). In the interim, such discourses can potentially provide "hidden transcripts" (Scott 1990, xii) of resistance, regard-less of whether they are articulated as public counterhegemonic challenges. In the end, the discursive space as well as the space on the court house lawn can be best described as contested terrains (Ed-wards 1979) with considerable transformative potential.

Conclusions, Reflections, and Second Thoughts

Periodically, social scientists rediscover the truth of the old adage that finding a good question is more difficult than answering it (see Hammersley and Atkinson 1983, 33–34; Merton 1959). This study not only confirms this observation, but also demonstrates that finding an answer—or at least a simple one—is no picnic in the woods, either. This Afterword provides a self-reflexive and self-critical overview of this ethnography: the questions it sought to answer, its partial success in addressing them, and its failings and shortcomings. This Afterword is not offered as an apology, defense, or atonement for my sins—real or imagined—but, rather, as an honest reflection upon some good ethnographic work that could have been better. Obviously, in writing this, I run the risks of discrediting my work or appearing self-indulgent. Nevertheless, I persist in this enterprise with the hopes that this proves, at the very least, to be interesting reading. But more importantly I hope that this will be of some assistance to workers tending adjacent intellectual fields. I also hope that it will be illuminating to my friends in Harlan County.

As indicated in the Foreword, I started this research project with two questions in mind. First, what accounts for the contradictory image of Appalachian residents as, on the one hand, militant working-class activists and, on the other hand, passive, clannish fatalists? The short answer to this question is that it should not be phrased as an "either-or" question and that, as academics, we should be advised of the risks associated with forcing the world and its inhabitants into neat categories and bipolar oppositions, particularly ones as one-dimensional and indefensible as the aforementioned examples. Nevertheless, some generalization and categorization is necessary if we are to participate and communicate in a coherent academic discipline. And at least my initial question concerning stereotypical oppositions does suggest some better ones: What can be said about the political ideology of Harlan miners and what accounts for the shifts in action, ideology, and consciousness among this group of social actors—people who obviously cannot be characterized as essentially passive or militant?

Much of this ethnography centers around the elucidation of the factors that help us to understand key transitions in the protest and union activity of Harlan County miners from 1920 to 1986. These include (1) changes in the organization of work and mechanization of mining that had influenced workers' experiences, identities, and relationships with management; (2) transformation of the characteristics and material requirements of coal production; (3) the dynamic relationship of the coal industry to other industries (particularly transport and alternative energy industries); (4) complex interactions between the regional, national, and global economic and political structures; (5) transitions in the structure of coal industry ownership; (6) the dynamic internal political turmoil of the UMW as well as its leadership's changing relationship to coal operators and government leaders; and (7) shifts in federal government policy toward labor unions and industrial regulation.

All of these factors helped make sense of a generational shift in local attitudes toward labor unions, a shift that is embodied and symbolized by Ernie Norton and his brother-in-law Bobby Carson. Ernie's memories of the Depression, of poverty and hunger, and of his father's stories of violent "gun thugs" and the authoritarian company-town system informed his loyalty to the UMW, a loyalty that he held in spite of the union's shortcomings and corruption. Bobby, on the other hand, came of age in an era when memories of the Depression had faded and the UMW's reputation had been tainted by corruption, murder, internal division, and wildcat strikes.

In "The Memory of Miners and the Conscience of Capital," Richard Couto (1993) argues that miners and their unions have drawn upon both personal and institutional "memory" in a series of recent struggles against an amoral, "amnestic" capitalistic system. In this system where profit motive ranks higher than community responsibility and the present is more important than the past, multinational corporations have a powerful incentive to escape contractual obligations that oblige them to pay for community costs or past social injustices. For example, throughout the 1980s, multinational energy corporations sought to scrap the miners' pension and health-care funds that had been established by their predecessors in UMW contract negotiations in 1950 and 1974.

Certainly my interviews with Harlan County's retired miners lend credence to Couto's argument. In them, miners drew upon these memories as they observed a recent increase in the level of greed among coal operators and complained about absentee ownership and outsider control: They were particularly suspicious and resentful of the coal industry's increasing domination by oil-controlled multinational corporations: And they also wondered why local Harlan County businessmen did not support the UMW more openly, since the UMW had contributed much financial well-being and stability to the community. Like coal operators, they believed free-enterprise capitalism to be a fair economic system, at least in theory. They also urged cooperation with their employers to increase production and profit. But, unlike the coal operators, miners recognized labor as the source of profit; they remembered decades of hard work and exploitation; and they continued to emphasize management's *debt* to their employees and to the communities in which they operated. In the miners' view, profit was only a necessary prerequisite to the companies' more important goal: providing for the well-being of their workers and communities. Profit was, in other words, the means to an end, not the end itself. This view stands in marked contrast to the view of most eastern Kentucky coal operators, who remind us, as did Ashland Coal Vice President William Ritchie, that coal companies "go into business for one reason . . . to make money. Jobs are a by-product of the original intent" (as quoted in Seltzer 1986, 62–63).

Much of this ethnography attempts to locate the sources and limitations of this "communitarian" ideology. In addition to a classical Marxian emphasis on shared work experiences—particularly the craft identity, cooperation, and camaraderie of work in this dangerous, masculine occupation—this ethnography also explores the relationship between kinship, community, religion, and class identity in Harlan County. Here is where matters become more complicated, as I advance the argument that kinship, community, and religion provide material, social, and ideological support for class solidarity, counterhegemonic resistance, and political protest while, at the same time, they compete with and undermine class identity and consciousness by providing alternative sources of identity, loyalty, and codes for behavior. This is particularly evident in the personalistic and paternalistic relationships that miners have enjoyed with local coal operators and community leaders.

The second question that animated this project—whether Harlan's miners are class conscious—is also problematic, if for no other reason than that the concept of consciousness refers to a variable, shifting, ideational phenomenon that is difficult to identify, isolate, and "pin down" for description. One obviously cannot see, touch, or measure consciousness but must deduce it from observations of political, ritual, and other forms of social action, interpretations of written texts and oral histories, and so forth. And, inasmuch as consciousness varies both from person to person and across time, it becomes difficult for a social researcher to offer generalization, contextualization, and explanation.

Furthermore, as Sean Wilentz (1984, 15–16) has so deftly pointed out, this question, like the first one, may be fundamentally flawed. It is based, for instance, upon "essentialist" assumptions and the definition of class consciousness as "an all-embracing (usually revolutionary) critique of capitalist wage-labor relations, held by the mass of proletarians and expressed in all consequential matters of public and private concern." In my Foreword, I admitted to carrying such a notion with me as I entered the field to interview Harlan miners for this ethnography. It took me a while to learn that, if I allowed myself to be "tyrannized" by such a concept, I would "short-circuit [my] attempts to understand the class perceptions that did exist" (Wilentz 1984, 16). After all, there is a very short answer to the question of whether Harlan miners are class conscious. The simple answer is no—or, at least, not many and not for long. In that sense, they are certainly no different from other American workers, who have been consistently characterized as less class conscious than their European counterparts.

Obviously, I had to find a more adequate question to pursue. In this case, I chose to explore the sort of political ideology and consciousness these miners did articulate, and to locate the material, social, and ideological factors that might account for its transformative and conservative tendencies as well as its historical ebbs and flow? I say this, not in an attempt to claim a moral or self-reflexive high ground, but rather to illustrate how much one can learn "in the field"—and, here, I define this field broadly, not just as ethnographic field research, but as in any methodological interchange between theory and data. In short, asking questions, even "bad" or poorly phrased ones, is always worthwhile when we allow them (and our theories) to be challenged and modified by our data and experiences.

The most regrettable shortcoming of this ethnography is its inattention to matters of race and ethnicity, particularly in light of the recent questioning of Corbin's (1981) claim that class unity overpowered racial and ethnic divisions in the coal towns of central Appalachia (see, for instance, Herrin 1985; Lewis 1987; Trotter 1990; Turner and Cabbell 1984) and a belated, but growing emphasis on the interpenetration of gender, race and class among feminists and other scholars. Many factors account for this myopia around matters of race and ethnicity. These include the fact that the ethnographer is a white (Anglo-Saxon, Protestant) who lived much of her life in a county with no African American residents, that she lived in an all-white enclave in Harlan County, and that she was working from a theoretical tradition that has been historically "color-blind." All of these factors contributed to my initial willingness to operate under the unfortunate, erroneous, and unrecognized assumption that one might regard white mining families as a people without race, or race-neutral bearers of working-class experience and consciousness.

Nothing could be farther from the truth. White miners, like Black ones, have a race. What is more, it did not take me long to realize that many of my friends and informants not only *had* race but were, in fact, racist. Some cautioned me against swimming in the public pool because it was frequented by African Americans, for instance. Once, upon seeing a child who apparently had one Black and one White parent, Ernie quipped, "Mixing a little cream with the coffee, I see." But most personally disturbing was the hostile glare I received from Bobby when I announced that I had to leave promptly in order to attend a Martin Luther King, Jr., Day program at the community college. His facial expression *seemed*, to me, to say, "Race traitor." But, perhaps, I misunderstood. I regret that I did not follow up questions concerning racism among Harlan miners and the relationship between race and class solidarity and division. At the time, I thought of several reasons why I should not: time and energy constraints, lack of contacts in the African American community, fear of alienating my White hosts and friends, and problems of establishing rapport in African American communities where I did not reside. In retrospect, none of them seem adequate.

While I cannot go back in time to correct this shortcoming now, I do take every opportunity to incorporate these issues in my teaching and certainly recommend that further research be done in this area. I can also point out the excellent, studies of African American miners and racial dynamics in the UMW and in Appalachian coal towns (Lewis 1987; Trotter 1990; Turner and Cabbell 1984) that can launch us on our way toward this long-overdue compensatory research. In regards to the Harlan County case, Alessandro Portelli (1991, 235–37) has documented a legacy of racial segregation, discrimination, and racially motivated violence in coal towns, most of which was submerged during the unionization struggles of the 1930s. Nevertheless, he pointed out, there were many ways in which racial segregation and racism undermined class solidarity in Harlan County. They provided local coal operators with tools in their struggle against the NMU, whose policy of racial integration and equality was used to discredit it among racist white coal miners. As Portelli and others have pointed out, then, color does matter.

The same can be said for gender, age, sexuality, and other forms of social differentiation that form the basis for inequality, exploitation, and conflict. This ethnography, because it focused upon class, offered only a glimpse of these other pertinent topics. I remain optimistic that this glimpse revealed a small sampling of the many different politically charged arenas in which social action— sometimes conflictual and sometimes cooperative—was carried out in Harlan County. And although activities within these arenas (from conflicts over snake-handling to school closures and hazardous waste cleanup to the Miners Memorial project) can teach us a lot about the nature and limitations of class consciousness in Harlan County, the meaning of these actions can not be reduced to questions of class conflict and identity.

ॐ

The process of writing this book has taken much longer than I, or my friends in Harlan County, ever anticipated. (Not to mention my long-suffering family.) It has spanned nearly a decade, from inception of the research to the dissertation to its publication as a book. During that time, all sorts of things have happened. Some of the people I knew in Harlan have died. Some married, some divorced, some moved away, and some had children. One of my dearest Harlan friends had a particularly dynamic decade: she married, divorced, moved to another town, remarried, and had two children. Like many of my friends, I left Harlan as well. And I, too, married, had a child, and lost people dear to me—most notably my paternal grandparents, Opal and Mallie Scott. In 1990, I returned home to Kentucky, with my husband and daughter; in order to assume a position on the faculty of the sociology department at the University of Kentucky.

Aside from becoming a parent, the process of researching, writing, and trying to publish this book has taught me more about myself and the world around me, than any other single experience. I have already discussed many of the lessons that these eighteen months in Harlan taught me. In the text itself, I highlighted this process by emphasizing my initial naivete, and by using humor and irony to point out potential pitfalls in even the most thoughtful, sympathetic, theoretically informed studies of the human condition. "What?," I complained. "Harlan Countians know as little about their family history and genealogy as I do?" Then, at a displaced miners' workshop, I noted my mistake in assuming that a battery of difficult exams would intimidate these men or send them into a tailspin of self-doubt, self-blame, and felt powerlessness. On the contrary, they remained quite capable of, at least temporarily, opening up a "free space" on the elite-dominated agenda. For a moment, at least, they took the floor and eloquently articulated their own critical, counterhegemonic position. My participation in the Harlan Miners Memorial Project taught me similar lessons about the potential for independent thought, public protest, and resistance among Harlan's working people; at the same time, it ultimately illustrated the strength of the opposition and constraints against them.

In the course of these descriptions, I have found geographic metaphors, like "free space" (Evans and Boyte 1986; see also Couto 1993), "contested terrain" (Edwards 1979), "took the floor," and "court house turf," to be useful. They call up almost military images of "territorial" struggles for control, resources, decision making, work conditions, use of time and labor, and other material factors. But these material struggles have a symbolic dimension as well. From the movement to democratize the UMW to the struggle to erect a miners monument and from the Small Branch debate over snake-handling to my informants' attempts to influence this book, much of the conflict chronicled here has been a cultural or discursive conflict.

As a neo-Marxian who has been influenced by feminist, poststructuralist, and postmodern thought, I have tried to argue against the false separation of these two facets of struggle and, instead, represent them in a dialectical and dialogical unity. This difficult task has been further complicated by my desire to make this text accessible to the nonacademic public, most notably my friends in Harlan, my family, neighbors, and students. It is more than a desire, really, it is a political commitment. Since my earliest undergraduate days, I have found academic writing to be unnecessarily elitist and antidemocratic.[1] Yet just as it took the experience of watching the film *Matewan* to make me understand the anxiety and alienation that my Harlan friends may feel as they read this book, it took the experience of writing and finding a willing and suitable publisher to make me aware of my own constraints and limitations, some personal and some structural. The most disheartening lesson I learned was that, as important as the opinions and feedback of Harlan Countians may have been to me, they were never as important as the ones expressed by my professors, colleagues, reviewers, and editors. Obviously, I respect these professionals for their knowledge, command of language, social position, and so forth. But, it would be dishonest not to point out that power—not friendship or respect—had the final word. Those who could most directly affect my career, were accorded more influence over the final product of this ethnography than my Harlan friends were. So, while it may be true that an ethnography is the product of multiple authors (see also Michael Frisch [1990] on "shared authority"), my experience suggests that all authors are not created equal. Some are more equal than others, as the saying goes.

In retrospect, I see some parallels between my position and experience in writing this book and the position and experiences of the Jaycees members who constructed the Miners Memorial. Both projects took more time, and ultimately cost us more, than we anticipated. In each case, we had something to say and had to claim a "free space" in which to say it. Some people supported us in our endeavors; others opposed us. We struggled, negotiated, and debated with both our opponents and ourselves. We alternatively shouted out and stayed silent, resisted and acquiesced. We often censored ourselves and engaged in impression management. And, in the end, we all compromised. If nothing else, we certainly learned a lot. In my view, both projects, this ethnography and the Miners Memorial, were worth the struggle. I hope my Harlan friends think so, too. But, if they do not, I can certainly respect their position. For, if Harlan Countians have taught me anything, it must be that "there are two sides to everything."

NOTES

FOREWORD

1. This is not to say that previous ethnographies of noncoal communities have ignored class struggle and or other forms of political conflict (see, for instance, Beaver 1986; Brown 1988; Bryant 1981; Foster 1988) or that studies of coal towns have failed to discuss religion and kinship (see, for instance, Corbin 1981). It is simply to say that the structural and ideological linkages between class, community, kinship, and religion have not constituted the primary focus of these works.

2. The inclusion of reproduction here is an important modification of the classical Marxian framework, intended to highlight the importance of nonwaged ("women's") work in the capitalist economy (see Barrett 1980 for a fuller discussion of this issue; also Chodorow 1978; Fraser 1989). While it is my hope that the depiction of women and theoretical recognition of gender in this ethnography compares favorably to other studies of Appalachian coal miners (see, for instance, Corbin 1981; Eller 1982; Lewis 1987; Shifflett 1991), I must emphasize that I did not initially make gender an explicit focus of this research.

3. These protective measures were not afforded to public figures whose words and deeds are a matter of common knowledge in Harlan County, with the exception of the political ads cited in Chapter 4.

CHAPTER 1

1. Appalachian tenancy and landlessness seem to have been more common than previously thought, as increasing numbers of historical researchers have called the region's preindustrial egalitarian image into question (see, for instance, Blee and Billings 1991; Dunaway 1993; Pudup 1986; Pudup, Billings, and Waller forthcoming).

2. Clarence's cousin signed a Kentucky "broad form deed," an arrangement that favored the mineral owner's rights over those of the surface owner. Luckily for him, early mining operations apparently never resulted in a major loss of property or livelihood to that line of the Brown family. Later, however, from the 1960s on, the "broad form deed" was to become a political bone of contention in eastern Kentucky as surface owners found themselves increasingly inconvenienced and victimized by mineral owners and leasees, particularly by strip mining. In 1988, a grassroots community organization called Kentuckians for the Common-

wealth led a successful statewide constitutional amendment campaign that prohibited strip mining without the permission of the landowner under "broad form" mineral deeds. Harlan Countians played a central role in this and several other political movements throughout the 1980s (see also chapter 3).

3. Their assessment, while broadly shared, was not unanimous. As a counterexample, see Crandall Shifflett's (1991) study of Stonega, Virginia, in which he argues that coal town residents preferred coal camps to the social isolation of their Appalachian farms (45–61). Obviously, there were pros and cons to coal camp life. And an interviewee's accentuation of one side over the other depends upon several factors, including her or his experiences in the coal camps as well as subsequent life events, general preferences and assessment, and political orientation. The community's past and its collective reconstruction of its history are at issue as well. Finally, the interviewer's research project, questions and probes, political orientation, and biases probably also play an important role. In sum, such memories are constructed and reconstructed through a complex series of social interactions, in which time and audience play a central role (see also Borland 1991; Frisch 1990; Portelli 1991; Stacey 1991).

4. At the time of these interviews, Joe Phipps was the president of the UMW District 19.

5. Working under the piece-rate system, families had a strong incentive to send their sons into the mines as soon as possible. Although there were laws prohibiting the employment of children, many parents lied about their sons' ages. Companies, as a rule, took them at their word.

6. Historian Crandall Shifflett (1991) also notes high rates of migration among newly proletarianized Appalachian workers (20–26), although his account emphasizes the importance of traditional cultural and social factors—the mountaineers' search for their "stable ideal" of a "kinship-based society in a communal setting" (11), to be exact—over the political economy of industrial coal mining.

7. This figure was computed by the Harlan Jaycees during the Harlan Miners Memorial Project, which constitutes the focus of Chapter 7. It was based upon their research of local health department death certificates, coal company fatality records, and a survey of Harlan County residents in 1985–86.

CHAPTER 2

1. These anecdotes are not exceptional but symptomatic of the problems that many Appalachian out-migrants have suffered (Philliber and McCoy 1981). In Cincinnati, a very popular destination for eastern Kentucky out-migrants during the 1950s and 1960s, the city council

adopted a human rights ordinance outlawing discimination in housing, employment, or public accommodations on the basis of Appalachian origin. This passed in November 1992 as part of a broader human rights measure extending protection to gays and lesbians. (For a discussion of this and other issues relating to the minority status of Appalachians, see the *Lexington Herald-Leader,* 20 February 1994 1, A16.)

CHAPTER 3

1.   Among the miners he has interviewed, Michael Yarrow (in progress) notes a similar unwillingness to discuss work with nonminers, particularly women. He goes on to say that miners' wives frequently participate in maintaining their ignorance about underground mine conditions in order to avoid worrying about their husbands' safety.

CHAPTER 4

1.   The practice of organizing a complex reality into a simplified bipolar opposition, privileging one end of the continuum over the other, and positing an evolutionary force pushing society/people toward the valued pole is a common feature of Western philosophical discourse, at least since the Enlightenment. Cressey is cited here primarily because he was writing specifically about Harlan County—*not* because he was unusually simplistic or dichotomous. If anything, his line of reasoning has been well accepted among Western scholars.

2.   Beaver (1986, 73–78) and Harvey (1993, 186–92) make a similar argument about the structural instability inherent in kin systems, which simultaneously value and operate on principles of extended kin reciprocity and conjugal family independence.

3.   I am alluding here to my own tendencies rather than to Marx, who more consistently recognized the sources of conflict and contradiction among industrial, rentier, and financial capitalists as well those among the proletariat (Harvey 1982).

4.   This does not set Harlan County apart from other Appalachian communities.

5.   I have used pseudononyms and removed the dates from these ads in order to protect the anonymity of those potential local leaders. While these ads are a matter of public record and these men are public indeed figures, I did not wish to single them out in a way which could prove harmful to their political careers.

6.   Once again, this does not set Harlan County apart from other Kentucky communities or the Kentucky State Legislature, several of

whose members were exposed, indicted, and convicted of bribery as the result of a 1990–91 FBI investigation.

7.   Bob Smith is a pseudonym.

CHAPTER 5

1.   There are important exceptions to this generalization. Joe Phipps and other union officials supported the proposed UMW merger with the oil workers' union, for example. And they participated in a boycott of Shell Oil Company, whose investments in South Africa supported apartheid. Also, several Harlan Countians were active in Kentuckians for the Commonwealth and other extracommunity coalitions aimed at protecting the environment, empowering local communities, restoring democracy, and achieving legislative reform (see also Fisher 1993; Gaventa et al. 1990).

2.   Michael Yarrow (1990, 49) notes a similar tendency in his interviews of central Appalachian miners, in which new hires from the 1970s have been, retrospectively, regarded as shirkers and tacitly blamed for the industry's 1980s decline. He further cites a shift in the cultural construction of masculinity from the 1970s, when the ability to "face down" one's boss was prized, to the 1980s, when hard work was valued as a sign of manliness.

CHAPTER 6

1.   It is no coincidence that most of the "sinners" who pursued this argument were also women and mothers.

2.   Although the Small Branch church had lost most of its women congregants, most county churches remained predominantly female.

3.   Their fashion and lifestyle choices symbolized their journey toward individualistic economic independence, romantic love, and sexual freedom, a journey that also included sexual danger, objectification, mindless consumerism, and the increased workload associated with combining wage employment with child care and household management (see also Hall 1986).

CHAPTER 7

1.   It might be difficult to identify the factors underlying this apparent improvement, but it seems likely that recession-inspired employee layoffs and increased mechanization in mining have played a more important role than have increased investment in safety programs or enforcement of mine safety regulations by the Reagan administration.

2. Kentucky's agricultural sector has also had comparatively high accident and death rates, sometimes surpassing those of mining. Historically, this issue has received little public attention, possibly because so many of the state's farmers are either owner-operators or non-union agricultural workers. (Increasingly, they are also non-U.S. born immigrant workers.) Over the last decade, however, agricultural health and safety have risen on the public policy and research agenda; the University of Kentucky and the state government are currently engaged in joint research projects investigating possible causes and solutions to this problem.

3. This lends credence to Ben Agger's (1991, 135–50) argument, following Marcuse (1955, 212–13), that "solidarity with the dead through memory helps restore public life" (Agger 1991, 151).

4. Later, I was informed that the original plaques had been found in the court house basement. Randy Head plans to donate them to the coal industry museum, which has been proposed as part of an economic plan to increase tourism to the county. The museum is currently under construction.

REFERENCES

BOOKS

Adler, Patricia A., and Peter Adler. 1987. *Membership Roles in Field Research*. Newbury Park, CA: Sage.

Agger, Ben. 1990. *The Decline of Discourse: Reading, Writing and Resistance in Postmodern Capitalism*. New York: Falmer Press.

Althusser, Louis. 1969. *For Marx*. Translated by B. Brews. New York: Pantheon Books.

Anderson, Robert M. 1979. *Vision of the Disinherited: The Making of American Pentecostalism*. New York: Oxford Univ. Press.

Annis, Sheldon. 1987. *God and Production in a Guatemalan Town*. Austin: Univ. of Texas Press.

Appalachian Land Ownership Task Force. 1980. *Who Owns Appalachia? Land Ownership and Its Impact*. Lexington: Univ. Press of Kentucky.

Argyle, Michael, and Benjamin Beit-Hallahmi. 1975. *The Social Psychology of Religion*. London: Routledge & Kegan Paul.

Baratz, Morton S. 1973. *The Union and the Coal Industry*. Port Washington, NY: Kennikat Press. Originally published in 1955.

Barrett, Michele. 1980. *Women's Oppression Today: Problems in Marxist Feminist Analysis*. London: New Left Books.

Batteau, Allen. 1990. *The Invention of Appalachia*. Tuscon: Univ. of Arizona Press.

Beaver, Patricia. 1986. *Rural Community in the Appalachian South*. Lexington: Univ. Press of Kentucky.

Bluestone, Barry, and Bennett Harrison. 1982. *The Deindustrialization of America: Plant Closings, Community Abandonment and the Dismantling of Basic Industry*. New York: Basic Books.

Braithwaite, John. 1985. *To Punish or Persuade: Enforcement of Coal Mine Safety*. New York: State Univ. of New York Press.

Bruce, Dicksen D., Jr. 1974. *And They All Sang Hallelujah: Plain Folk Camp Meeting Religion, 1800–45*. Knoxville: Univ. of Tennessee Press.

Bryant, F. Carlene. 1981. *We're All Kin: A Cultural Study of a Mountain Neighborhood*. Knoxville: Univ. of Tennessee Press.

Brown, James S. 1988. *Beech Creek: A Study of a Kentucky Neighborhood*. Berea, KY: Berea College Press. Originally published in 1950.

Burawoy, Michael. 1991. *Ethnography Unbound: Power and Resistance in the Modern Metropolis*. Berkeley: Univ. of California Press.

Calhoun, Craig. 1982. *The Question of Class Struggle: The Social Foundations of Popular Radicalism during the Industrial Revolution.* Chicago: Univ. of Chicago Press.

Caudill, Harry. 1962. *Night Comes to the Cumberlands: A Biography of a Depressed Area.* Baltimore: Little, Brown.

Caudill, Harry. 1983. *Theirs Be the Power: The Moguls of Eastern Kentucky.* Urbana: Univ. of Illinois Press.

Chandler, Betsy. 1987. *How Are Kentucky's Children Stacking Up? A County by County Analysis.* Frankfort, KY: Kentucky Youth Advocates.

Chodorow, Nancy. 1978. *The Reproduction of Mothering.* Berkeley: Univ. of California Press.

Clark, Paul F. 1981. *The Miners' Fight for Democracy: Arnold Miller and the Reform of the United Mine Workers.* Ithaca, NY: Cornell Univ. Press.

Clifford, James, and George Marcus, eds. 1986. *Writing Culture: The Poetics and Politics of Ethnography.* Berkeley: Univ. of California Press.

Coleman, McAlister. 1943. *Men and Coal.* New York: Farrar & Rinehart.

Corbin, David. 1981. *Life, Work and Rebellion in the Coal Fields: The Southern West Virginia Miners, 1880–1922.* Urbana: Univ. of Illinois Press.

Deaton, John, Jr. 1978. *Factual Poems.* Published by the author.

Dieter, Melvin. 1980. *Holiness Revival of the Nineteenth Century.* New Princeton, NJ: Scarecrow Press.

Dix, Keith. 1988. *What's a Coal Miner to Do? The Mechanization of Coal Mining.* Pittsburgh: Univ. of Pittsburgh Press.

Dorgan, Howard. 1987. *Giving Glory to God in Appalachia: Worship Practices of Six Baptist Subdenominations.* Knoxville: Univ. of Tennessee Press.

Dreiser, Theodore. 1932. *Harlan County Miners Speak.* New York: Da Capo Press.

Dunn, Durwood. 1988. *Cades Cove: The Life and Death of a Southern Appalachian Community, 1818–1937.* Knoxville: Univ. of Tennessee Press.

Durkheim, Emile. 1965. *The Elementary Forms of Religious Life.* J. W. Swain Translated by. New York: Free Press.

Edwards, Richard. 1979. *Contested Terrain.* New York: Basic Books.

Egerton, John. 1983. *Generations: An American Family.* Lexington: Univ. Press of Kentucky.

Eller, Ronald D. 1982. *Miners, Millhands, and Mountaineers: Industrialization of the Appalachian South, 1880–1930.* Knoxville: Univ. of Tennessee Press.

Evans, Sara M., and Harry Boyte. 1986. *Free Spaces: The Sources of Democratic Change in America.* New York: Harper & Row.

Ewen, Lynda Ann. 1979. *Which Side Are You On? The Brookside Mine Strike in Harlan County, Kentucky, 1973–74.* Chicago: Vanguard Books.

Fantasia, Rick. 1988. *Cultures of Solidarity: Consciousness, Action, and Contemporary American Workers.* Berkeley: Univ. of California Press.

Fisher, Steve. 1993. *Fighting Back in Appalachia.* Philadelphia: Temple Univ. Press.

Forester, W. D. 1986. *Harlan County The Turbulent Thirties.* Publishing house unknown.

Foster, Stephen. 1988. *The Past Is Another Country: Representation, Historical Consciousness and Resistance in the Blue Ridge.* Berkeley: Univ. of California Press.

Fraser, Nancy. 1989. *Unruly Practices: Power, Discourse and Gender in Contemporary Social Theory.* Minneapolis: Univ. of Minnesota Press.

Frisch, Michael, ed. 1990. *A Shared Authority: Essays on the Craft and Meaning of Oral and Public History.* Albany: State Univ. of New York Press.

Garland, Jim. 1983. *Welcome the Traveller Home.* Lexington: Univ. Press of Kentucky.

Gaventa, John. 1980. *Power and Powerlessness: Quiescence and Rebellion in an Appalachian Valley.* Urbana: Univ. of Illinois Press.

Gaventa, John, Barbara Ellen Smith, and Alex Willingham, eds. 1990. *Communities in Economic Crisis: Appalachia and the South.* Philadelphia: Temple Univ. Press.

Genovese, Eugene. 1974. *Roll, Jordan, Roll: The World the Slaves Made.* New York: Random House.

Gerstle, Gary. 1989. *Working-Class Americanism: The Politics of Labor in a Textile City, 1914–1960.* New York: Cambridge Univ. Press.

Goffman, Ervin. 1959. *The Presentation of Self in Everyday Life.* Garden City, NY: Doubleday.

Gouldner, Alvin W. 1970. *The Coming Crisis of Western Sociology,* New York: Avon.

Gramsci, Antonio. 1971. *Selections from the Prison Notebooks.* Edited and translated by Q. Hoare and G. N. Smith. New York: International Universities.

Green, Archie. 1972. *Only a Miner: Studies in Coal Miners.* Urbana: Univ. of Illinois Press.

Greenhouse, Carol J. 1986. *Praying for Justice: Faith, Order and Community in an American Town.* Ithaca: Cornell Univ. Press.

Greenway, John. 1953. *American Folksongs of Protest.* New York: Octagon Books.

Gutman, Herbert. 1976. *Work, Culture and Society in Industrializing Society.* New York: Vintage.

Habermas, Jürgen. 1987. *The Theory of Communicative Action.* Vol. 2. Boston: Beacon Press.

Hall, Stuart, and T. Jefferson, eds. 1976. *Resistance through Rituals.* London: Hutchinson.

Halperin, Rhoda H. 1990. *The Livelihood of Kin: Making Ends Meet the Kentucky Way.* Austin: Univ. of Texas Press.

Hammersley, Martyn, and Paul Atkinson. 1983. *Ethnography Principles in Practice.* New York: Routledge.

Harvey, David. 1982. *The Limits to Capital.* Chicago: Univ. of Chicago Press.

Harvey, David L. 1993. *Potter Addition: Poverty, Family and Kinship in a Heartland Community.* New York: Aldine de Gruyter.

Hevener, John. 1978. *Which Side Are You On? The Harlan County Coal Miners, 1931–39.* Urbana Univ. of Illinois Press.

Hicks, George. 1976. *Appalachian Valley.* New York: Holt, Rinehart and Winston.

Hochschild, Arlie. 1989. *The Second Shift.* New York: Viking.

Ireland, Robert. 1977. *The County in Kentucky History.* Lexington: Univ. Press of Kentucky.

Jones, George C. 1985. *Growin' Up Hard in Harlan County.* Lexington: Univ. Press of Kentucky.

Kephart, Horace. 1913. *Our Southern Highlanders.* Knoxville: Univ. of Tennessee Press.

LaBarre, Weston. 1962. *They Shall Take Up Serpents.* New York: Schocken Books.

Lancaster, Roger N. 1988. *Thanks to God and the Revolution: Religion and Class Consciousness in the New Nicaragua.* New York: Columbia Univ. Press.

Lawless, Elaine J. 1988a. *God's Peculiar People: Women's Voices and Folk Tradition in a Pentecostal Church.* Lexington: Univ. of Kentucky Press.

Lawless, Elaine J. 1988b. *Handmaidens of the Lord: Pentecostal Women Preachers and Traditional Religion.* Philadelphia: Univ. of Pennsylvania Press.

Lerner, Gerda. 1986. *The Creation of Patriarchy.* New York: Oxford Univ. Press.

Lewis, Helen, Linda Johnson, and Donald Askins, eds. 1978. *Colonialism in Modern America: The Appalachian Case.* Boone, NC: Appalachian Consortium Press.

Lewis, Ronald L. 1987. *Black Coal Miners in America: Race, Class and Community Conflict.* Lexington: Univ. Press of Kentucky.

Lipset, Seymour. 1963. *Political Man.* Garden City, NY: Anchor Books.

Lukacs, Georg. 1971. *History and Class Consciousness: Studies in Marxist Dialectics.* Translated by R. Livingstone. Cambridge: MIT Press.

Mann, Michael. 1987. *Consciousness and Action among the Western Working Class.* 2d ed. Atlantic Heights, NJ: Humanities Press.

Marcus, George E., and Michael J. Fischer. 1986. *Anthropology as Cultural Critique: An Experimental Moment in the Human Sciences.* Chicago: Univ. of Chicago Press.

Marx, Karl, and Friedrich Engels. 1942. *German Ideology.* Translated by R. Pasqual. London: Lawrence & Wisehart.

Michrina, Barry P. 1993. *Pennsylvania Mining Families: The Search for Dignity in the Coalfields.* Lexington: Univ. Press of Kentucky.

Mills, C. Wright. 1959. *The Sociological Imagination.* London: Oxford Univ. Press.

Nash, June. 1979. *We Eat the Mines and the Mines Eat Us.* New York: Columbia Univ. Press.

Okley, Judith and Helen Callaway, eds. 1992. *Anthropology and Autobiography.* New York: Routledge.

Owsley, Frank Lawrence. 1949. *Plain Folk of the Old South.* Baton Rouge: Louisiana State Univ. Press.

Pearsall, Marion. 1959. *Little Smoky Ridge.* Tuscaloosa: Univ. of Alabama Press.

Philliber, William W., and Clyde B. McCoy. 1981. *The Invisible Minority.* Lexington: Univ. Press of Kentucky.

Pope, Liston. 1942. *Millhands and Preachers: A Study of Gastonia.* New Haven: Yale Univ. Press.

Pudup, Mary Beth, Dwight Billings, and Altina Waller, eds. forthcoming. *Mountain Life and Work: Appalachia and the Road to Capitalist Underdevelopment.* Chapel Hill: Univ. of North Carolina Press.

Rabinow, Paul. 1977. *Reflections on Fieldwork in Morocco.* Berkeley: Univ. of California Press.

Sayers, Sean. 1985. *Reality and Reason: Dialectic and the Theory of Knowledge.* Oxford: Basil Blackwell.

Scott, James C. 1990. *Domination and the Arts of Resistance: Hidden Transcripts.* New Haven: Yale Univ. Press.

Schneider, David M. 1968. *American Kinship: A Cultural Account.* Chicago: Univ. of Chicago Press.

Schwarzweller, H. K., J. S. Brown and J. J. Mangalam. 1971. *Mountain Families in Transition.* University Park: Pennsylvania State Univ. Press.

Seltzer, Curtis. 1985. *Fire in the Hole: Miners and Managers in the American Coal Industry.* Lexington: The Univ. Press of Kentucky.

Shapiro, Henry D. 1978. *Appalachia on Our Mind: The Southern Mountains and Mountaineers in the American Consciousness, 1870–1920.* Chapel Hill: Univ. of North Carolina Press.

Shifflett, Crandall A. 1991. *Coal Towns: Life, Work and Culture in Company Towns of Southern Appalachia, 1880–1960*. Knoxville: Univ. of Tennessee Press.

Sontag, Susan. 1978. *Illness As Metaphor*. New York: Farrar, Strauss & Giroux.

Stack, Carol. 1974. *All Our Kin*. New York: Harper & Row.

Stephenson, John. 1968. *Shiloh*. Lexington: Univ. Press of Kentucky.

Taussig, Michael T. 1980. *The Devil and Commodity Fetishism in South America*. Chapel Hill: Univ. of North Carolina Press.

Taylor, Paul F. 1990. *Bloody Harlan: The United Mine Workers of America in Harlan County, Kentucky, 1931–41*. New York: Univ. Press of America.

Thompson, Edward P. 1966. *The Making of the English Working Class*. New York: Vintage Books.

Titler, George. n.d. *Hell in Harlan*. Beckley, WV: BJW Printers.

Titon, Jeff. 1988. *Powerhouse for God: Speech, Chant and Song in an Appalachian Baptist Church*. Austin: Univ. of Texas Press.

Trotter, Joe William, Jr. 1990. *Coal, Class and Color: Blacks in Southern West Virginia, 1915–32*. Urbana: Univ. of Illinois Press.

Turner, William H., and Edward C. Cabbell, eds. 1984. *Blacks in Appalachia*. Lexington, KY: Univ. Press of Kentucky.

Waller, Altina L. 1988. *Feud: Hatfields, McCoys and Social Change in Appalachia, 1860–1900*. Chapel Hill: Univ. of North Carolina Press.

Weber, Max. 1976. *The Protestant Ethic and the Spirit of Capitalism*. New York: Charles Scribner's.

Weller, Jack. 1965. *Yesterday's People: Life in Contemporary Appalachia*. Lexington: Univ. Press of Kentucky.

Whisnant, David. 1983. *All That Is Native and Fine: The Politics of Culture in an American Region*. Chapel Hill: Univ. of North Carolina Press.

Wilentz, Sean. 1984. *Chants Democratic: New York City and the Rise of the American Working Class, 1788–1850*. New York: Oxford Univ. Press.

Willis, Paul E. 1977. *Learning to Labour: How Working Class Kids Get Working Class Jobs*. Westmead: Saxon House.

Wooley, Bryan, and Ford Reid. 1974. *We Be Here When the Morning Comes*. Lexington: Univ. Press of Kentucky.

UNPUBLISHED DISSERTATIONS, THESES, AND PAPERS

Beaver, Patricia D. 1976. "Symbols and Social Organization in an Appalachian Mountain Community." Doctoral dissertation. Duke Univ.

Billings, Dwight, and Kathleen Blee. 1991. "Appalachian Inequality in the Nineteenth Century: The Case of Beech Creek, Kentucky." Paper delivered at the Fourteenth Annual Appalachian Studies Conference, Berea, KY.

Blee, Kathleen M., and Dwight B. Billings. 1992. "Appalachian Feuding: A Longitudinal Case Study of Violent Disputing." Report for the Fund for Research on Dispute Resolution."

Dotson, John A. 1943. "Socio-Economic Background and Changing Education in Harlan County, Kentucky." Doctoral dissertation. George Peabody College for Teachers.

Dunaway, Wilma A. 1993. "Debunking Sacred Myths: New Research Findings About Landholding in Southern Appalachia, 1790–1900." Paper delivered at the Sixteenth Annual Appalachian Studies Conference, Johnson City, TN.

Foster, Stephen William. 1977. "Identity as Symbolic Construction." Doctoral Dissertation. Princeton Univ., Princeton, NJ.

Graves, Glenna. 1993. "In the Morning We Had Bulldog Gravy: Women in the Coal Camps of the Appalachian South." Doctoral dissertation; Univ. of Kentucky.

Kimbrough, David. 1992. "Park Saylor and the Eastern Kentucky Snake Handlers: A Religious History." Doctoral dissertation. Indiana Univ.

Maggard, Sally. 1988. "Eastern Kentucky Women on Strike: A Study of Gender, Class and Political Action in the 1970s." Doctoral dissertation. Univ. of Kentucky.

Pudup, Mary Beth. 1986. "Land Before Coal." Doctoral dissertation. Univ. of California, Berkeley.

Pudup, Mary Beth. 1988. "Appalachia and the Regional Question." Unpublished paper.

Scott, Shaunna L. 1988. "Where There is No Middle Ground: Community and Class Consciousness in Harlan County, Kentucky." Doctoral dissertation. Univ. of California, Berkeley.

Scott, Shaunna L. 1991. "You Can Put That in Your Book!: History and Reality in Harlan County, Kentucky." Meetings of the Southern American Studies Association, Williamsburg, VA.

Silver, Roy. 1991. "The Struggle Against the Poisoning of Harlan County's Dayhoit: Fighting the Good Fight." Paper presented at the American Sociological Association Meetings, Cincinnati, Ohio.

Yarrow, Michael. 1982. "How Good Strong Union Men Line It Out: Exploration of the Structure and Dynamics of Coal Miners' Class Consciousness." Doctoral dissertation, Rutgers University.

Yarrow, Michael. in progress. "Voices from the Mines: Class and Gender in the Consciousness of Mining Families Families." Book manuscript.

Yount, Kristen. 1986. "Women and Men Coal Miners: Coping with

Gender Integration Underground." Doctoral dissertation. Univ. of Colorado.

ESSAYS AND ARTICLES

Anglin, Mary K. 1992. "A Question of Loyalty: Nationalism and Regional Identity in Workers' Narratives." *Anthropology Quarterly* 65:105–16.

Anglin, Mary K. 1993. "Engendering the Struggle: Women's Labor and Traditions of Resistance in Southern Appalachia." In *Fighting Back in Appalachia: Traditions of Resistance and Change*, edited by S. L. Fisher. pp. 263–82. Philadelphia: Temple Univ. Press.

Arcury, Thomas A. 1990. "Appalachian Agricultural Diversity." *Human Ecology* 18 no. 1:105–30.

Banks, Alan. 1983–84. "Coal Miners and Firebrick Workers: The Structure of Work Relations in Two Eastern Kentucky Communities." *Appalachian Journal* 2:85–102.

Batteau, Allen. 1982a. "The Contradictions of a Kinship Community." In *Holding on to the Land and the Lord*, edited by R. Hall and C. Stack, eds. Southern Anthropological Proceedings No. 15, 25–40. Athens: Univ. of Georgia Press.

Batteau, Allen. 1982b. "Mosbys to Broomsedge: The Semantics of Class in an Appalachian Kinship System." *American Ethnologist*. 9 no. 3:445–66.

Batteau, Allen. 1983. "Rituals of Dependence in Appalachian Kentucky." In *Appalachia and America: Autonomy and Regional Dependence*, edited by A. Batteau, 142–67. Lexington: Univ. Press of Kentucky.

Bethell, Thomas, N. 1983. "Forword." In *Welcome the Traveler Home: Jim Garland's Story of the Kentucky Mountains*, edited by Julia S. Ardery, vii-xxix. Lexington: Univ. of Kentucky Press.

Billings, Dwight B. 1990. "Religion as Opposition: A Gramscian Analysis." *American Journal of Sociology* 96, no. 1:1–31.

Billings, Dwight B., Kathleen M. Blee, and Louis Swanson. 1986. "Culture, Family and Community in Preindustrial Appalachia." *Appalachian Journal* 13:154–70.

Billings, Dwight B., and Shaunna L. Scott. 1994. "Religion and Political Legitimation." *Annual Review of Sociology* 20:173–201.

Bishop, Bill. 1976. "1931: The Battle of Evarts." *Southern Exposure* 4, nos. 1–2:91–101.

Borland, Katherine. 1991. "That's Not What I Said: Interpretive Conflict in Oral Narrative Research." In *Women's Words: The Feminist Practice of Oral History*, edited by S. B. Gluck and D. Patai, 63–76. New York: Routledge.

Brown, James S. 1952. "The Conjugal Family and the Extended Family Group." *American Sociological Review* 17:297–306.

Brown, James S. 1971. "Population and Migration Changes." In *Change in Rural Appalachia: Implications for Action Programs*, edited by J. D. Photiadis and H. K. Schwarzwellar, pp. 85–98. Philadelphia: Univ. of Pennsylvania Press.

Brown, James S., Harry K. Schwarzweller, and Joseph J. Mangalam. 1963. "Kentucky Mountain Migration and the Stem Family: An American Variation on a Theme by LePlay." *Rural Sociology* 28:48–69.

Bubka, Tony. 1970. "The Harlan County Coal Strike of 1931." In *Hitting Home: The Great Depression in Town and Country*, edited by B. Sternsher, 181–99. Chicago: Quadrangle Books.

Caudill, Harry M. 1977. "Dead Laws and Dead Men: Manslaughter in a Coal Mine." *The Nation*, 23 April, 492–97.

Clifford, James. 1986. "Introduction: Partial Truths." In *Writing Culture: The Poetics and Politics of Ethnography*, edited by James Clifford and George E. Marcus, 1–26. Berkeley: Univ. of California Press.

Couto, Richard A. 1993. "The Memory of Miners and the Conscience of Capital: Coal Miners' Strikes As Free Spaces." In *Fighting Back in Appalachia: Traditions of Resistance and Change*, edited by S. Fisher, 165–94. Philadelphia: Temple Univ. Press.

Cressey, Paul Frederick. 1949. "Social Disorganization and Reorganization in Harlan County, Kentucky." *American Sociological Review* 14:389–94.

Cucchiari, Salvatore. 1990. "Between Shame and Sanctification: Patriarchy and Its Transformations in Sicilian Pentecostalism." *American Ethnologist* 17, no. 4:687–797.

Eller, Ronald D. 1979. "Land and Family: An Historical View of Preindustrial Appalachia." *Appalachian Journal* 6, no. 2:83–109.

Feine, Judith Ivy. 1990. "Snobby People and Just Plain Folks: Social Stratification and Rural, Low-Status Women." *Sociological Spectrum* 10:527–39.

Fitzpatrick, John S. 1980. "Adapting to Danger: A Participant Observation Study of an Underground Mine." *Sociology of Work and Occupations*, 7:131–58.

Foley, Douglas E. 1989. "Does the Working Class Have a Culture?" *Cultural Anthropology* 4, no. 2:137–62.

Foster, George M. 1967. "The Dyadic Contract: A Model for the Social Structure of a Mexican Village." In *Peasant Society: A Reader*, edited by J. Potter, M. Diaz, and G. Foster, 213–30. Boston: Little, Brown.

Foucault, Michel. 1982. "The Subject and Power." In *Michel Foucault Beyond Structuralism and Hermeneutics*, edited by Hubert Dreyfus and Paul Rabinow, 208–26. New York: Pantheon.

Fowler, George. 1904. "Social and Industrial Conditions in the Pocahontas Coal Field." *Engineering Magazine,* June, 383–96.

Garkovitch, Lorraine. 1982. "Kinship and Return Migration in Eastern Kentucky." *Appalachian Journal* 10, no. 1:62–70.

Gaventa, John. 1990. "From the Mountains to the *Maquiladoras:* A Case Study of Capital Flight and Its Impact on Workers." In *Communities in Economic Crisis: Appalachia and the South,* edited by J. Gaventa, B. E. Smith, and A. Willingham, 85–94. Philadelphia: Temple Univ. Press.

Gerlach, Luther P. 1974. "Pentecostalism: Revolution or Counter-Revolution." In *Religious Movements in Contemporary America,* edited by I. L. Zaretsky, 669–700. Princeton, NJ: Princeton Univ. Press.

Gerrard, Nathan L. 1970. "Churches of the Stationary Poor." In *Change in Rural Appalachia: Implications for Action Programs,* edited by J. Photiadis and H. Scharzwellar, 99–114. Philadelphia: Univ. of Pennsylvania Press.

Gill, Lesley. 1990. "Like a Veil to Cover Them: Women and the Pentecostal Movement in La Paz." *American Ethnologist* 17, no. 4:708–21.

Greenhouse, Carol J. 1992. "Signs of Quality: Individualism and Hierarchy in American Culture." *American Ethnologist* 19, no. 2:233–54.

Hall, Jacqueline Dowd. 1986. "Disorderly Women: Gender and Labor Militancy in the Appalachian South." *Journal of American History* 73, no. 2:354–82.

Hastrup, Kirsten. 1992. "Writing Ethnography: State of the Art." In *Anthropology and Autobiography,* edited by Judith Okley and Helen Callaway, 116–33. New York: Routledge.

Herrin, Dean. 1985. "The Impact of the Company Town on Traditional Life." *Proceedings of the Eighth Annual Appalachian Studies Conference,* 166–74. Boone, NC: Appalachian Consortium Press.

Holt, John B. 1940. "Holiness Religion: Culture Shock and Reorganization." *American Sociological Review* 5, no. 5:740–47.

Hopkins, Nicholas S. 1986. "Class Consciousness and Political Action in Testour." *Dialectical Anthropology* 11, no. 1:73–92.

Inglis, Ken. 1987. "Men, Women and War Memorials: Anzac Australia." *Daedalus* 116, no. 4:35–59.

Kane, Steven M. 1974. "Holy Ghost People: The Snake Handlers of Southern Appalachia." *Appalachian Journal* 1, no. 3:252–62.

Kerr, Clark, and Abraham Siegal. 1954. "The Inter-Industry Propensity to Strike: An International Compass." In *Industrial Conflict,* edited by A. Kornhauser, R. Dubin and A. M. Ross. 189–212. New York: McGraw-Hill.

Lears, T. J. Jackson. 1985. "The Concept of Cultural Hegemony: Problems and Possibilities." *American Historical Review* 90:567–93.

Lewis, Helen, Sue Koback, and Linda Johnson. 1978. "Family, Religion and Colonialism." In *Colonialism in Modern America: The Appala-*

chian Case, edited by H. Lewis, L. Johnson and D. Askins, 15–26. Boone, NC: Appalachian Consortium Press.

Maggard, Sally Ward. 1983–84. "Cultural Hegemony: The News Media and Appalachia." *Appalachian Journal* 11, nos. 1–2:67–83.

Maggard, Sally Ward. 1985. "Class and Gender: New Theoretical Priorities in Appalachian Studies." *Journal of the Appalachian Studies Association* 8:100–111.

Maggard, Sally Ward. 1990. "Gender Contested: Women's Participation in the Brookside Coal Strike." In *Women and Social Protest,* edited by G. West and R. Blumberg, 75–98. New York: Oxford Univ. Press.

Mann, Ralph. 1992. "Mountains, Land and Kin Networks: Burkes Garden, Virginia, in the 1840s and 1850s." *Journal of Southern History* 58, no. 3:411–34.

Marx, Karl. 1967. "The Holy Family." In *Writings of the Young Marx on Philosophy and Society,* edited by L. D. Easton and K. H. Guddat. Garden City, NY: Doubleday-Anchor Books.

Marx, Karl. 1975. "Introduction to a Critique of Hegel's Philosophy of Right." In *Karl Marx: Early Writings,* 243–58. New York: Vintage Books.

McCoy, Clyde B., and Virginia McCoy Watkins. 1981. "Stereotypes of Appalachian Migrants." In *The Invisible Minority: Urban Appalachians,* edited by W. Philliber, and C. McCoy, 20–34. Lexington: Univ. Press of Kentucky.

Merton, Robert K. 1959. "Introduction: Notes on Problem-Finding in Sociology." In *Sociology Today,* vol. 1, edited by R. K. Merton, L. Broom, and L. S. Cottrell, Jr., ix–xxxiv. New York: Harper & Row.

Murphy, William P. 1990. "Creating the Appearance of Consensus in Mende Political Discourse." *American Anthropologist* 92, no. 1:24–41.

Ollman, Bertell. 1987. "How to Study Class Consciousness and Why We Should." *Insurgent Sociologist* 14, no. 1:57–98.

Portelli, Alessandro. 1990. "Patterns of Paternalism in Harlan County." *Appalachian Journal* 17, no. 2:140–55.

Portelli, Alessandro. 1991. "No Neutrals There: The Cultural Class Struggle in the Harlan Miners' Strike of 1931–32." In *The Death of Luigi Trastulli and Other Stories,* 216–40. Albany: State Univ. of New York Press.

Pudup, Mary Beth. 1989. "The Boundaries of Class in Preindustrial Appalachia." *Journal of Historical Geography* 15, no. 2:139–62.

Pudup, Mary Beth. 1990a. "The Limits of Subsistence: Agriculture and Industry in Central Appalachia." *Agricultural History* 64, no. 1:61–89.

Pudup, Mary Beth. 1990b. "Women's Work in the West Virginia Economy." *West Virginia History* 49:7–10.

Pudup, Mary Beth. 1991. "Social Class and Economic Development in Southeast Kentucky, 1820–1880." In *Appalachian Frontiers: Settlement, Society and Development in the Preindustrial Era,* edited by R. D. Mitchell, 235–60. Lexington: Univ. Press of Kentucky.

Roberts, Bryan. 1968. "Protestant Groups and Coping with Urban Life in Guatamala City." *American Journal of Sociology.* 73:735–67.

Sandage, Scott A. 1993. "A Marble House Divided: The Lincoln Memorial, the Civil Rights Movement, and the Politics of Memory, 1939–63." *Journal of American History* 80, no. 1:135–67.

Schockel, B. H. 1916. "Changing Conditions in the Kentucky Mountains." *Scientific Monthly* 111, no. 8:105–31.

Schwarzweller, Harry K., and James S. Brown. 1967. "Social Class Origins, Rural Urban Migration, and Economic Life Chances: A Case Study." *Rural Sociology* 32:5–19.

Schwartz, Barry. 1982. "The Social Context of Commemoration: A Study in Collective Memory." *Social Forces* 61, no. 2:374–402.

Scott, Shaunna L. 1993. "Gone Away from God: Economic Transformation and Religious Discourse during a Pentecostal Revival." *Journal of the Appalachian Studies Association* 5:100–09.

Scott, Shaunna L. 1994. "They Don't Have to Live by the Old Traditions: Saintly Men, Sinner Women and an Appalachian Pentecostal Revival." *American Ethnologist* 21, no. 2:227–44.

Sovine, Melanie. 1979. "On the Study of Religion in Appalachia: A Review/Essay." *Appalachian Journal* 6:239–44.

Stacey, Judith. 1991. "Can There Be a Feminist Ethnography?" In *Women's Words: The Feminist Practice of Oral History,* edited by S. Gluck and D. Patai, 11–20. New York: Routledge.

Steinberg, Marc W. 1991. "The Re-Making of the English Working Class?" *Theory and Society* 20:173–97.

Stekert, Ellen. 1963. "The Snake-Handling Cult of Harlan County, Kentucky." *Southern Folklore Quarterly* 27:316–22.

Tickamyer, Ann, and Cecil Tickamyer. 1991. "Gender, Family Structure and Poverty in Central Appalachia." In *Appalachia Social Context: Past and Present,* 2d ed., edited by B. Ergood and B. Kuhre, 307–14. Dubuque: Kendall/Hunt.

Wagner-Pacifici, Robin, and Barry Schwartz. 1991. "The Vietnam Veterans Memorial: Commemorating a Difficult Past." *American Journal of Sociology* 97, no. 2:376–420.

Wallace, Michael. 1987. "Dying for Coal: The Struggle for Health and Safety Conditions in American Coal Mining, 1930–82." *Social Forces* 66, no. 2:336–64.

Weingartner, Paul, Dwight Billings, and Kathleen Blee. 1989. "Agricultural in Preindustrial Appalachia: Subsistence Farming in Beech

Creek, 1850–1880." *Journal of the Appalachian Studies Association* 1:74–78.

White, Stephen E. 1987. "Return Migration to Eastern Kentucky and the Stem Family Concept." *Growth and Change* 18, no. 2:38–52.

Yarrow, Michael. 1979. "The Labor Process in Coal Mining: Struggle for Control." In *Case Studies in the Labor Process,* edited by A. Zimbalist. New York: Monthly Review Press.

Yarrow, Michael. 1985. "Capitalism, Patriarchy and 'Men's Work': The System of Control of Production of Coal Mining." *Proceedings of the 8th annual Appalachian Studies Conference.* Boone, NC: Appalachian Consortium Press.

Yarrow, Michael. 1990. "Voices from the Coalfields: How Miners' Families Understand the Crisis of Coal." In *Communities in Economic Crisis: Appalachia and the South,* edited by J. Gaventa, B. E. Smith, and A. Willingham, 38–52. Philadelphia: Temple Univ. Press.

GOVERNMENT DOCUMENTS

Census of Agriculture. 1830. Manuscript schedules. Harlan County, Kentucky.

Census of Agriculture. 1880. Table V: Number and Size of Farms by Tenancy.

Census of Population. 1830. Manuscript schedules. Harlan County, Kentucky.

Census of Population. 1860. Manuscript schedules. Harlan County, Kentucky.

Census of Population. 1880. Manuscript schedules. Harlan County, Kentucky.

Census of Population. 1900. Vol. 1. Part 1. Table 5: Population, 1890 and 1900.

Census of Population. 1910. Vol. 3. Part 1. Table 1: Population Characteristics.

Census of Population. 1920. Vol. 3. Part 1. Table 9: Population Characteristics.

Census of Population. 1930. Vol. 3. Part 1. Table 11: Population Characteristics.

Census of Population. 1950. Vol. 2. Part 17. Table 17: Population, 1930–50.

Census of Population. 1960. Vol. 1. Part 19. Table 13: Population Characteristics.

Census of Population. 1970. Vol. 1. Part 19. Table 121: Labor Force Status.

Census of Population. 1980. No. C19. Table 176: Labor Force Status.

Kentucky Cabinet for Human Resources. 1985. Labor Force Estimate, Annual Averages.

Kentucky Department of Economic Development. 1986. Resources for Economic Development: Harlan County. Department of Economic Development. Division of Research and Planning.

Kentucky Department of Mines and Minerals. 1985. Annual report. December 31.

Kentucky Department of Mines and Minerals. 1986. Annual report. December 31.

Kentucky Department of Mines and Minerals. 1990. Annual report. December 31.

Bureau of Economic Analysis. 1991. U.S. Department of Commerce. Table CA35.

County Business Patterns. 1970. U.S. Department of Commerce. Bureau of Census. Table 2.

County Business Patterns. 1986. U.S. Department of Commerce. Bureau of Census. Table 2.

U.S. Department of Labor. 1985. Bureau of Labor Statistics. June. Bulletin 2217. Tables 75 and 76.

U.S. Department of Labor. 1988. Annual Report to the Secretary of Labor. Mine Safety and Health Administration. Table 4: Coal Mine Fatalities.

REPORTS

Eller, Ronald D., Phil Jenks, Chris Jasparro, and Jerry Napier. 1994. *Kentucky's Distressed Communities: A Report on Poverty in Appalachian Kentucky.* The Appalachian Center of the University of Kentucky. (April).

National Council of Churches of Christ in the USA. 1980. *Churches and Church Membership in the US, 1980.*

Seltzer, Curtis. 1986. "The Coal Industry after 1970: Cost Internalization, Good Works, and Public Planning for Development." *Mountain Association for Community Economic Development* 5:1–115.

State Data Center. 1991. *Report on Single-Parent Households.* University of Louisville. August.

HISTORICAL COLLECTIONS

Burns, Annie Walker. 1870. Family Bible Records of Harlan County, Kentucky, People.

Southeast Community College (SECC-OHP). Oral History Project. Cumberland, KY. James C. Goode, curator.

NEWSPAPERS AND NEWSLETTERS

Coal Employment Project. 1990. *Coal Mining Women's Support Team News*. Vol. 1. issue 4, p. 1.

Harlan Daily Enterprise (HDE)

Lexington Herald-Leader

Louisville Courier-Journal

SUBJECT INDEX

NAME INDEX

PLACE INDEX